Introducing
Grunge Geometric
TEXTURES VOL.1

I have a dualistic theory of style and art and this allows me to determine one style as opposed to another.
This book develops designs in the geometric world with a particular imprint called "grunge" in opposition to a synthetic, iconographic, linear vision.

I could represent the geometries differently with regular lines in a minimal way as in GEOMETRIC TEXTURES FOR FASHION or in a simple but stylish synthesis as in TECNO POP or lines complex with an inner vision as in STRUCTURED TEXTURES VOL.1
In this volume instead I have created designs where the broken, smudged, sketchy sign is predominant and the backgrounds are irregular to the limit of abstraction.
In this gallery I have also included images with fresh strokes and watercolour stains because they express a touch of irregularity that is included in this new concept.

Indeed, expanding the initial concept of "grunge" helps to find a common way of classifying a design within a larger family as opposed to the rational, minimalist and techno style prevailing in the world today.
But it is a dual world that opposes rational to irrational, regular to irregular, geometric to abstract, linear-precise to "grunge".

Both styles are now functional to our need of representation and our way of being contemporary.

Vincenzo Sguera

Published by
ARKIVIA BOOKS srl

Borgo Allegri, 60r
50122 FIRENZE - FI (Italy)
Phone:
(0039) 3392349130
web:
www.arkiviabooks.com
www.vincenzosguera.com
e-mail:
info@arkiviabooks.com
info@vincenzosguera.com

The 2 DVDs included are an integral part of this publication and cannot be sold separately.

Copyright and Rights to Use

The use of designs included in this book and the DVD is free. However the copyright of the designs belongs to Vincenzo Sguera, who does not transfer an exclusive use of the designs.
Include a line indicating the copyright:
© 2016 Vincenzo Sguera.

The republication of the book in part or in whole and with any kind of medium (paper, CD, DVD, photocopier, internet etc.) is forbidden except by a reviewer who may quote brief passages in a review.

The creation of designs is a continuously evolving activity. Any resemblance between the designs in this book and other designs subject to intellectual-property copyright results from ignorance of the existence of said copyright or is purely coincidental.

If, unknown to the author and the publisher, any design contained in this book is already registered, they do not authorize the use of such design by book buyers.
They decline all responsability since they cannot be aware of all the designs registered or used previous to this publication in all countries.

ARKIVIA BOOKS is not responsible for the use of its designs where this does not conform to the laws in force to which the user is subject. Users assume full responsibility and should verify the real possibilities of use in their own territory of production, distribution and sales.

Those who buy this book can use freely the designs inside with only 3 reserves:

1)
the designs cannot to be used to produce a book, an ebook or a CD/DVD with the same purpose as this book, or to sell these designs in any way, including through internet, or give them away for free both individually and in groups or in whole. It is possible to sell products derived from these designs but not the designs themselves.

2)
Each design must not already have been registered before this publication by others, as mentioned above.

3 - The destination of the designs must be respected: so if a design is a texture, a different use is not authorized, such as a trademark; the same is valid for characters or graphics.

Copyright belongs to Vincenzo Sguera who in this case cedes the use, for this, mention the copyright © 2016 Vincenzo Sguera

DVD info / Technical Details

The Book contains 2 DVDs suitable for WINDOWS® and MACINTOSH® with 250 files so divided: the first 125 files are in DVD-1, the second in DVD-2.
Each DVD contains 2 Folders: one for the high resolution files to 300 ppi and the other for the files to 72 ppi.

It was necessary to use 2 DVDs since all the 250 high-resolution files and large formats fit only into 2 DVDs. I made this choice to not decrease the quality of the designs that remains one of my standards along with creative variety even at the expense of a minor stylistic compliance.

FORMAT
I have chosen the format JPG as the files are very large, both in cm. and bites.
If I used a PDF file, for example, it would need as many as 4 or 5 DVDs.
I preferred a large size, near to their real use and a final resolution which is quite high and professional = 300 ppi.
In addition to this folder (300 ppi CMYK) I have also added a folder with the same files at 72 ppi in RGB for easy reference.

Each of the two folders contains the same designs but with a different resolution and different colour scale.
These are the FOLDERS:

JPG 300 ppi - CMYK
These Files are in JPG Format saved at 300 ppi resolution and in CMYK.

JPG 72 ppi - RGB
Here you find Low Resolution BITMAP Files in JPG format (72 ppi in colour scale RGB), that can be used to develop projects with lighter Files and are for quick vision.

TYPE OF FILES
The Files in the DVD are all BITMAP: this means in the first place that they can be opened by all softwares that use BITMAP Format.

SOFTWARE
The main BITMAP software is: PHOTOSHOP but it is possible to open these files in software such as CORELPAINT, PAINTSHOP, COREL PAINTER etc.

SIZES
The size of the files is listed both in centimetres and in pixels at 300 ppi.

COLOURS
In BITMAP files the colours can be in RGB (Red, Green and Blue), more useful for video and internet use, or in CMYK (Cyan, Magenta, Yellow and Black) normally used for printing needs.

The copyright of WINDOWS, MACINTOSH, PHOTOSHOP, CORELPAINT, PAINTSHOP, COREL PAINTER belongs to the owners.

page 004

GGT0001
pattern size
50 cm x 50 cm
5906 x 5906 pixels
at 300 ppi in CMYK

page 005

GGT0002
pattern size
47 cm x 50 cm
5552 x 5906 pixels
at 300 ppi in CMYK

GGT0003
pattern size
47 cm x 50 cm
5552 x 5906 pixels
at 300 ppi in CMYK

page 006

GGT0004
pattern size
45 cm x 60 cm
5315 x 7087 pixels
at 300 ppi in CMYK

page 007

GGT0005
pattern size
45 cm x 50 cm
5315 x 5906 pixels
at 300 ppi in CMYK

GGT0006
pattern size
45 cm x 60 cm
5315 x 7087 pixels
at 300 ppi in CMYK

page 008

GGT0007
pattern size
42 cm x 50 cm
4961 x 5906 pixels
at 300 ppi in CMYK

GGT0008
pattern size
42 cm x 50 cm
4961 x 5906 pixels
at 300 ppi in CMYK

page 009

GGT0009
pattern size
45 cm x 50 cm
5315 x 5906 pixels
at 300 ppi in CMYK

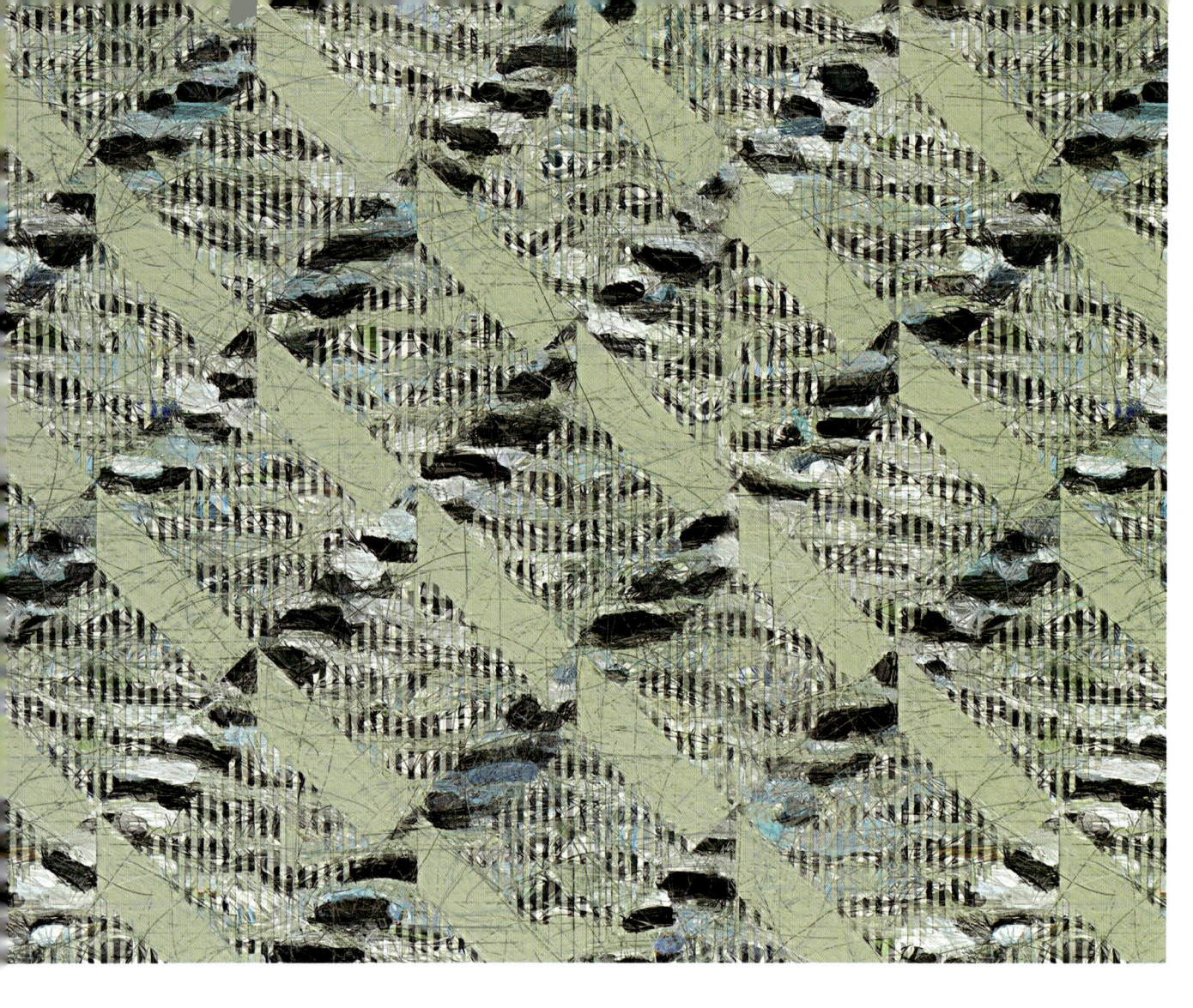

page 010

GGT0010
pattern size
45 cm x 60 cm
5315 x 7087 pixels
at 300 ppi in CMYK

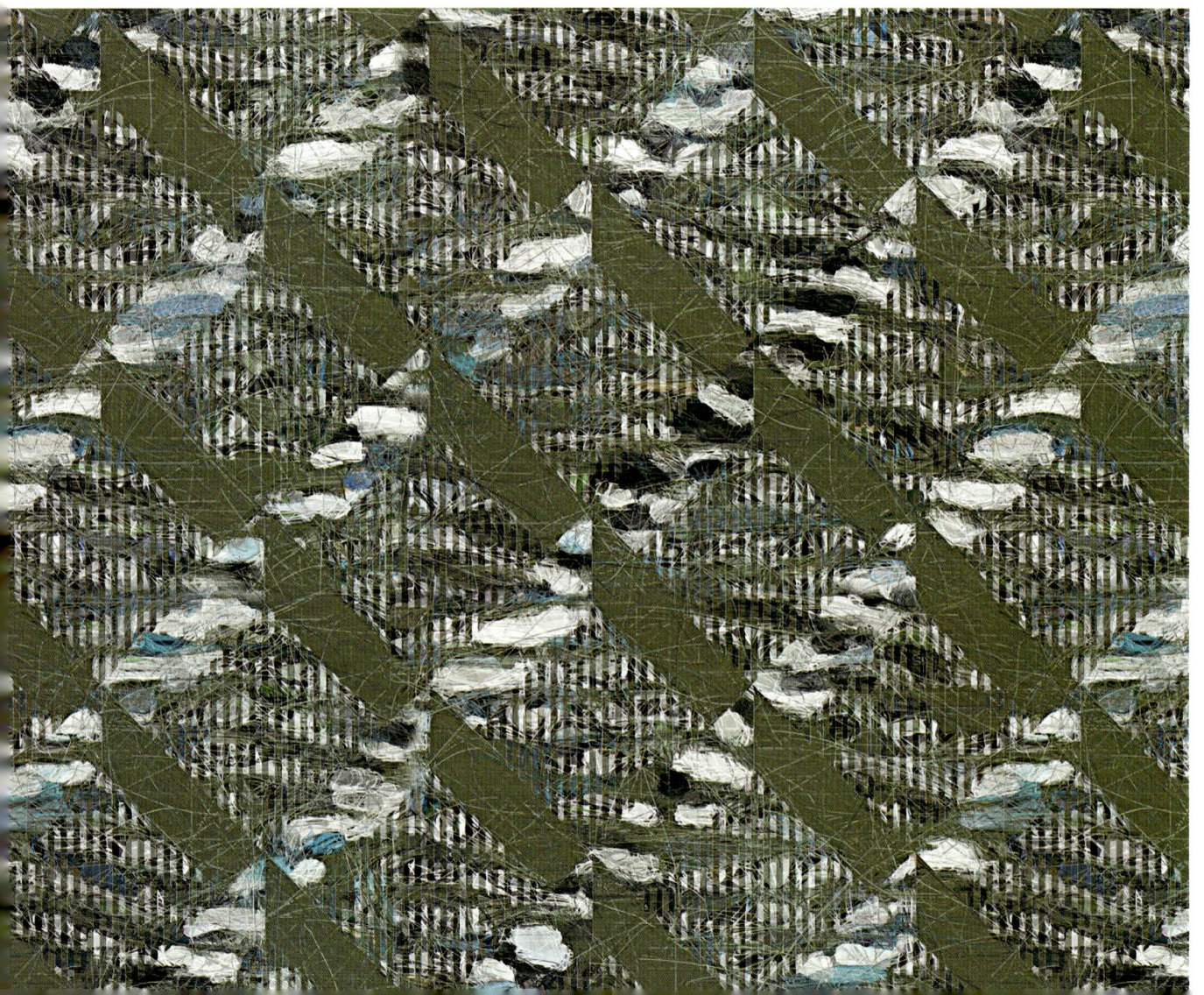

GGT0011
pattern size
45 cm x 60 cm
5315 x 7087 pixels
at 300 ppi in CMYK

page 011

GGT0012
pattern size
45 cm x 60 cm
5315 x 7087 pixels
at 300 ppi in CMYK

page 012

GGT0013
pattern size
43 cm x 50 cm
5079 x 5906 pixels
at 300 ppi in CMYK

GGT0014
pattern size
30 cm x 40 cm
3544 x 4725 pixels
at 300 ppi in CMYK

page 013

GGT0015
pattern size
54 cm x 60 cm
6368 x 7087 pixels
at 300 ppi in CMYK

page 014

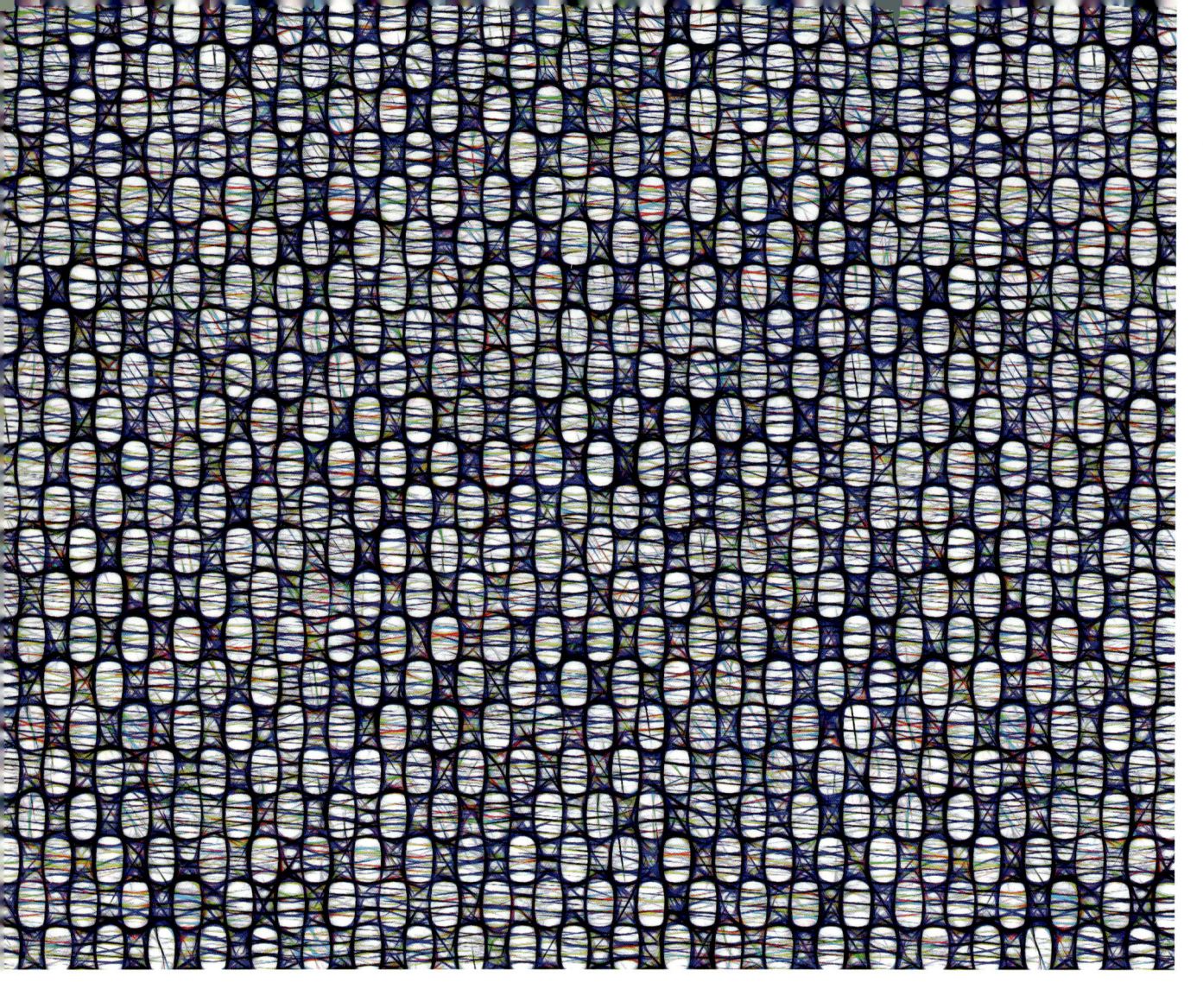

GGT0016
pattern size
28 cm x 30 cm
3308 x 3544 pixels
at 300 ppi in CMYK

GGT0017
pattern size
28 cm x 30 cm
3308 x 3544 pixels
at 300 ppi in CMYK

page 015

GGT0018
pattern size
60 cm x 60 cm
7087 x 7087 pixels
at 300 ppi in CMYK

page 016

GGT0019
pattern size
42 cm x 70 cm
4961 x 8268 pixels
at 300 ppi in CMYK

page 017

GGT0020
pattern size
50 cm x 50 cm
5906 x 5906 pixels
at 300 ppi in CMYK

GGT0021
pattern size
50 cm x 50 cm
5906 x 5906 pixels
at 300 ppi in CMYK

page 018

GGT0022
pattern size
50 cm x 44 cm
5906 x 5197 pixels
at 300 ppi in CMYK

GGT0023
pattern size
50 cm x 44 cm
5906 x 5197 pixels
at 300 ppi in CMYK

page 019

GGT0024
pattern size
40 cm x 40 cm
4725 x 4725 pixels
at 300 ppi in CMYK

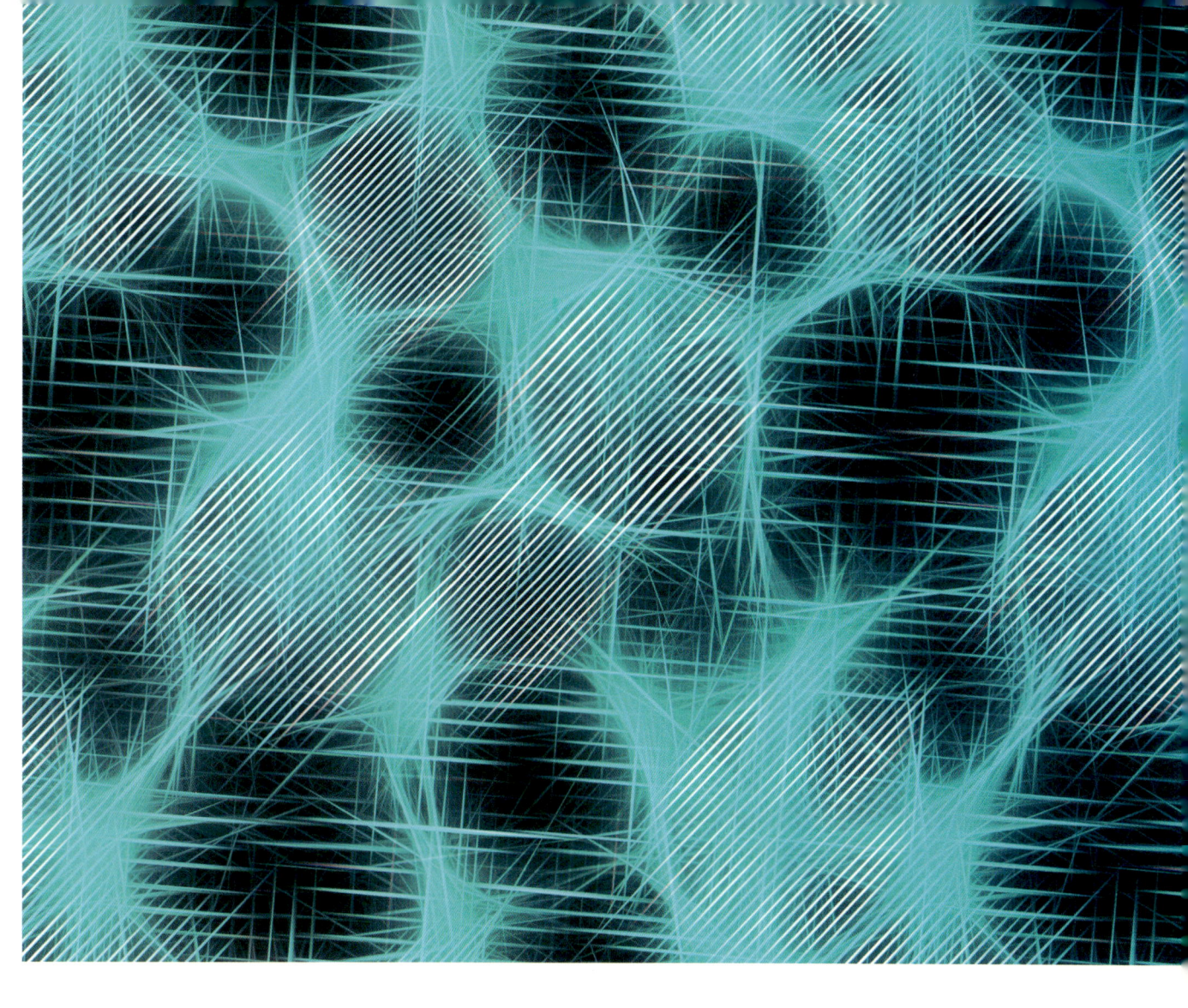

GGT0025
pattern size
50 cm x 50 cm
5906 x 5906 pixels
at 300 ppi in CMYK

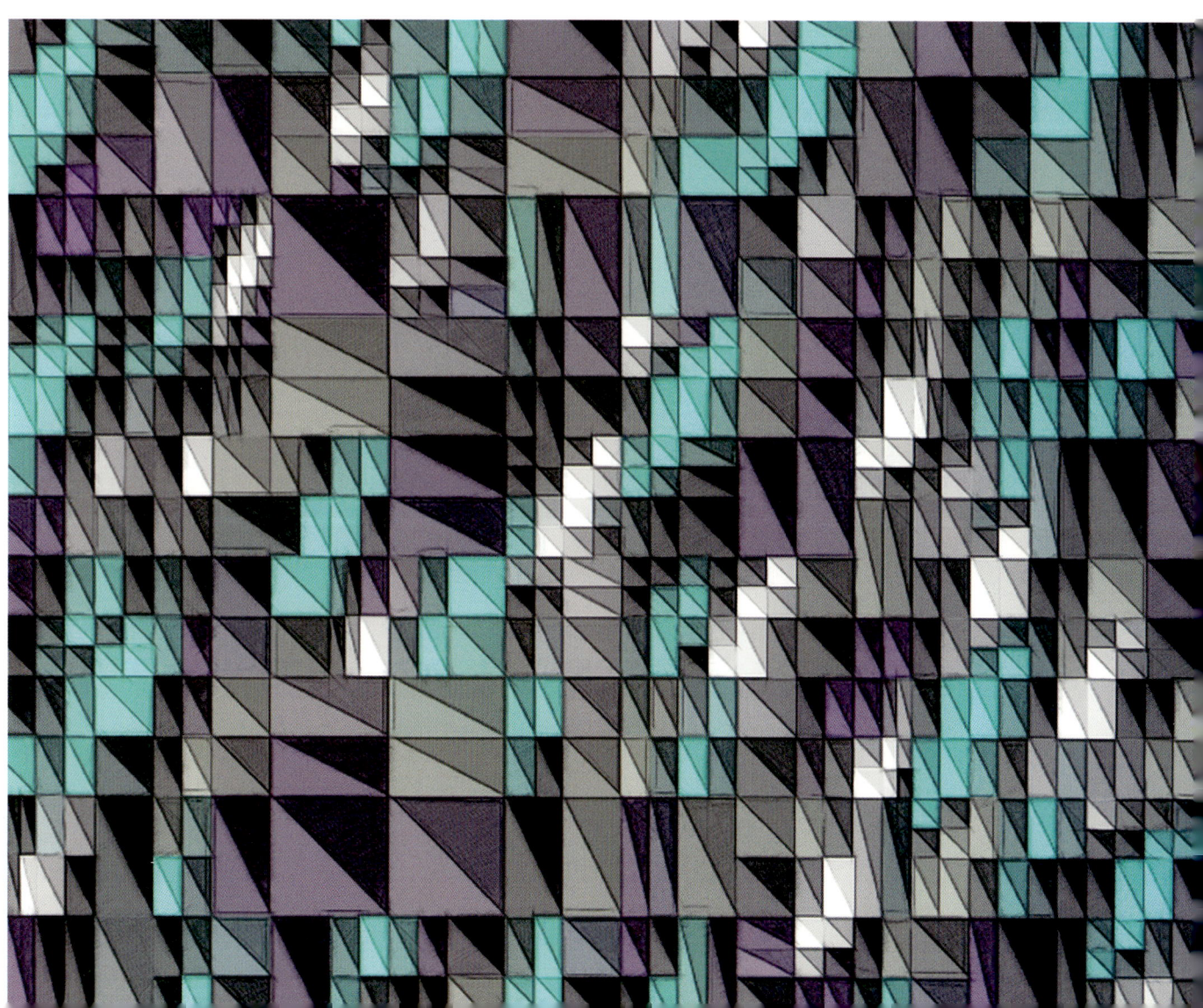

page 020

GGT0026
pattern size
45 cm x 50 cm
5315 x 5906 pixels
at 300 ppi in CMYK

page 021

GGT0027
pattern size
45 cm x 60 cm
5315 x 7087 pixels
at 300 ppi in CMYK

GGT0028
pattern size
50 cm x 60 cm
5906 x 7087 pixels
at 300 ppi in CMYK

page 022

GGT0029
pattern size
40 cm x 60 cm
4725 x 7087 pixels
at 300 ppi in CMYK

page 023

GGT0030
pattern size
50 cm x 60 cm
5906 x 7087 pixels
at 300 ppi in CMYK

GGT0031
pattern size
50 cm x 64 cm
5906 x 7560 pixels
at 300 ppi in CMYK

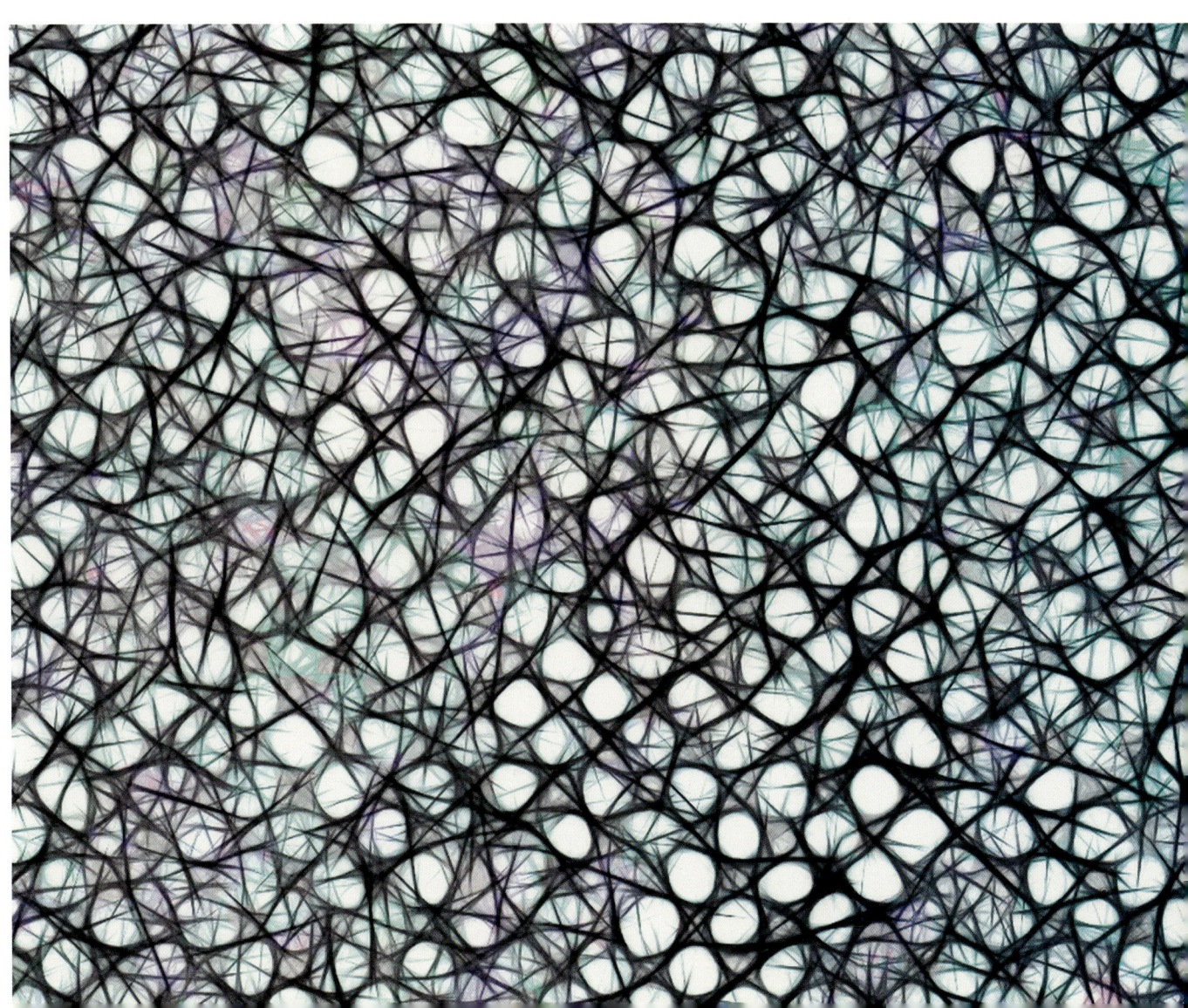

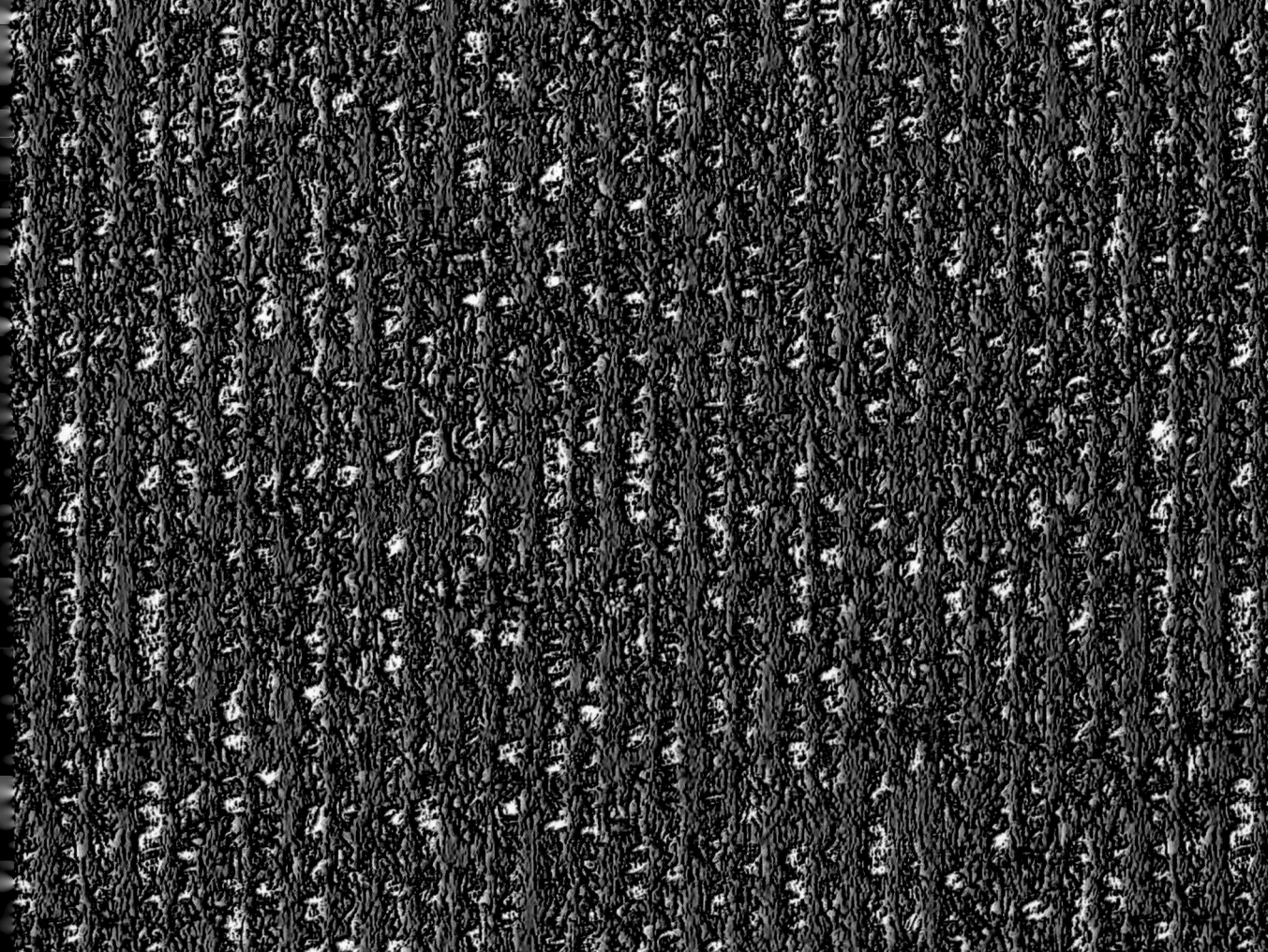

page 024

GGT0032

pattern size
32 cm x 40 cm
3780 x 4724 pixels
at 300 ppi in CMYK

GGT0033

pattern size
32 cm x 40 cm
3780 x 4724 pixels
at 300 ppi in CMYK

page 025

GGT0034
pattern size
48 cm x 60 cm
5670 x 7087 pixels
at 300 ppi in CMYK

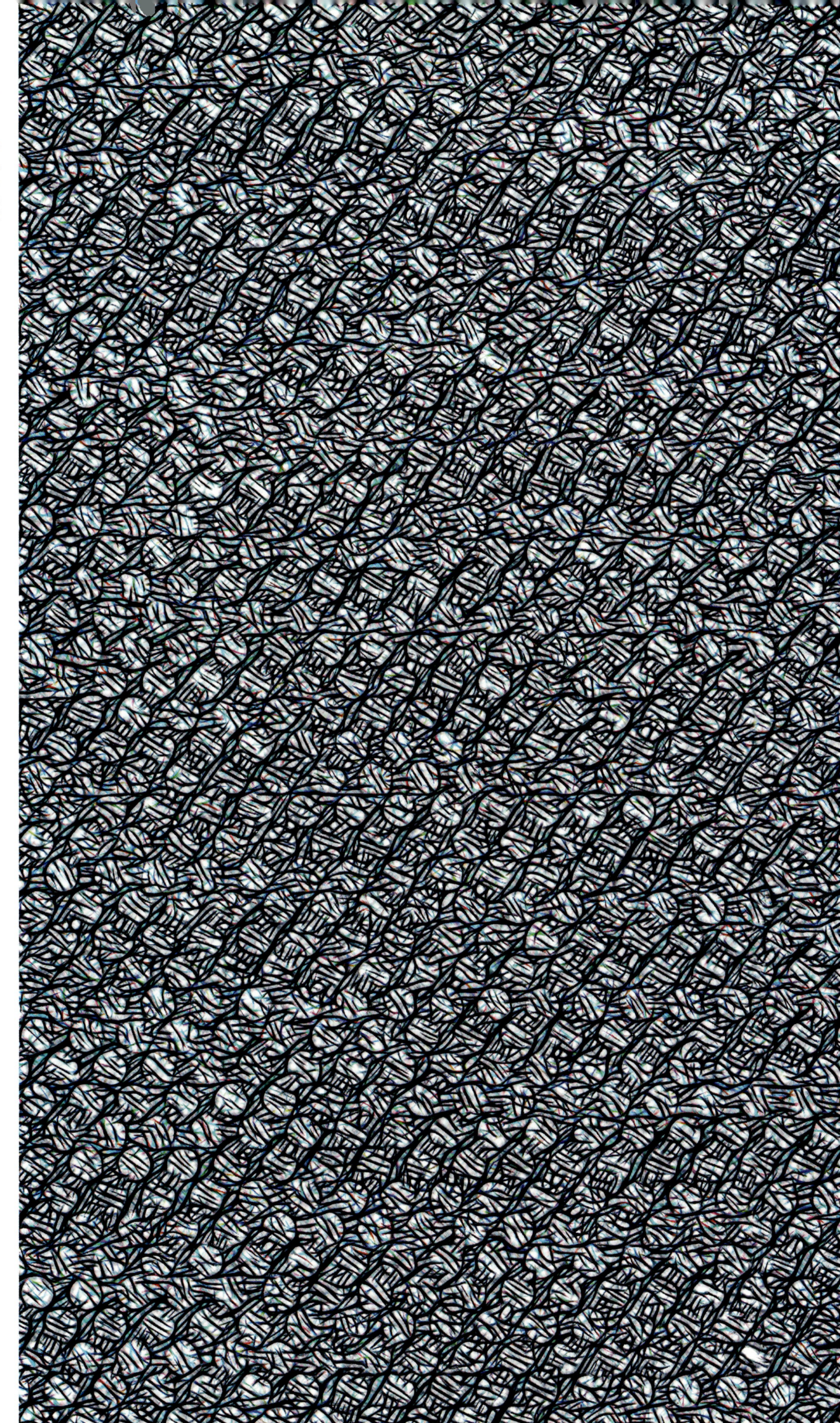

page 026

GGT0035
pattern size
60 cm x 60 cm
7087 x 7087 pixels
at 300 ppi in CMYK

page 027

GGT0036
pattern size
56 cm x 60 cm
6615 x 7087 pixels
at 300 ppi in CMYK

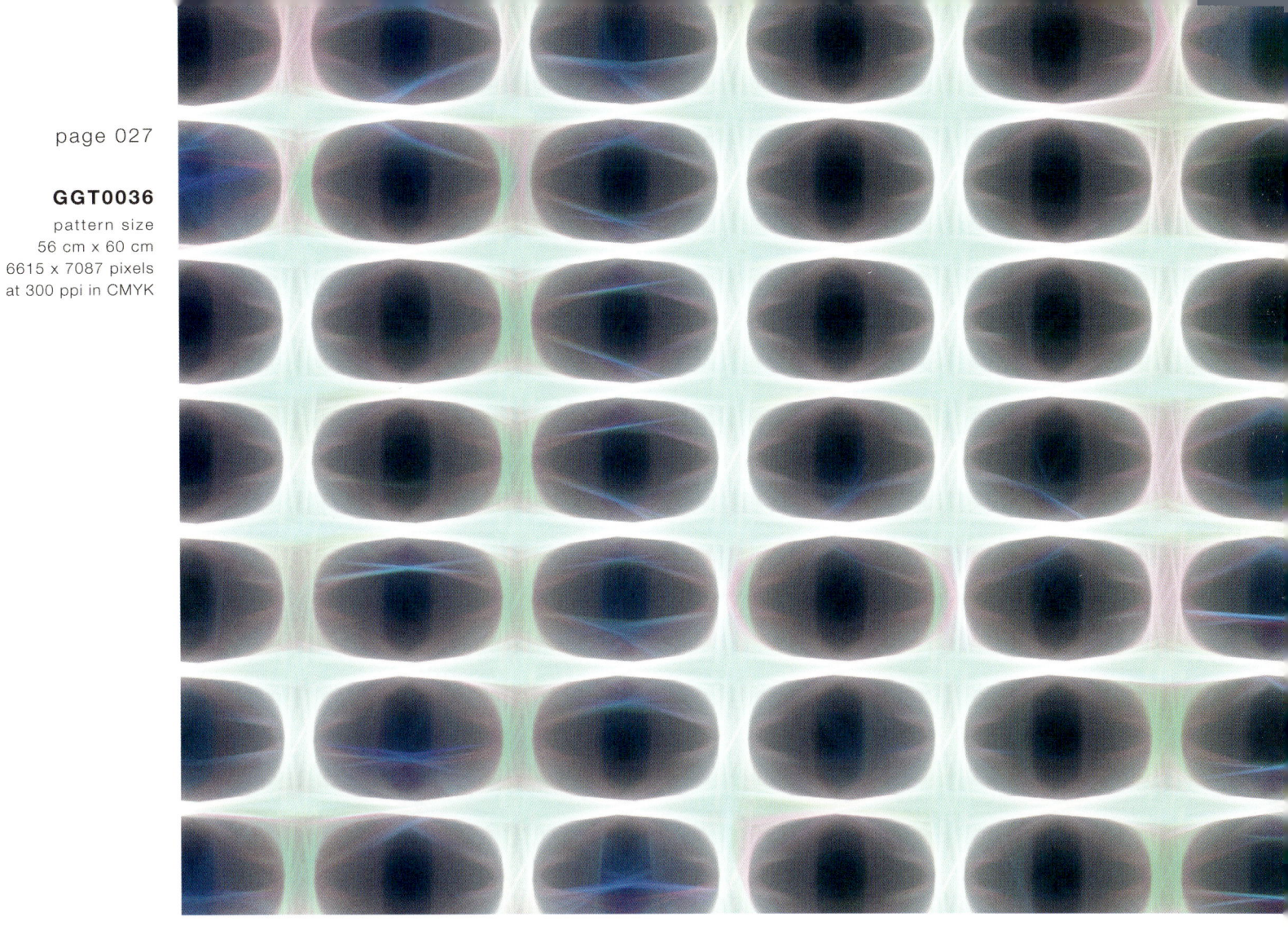

GGT0037
pattern size
70 cm x 70 cm
8268 x 8268 pixels
at 300 ppi in CMYK

page 028

GGT0038
pattern size
70 cm x 70 cm
8268 x 8268 pixels
at 300 ppi in CMYK

page 029

GGT0039
pattern size
40 cm x 35 cm
4725 x 4134 pixels
at 300 ppi in CMYK

GGT0040
pattern size
50 cm x 50 cm
5906 x 5906 pixels
at 300 ppi in CMYK

page 030

GGT0041
pattern size
70 cm x 70 cm
8268 x 8268 pixels
at 300 ppi in CMYK

page 031

GGT0042
pattern size
60 cm x 45 cm
7087 x 5315 pixels
at 300 ppi in CMYK

GGT0043
pattern size
70 cm x 66 cm
8268 x 7796 pixels
at 300 ppi in CMYK

page 032

GGT0044
pattern size
60 cm x 60 cm
7087 x 7087 pixels
at 300 ppi in CMYK

page 033

GGT0045
pattern size
60 cm x 60 cm
7087 x 7087 pixels
at 300 ppi in CMYK

GGT0046
pattern size
30 cm x 50 cm
3544 x 5906 pixels
at 300 ppi in CMYK

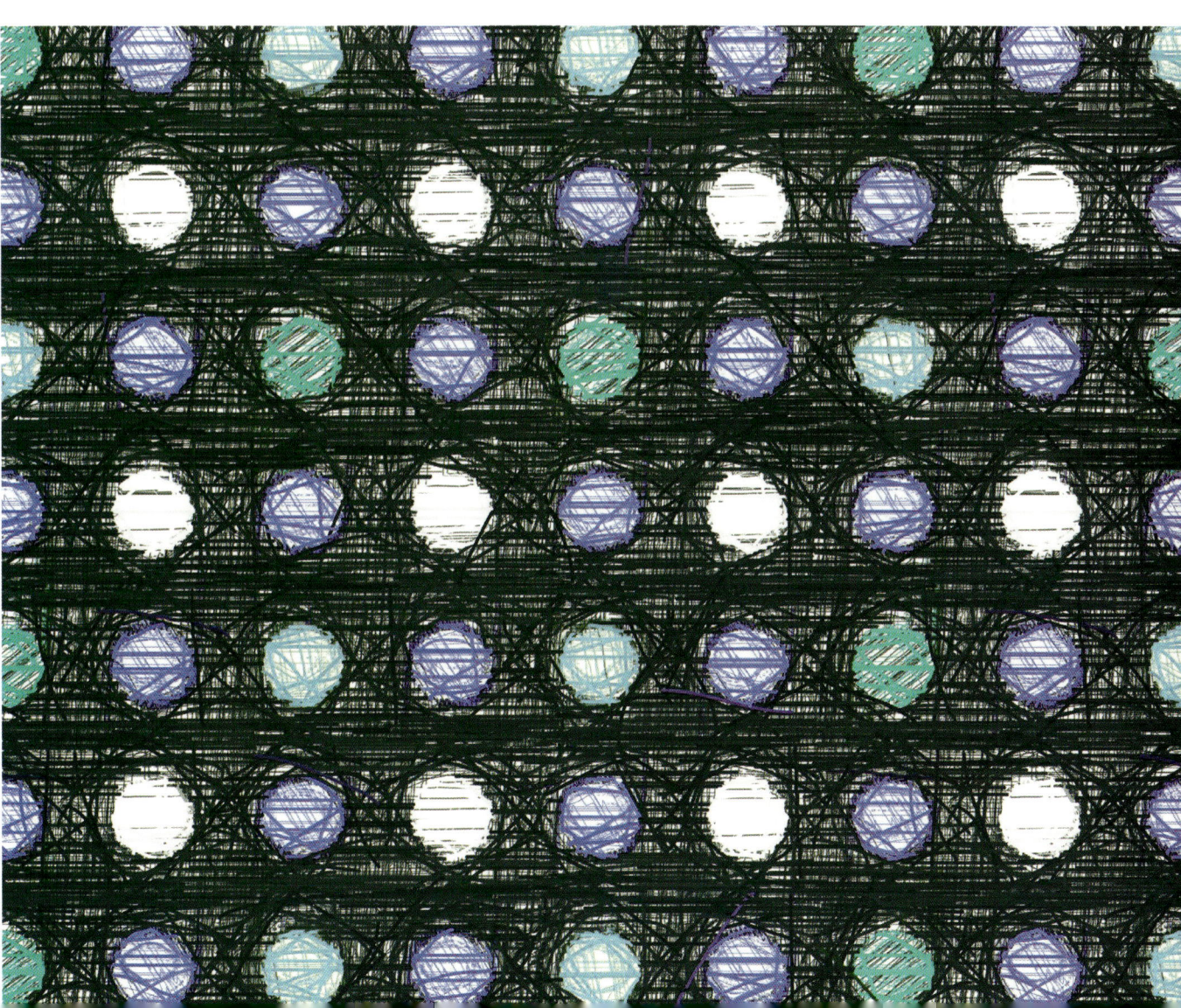

page 034

GGT0047
pattern size
50 cm x 50 cm
5906 x 5906 pixels
at 300 ppi in CMYK

page 035

GGT0048
pattern size
48 cm x 60 cm
5670 x 7087 pixels
at 300 ppi in CMYK

GGT0049
pattern size
52 cm x 60 cm
6142 x 7087 pixels
at 300 ppi in CMYK

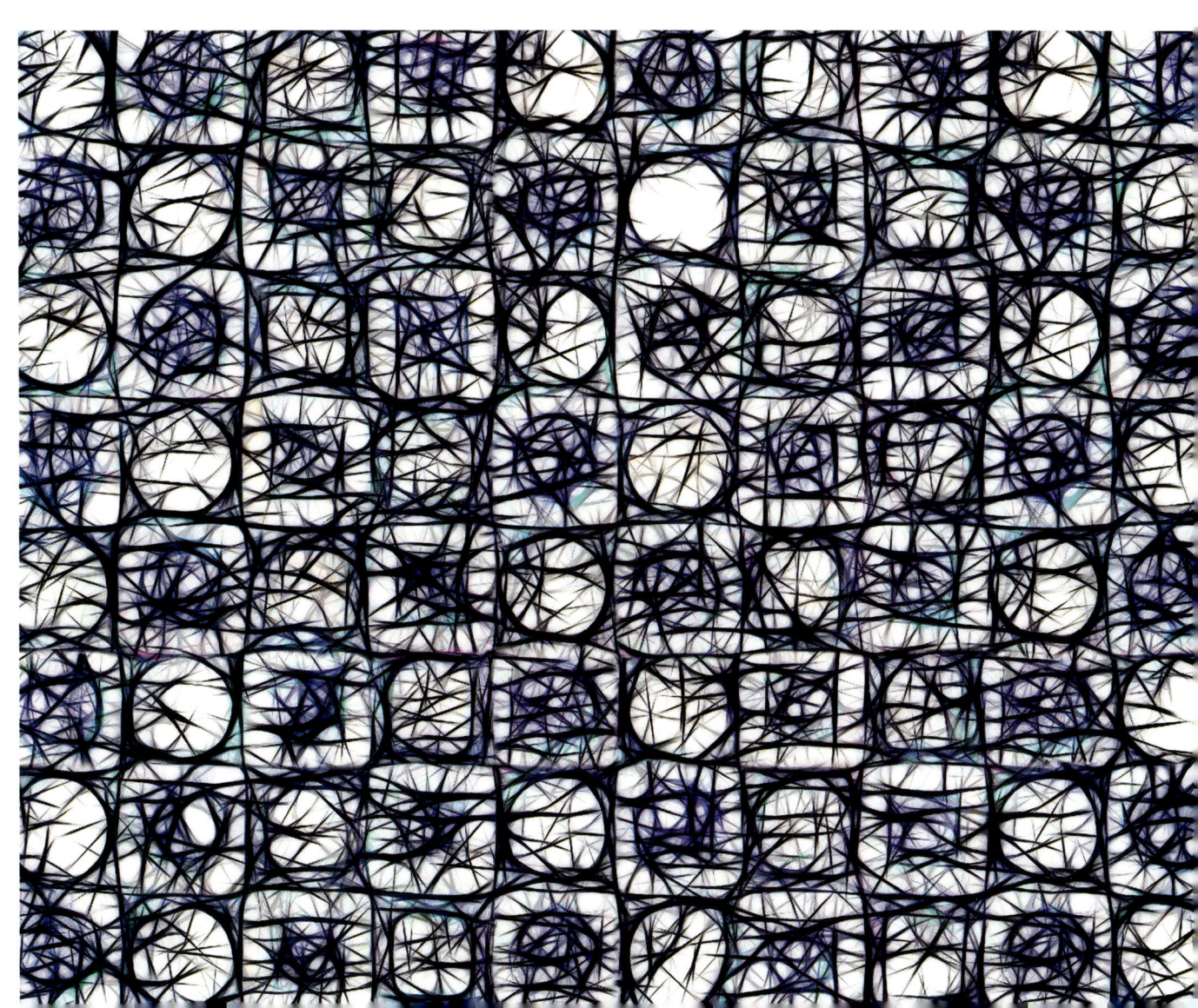

page 036

GGT0050
pattern size
60 cm x 60 cm
7087 x 7087 pixels
at 300 ppi in CMYK

GGT0051
pattern size
70 cm x 66 cm
8268 x 7796 pixels
at 300 ppi in CMYK

page 037

GGT0052
pattern size
60 cm x 60 cm
7087 x 7087 pixels
at 300 ppi in CMYK

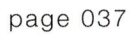

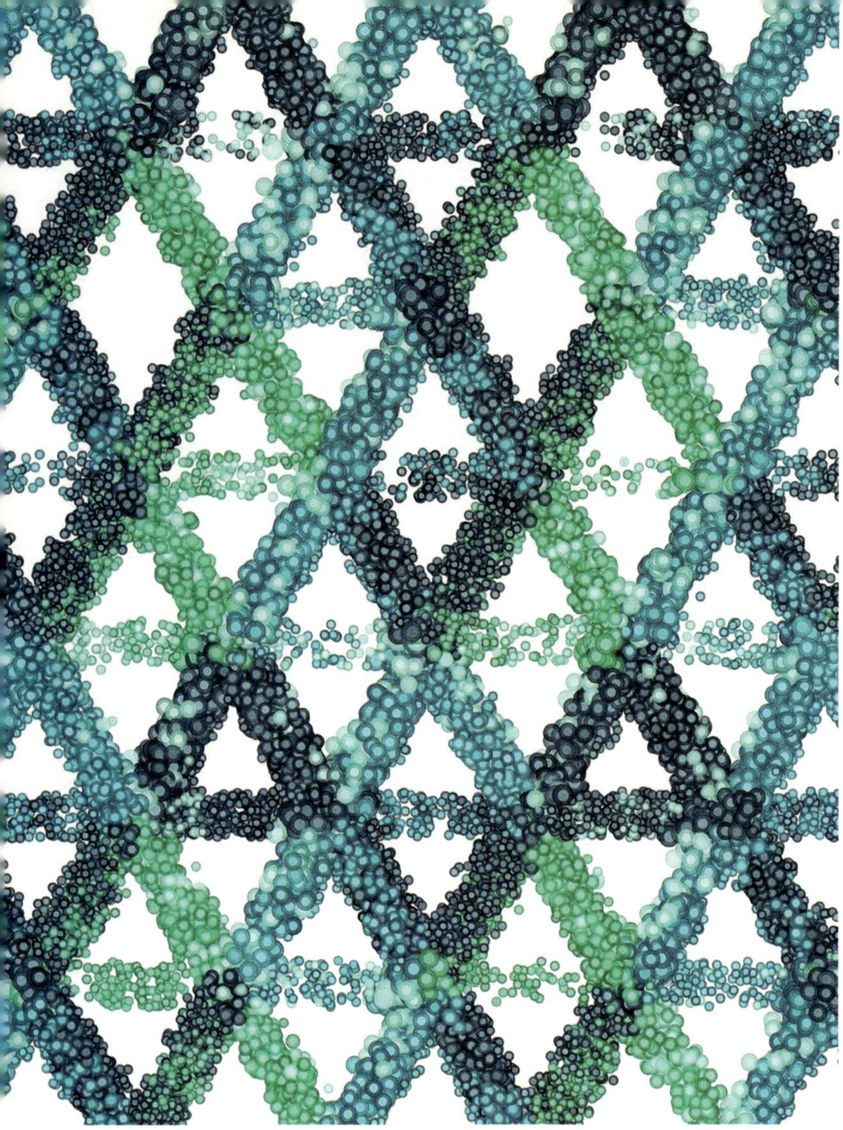
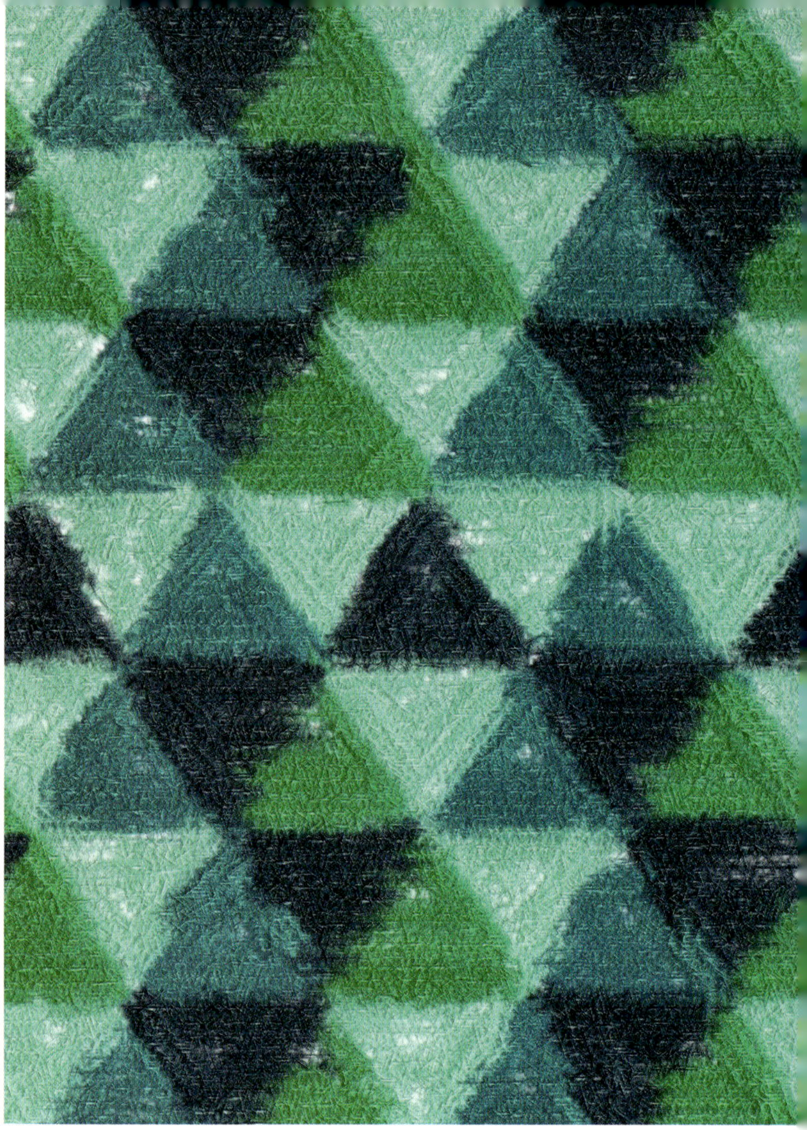
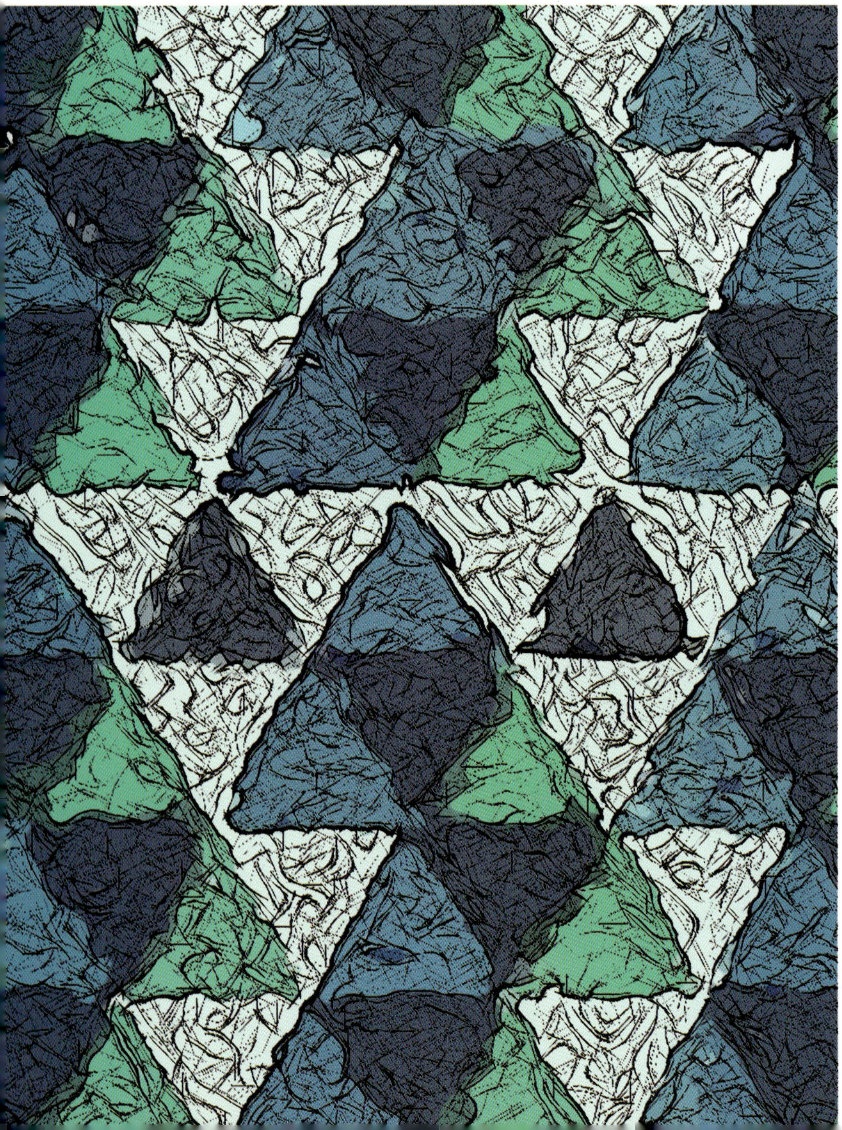
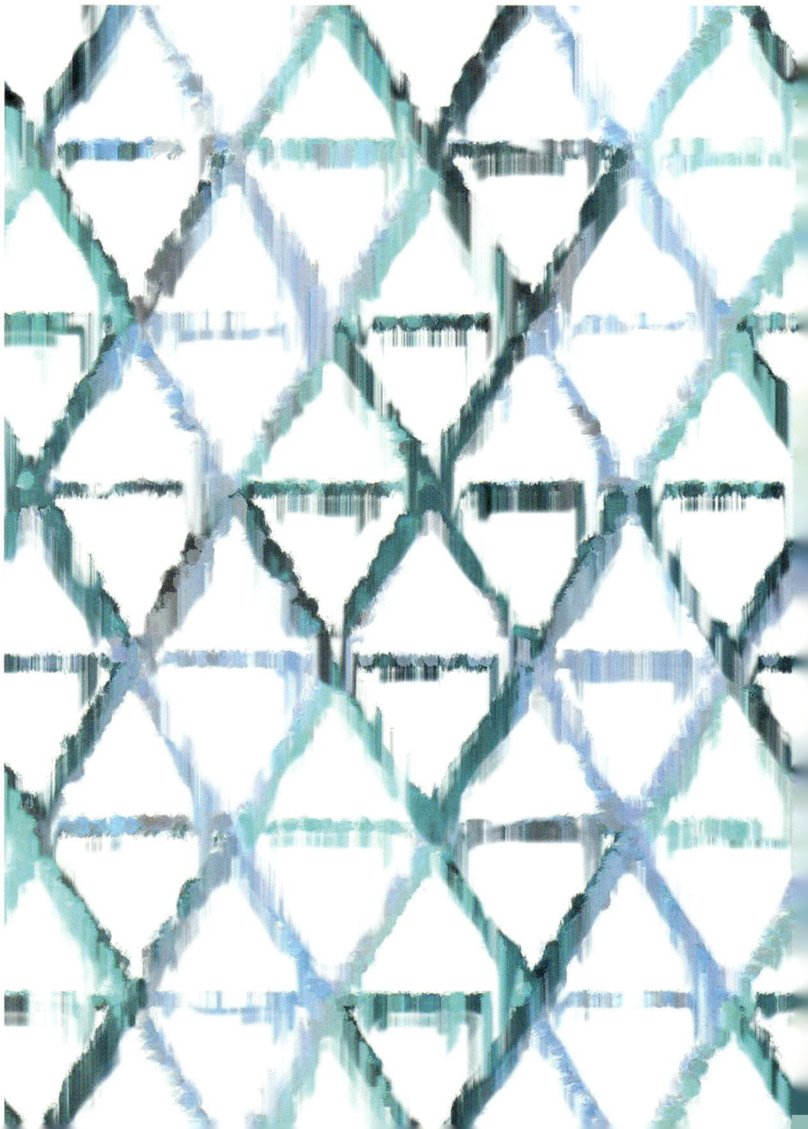

page 039

GGT0057
pattern size
60 cm x 60 cm
7087 x 7087 pixels
at 300 ppi in CMYK

GGT0053
pattern size
54 cm x 60 cm
6378 x 7087 pixels
at 300 ppi in CMYK

GGT0054
pattern size
60 cm x 50 cm
7087 x 5906 pixels
at 300 ppi in CMYK

GGT0055
pattern size
60 cm x 50 cm
7087 x 5906 pixels
at 300 ppi in CMYK

GGT0056
pattern size
60 cm x 50 cm
7087 x 5906 pixels
at 300 ppi in CMYK

< page 038

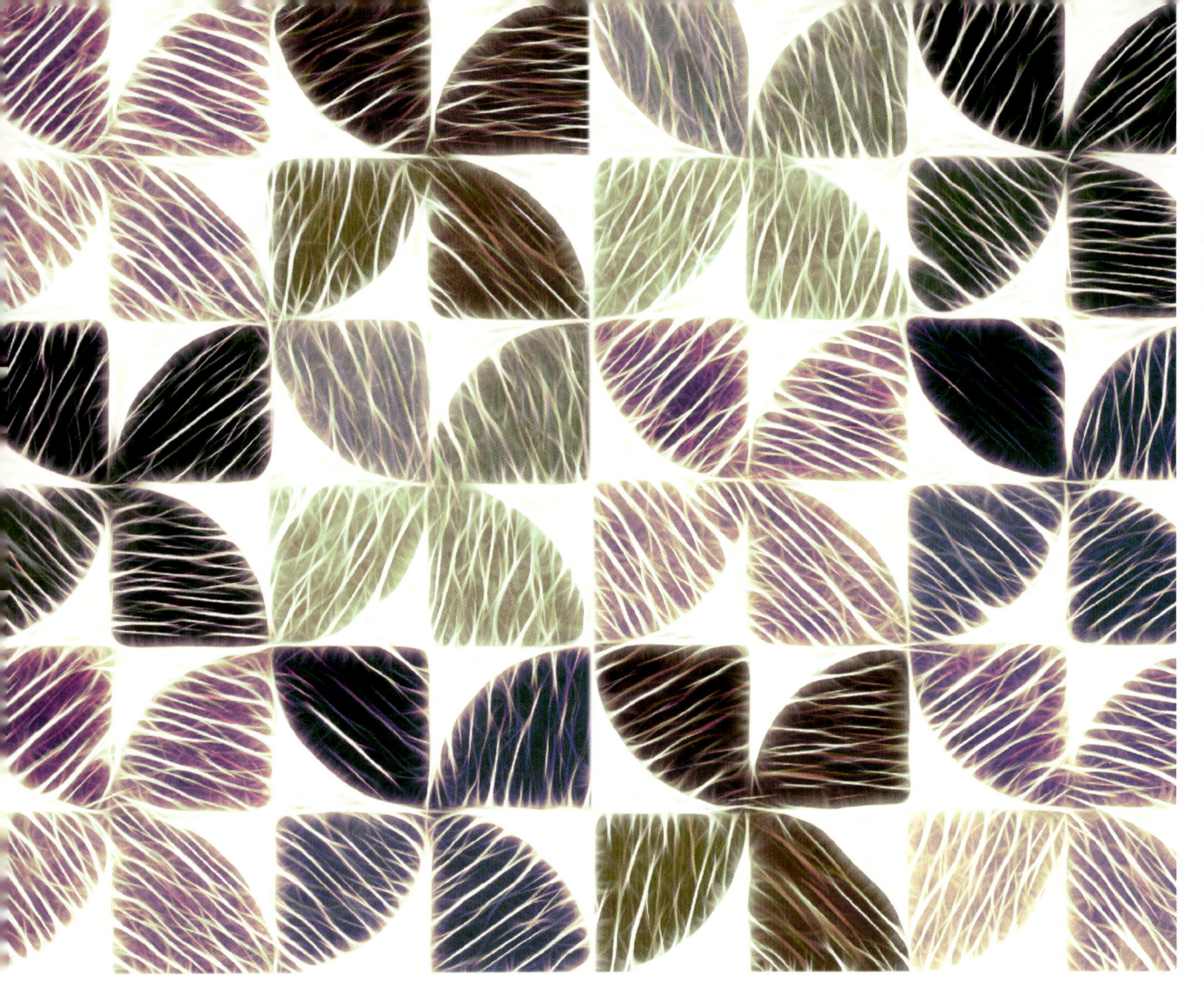

page 040

GGT0058
pattern size
50 cm x 70 cm
5906 x 8268 pixels
at 300 ppi in CMYK

GGT0059
pattern size
50 cm x 50 cm
5906 x 5906 pixels
at 300 ppi in CMYK

page 041

GGT0060
pattern size
80 cm x 80 cm
9449 x 9449 pixels
at 300 ppi in CMYK

page 042

GGT0061
pattern size
45 cm x 60 cm
5315 x 7087 pixels
at 300 ppi in CMYK

GGT0062
pattern size
45 cm x 60 cm
5315 x 7087 pixels
at 300 ppi in CMYK

page 043

GGT0063
pattern size
45 cm x 60 cm
5315 x 7087 pixels
at 300 ppi in CMYK

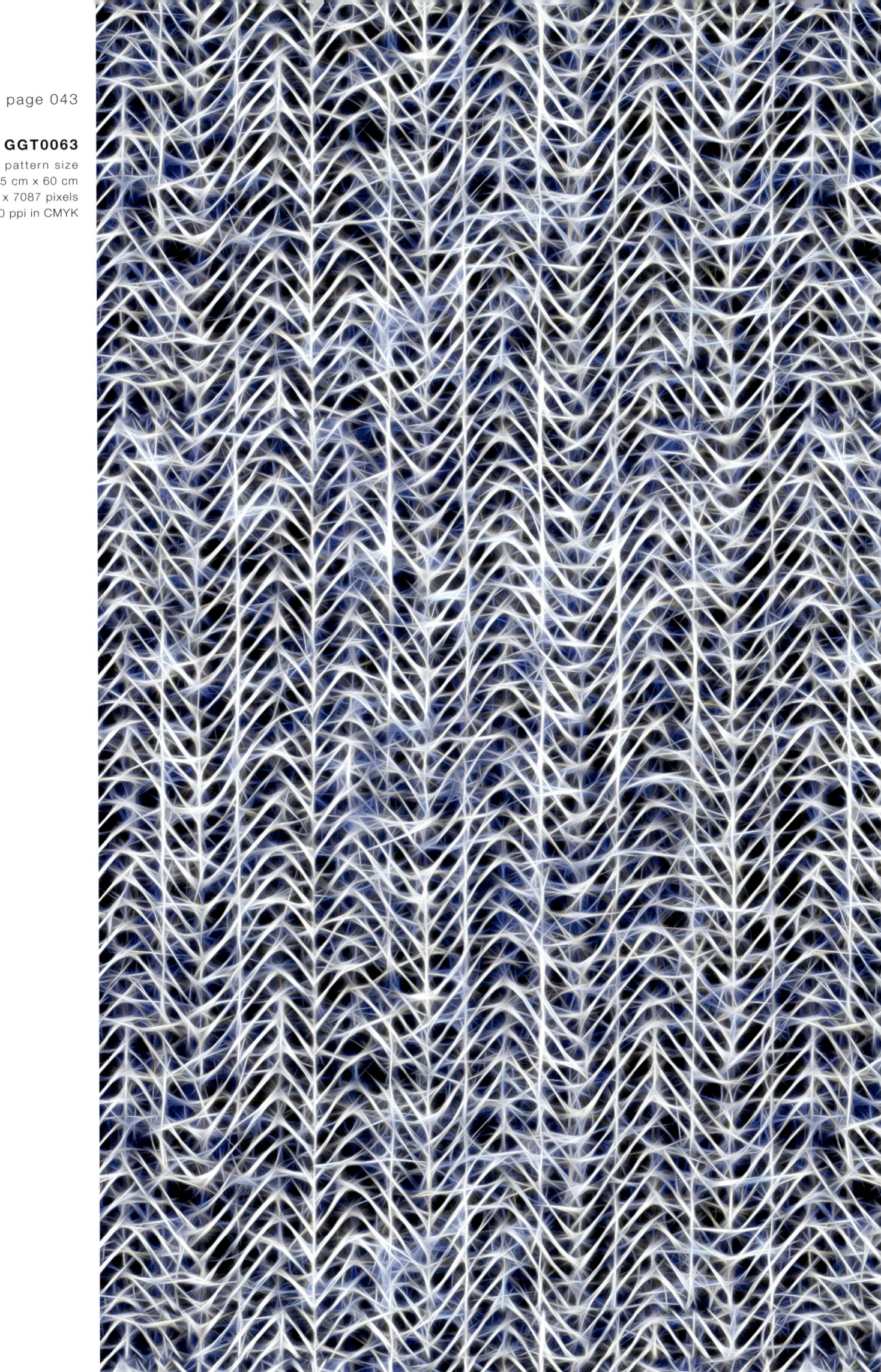

page 044

GGT0064

pattern size
50 cm x 50 cm
5906 x 5906 pixels
at 300 ppi in CMYK

GGT0065

pattern size
50 cm x 50 cm
5906 x 5906 pixels
at 300 ppi in CMYK

GGT0066

pattern size
50 cm x 50 cm
5906 x 5906 pixels
at 300 ppi in CMYK

GGT0067

pattern size
50 cm x 50 cm
5906 x 5906 pixels
at 300 ppi in CMYK

GGT0068

pattern size
50 cm x 50 cm
5906 x 5906 pixels
at 300 ppi in CMYK

page 045 >

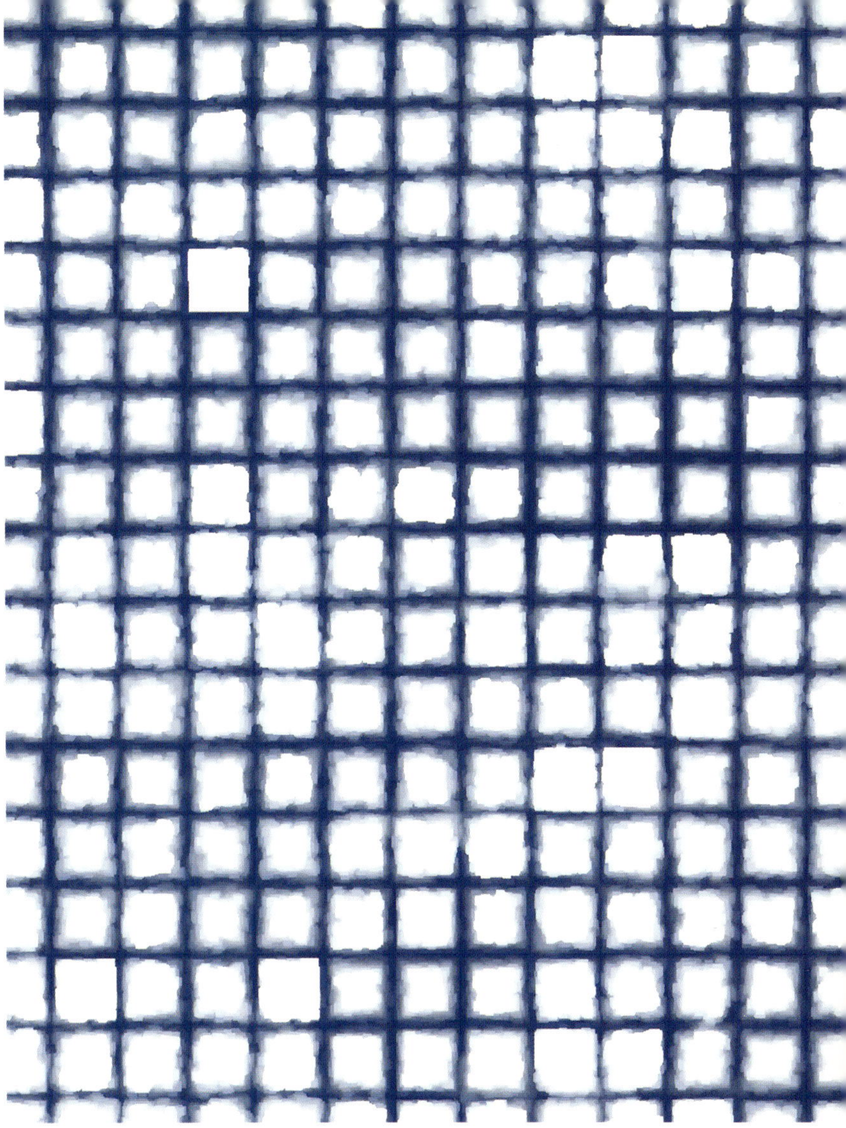
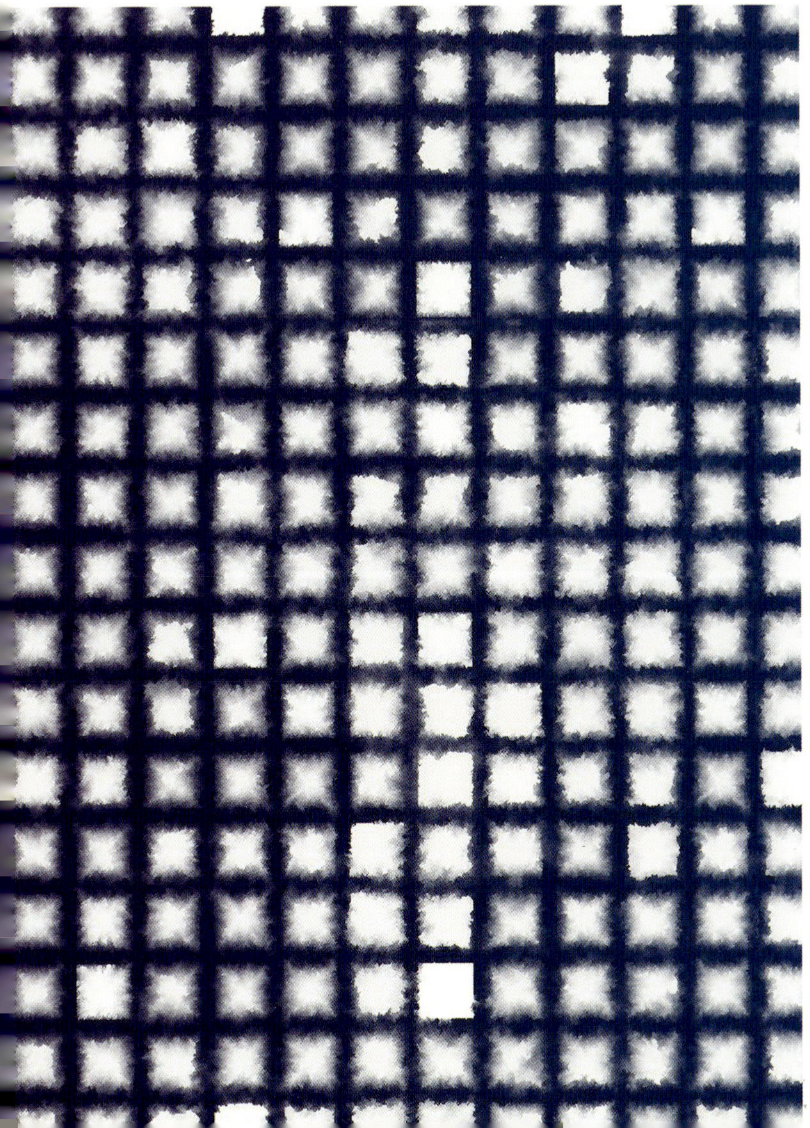
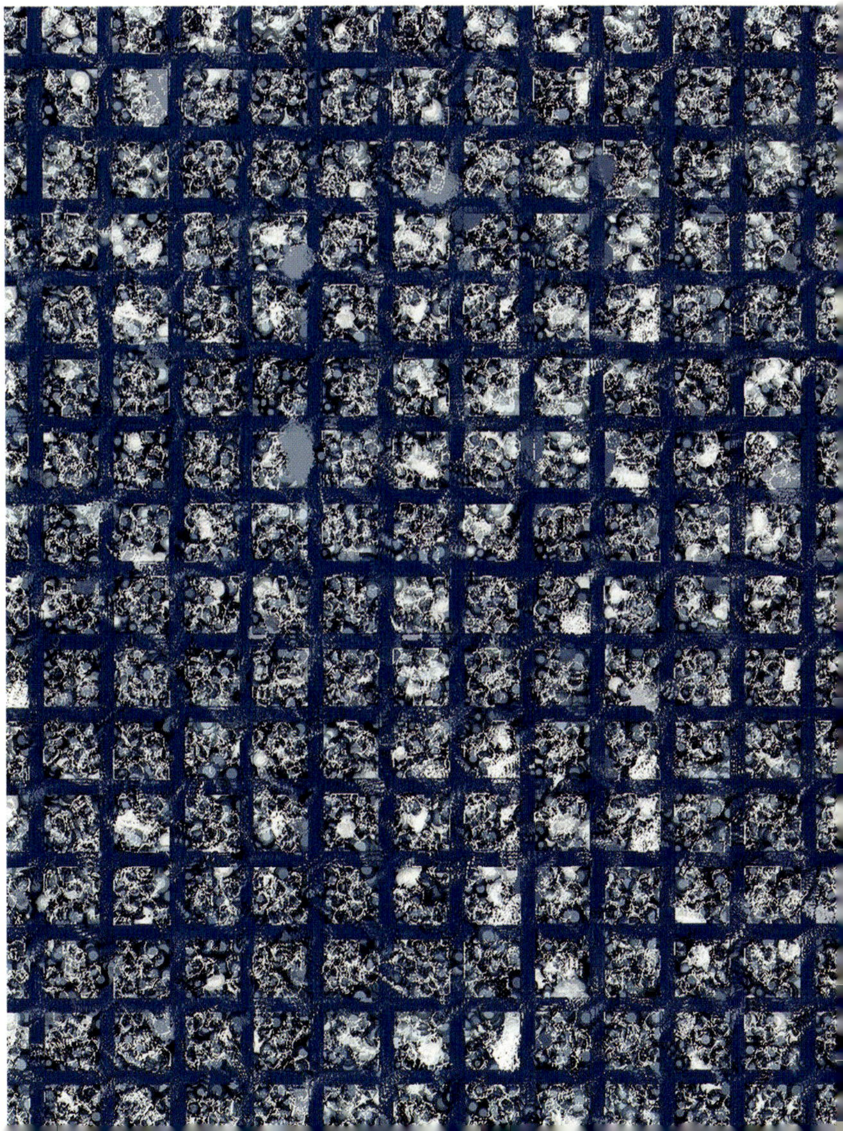

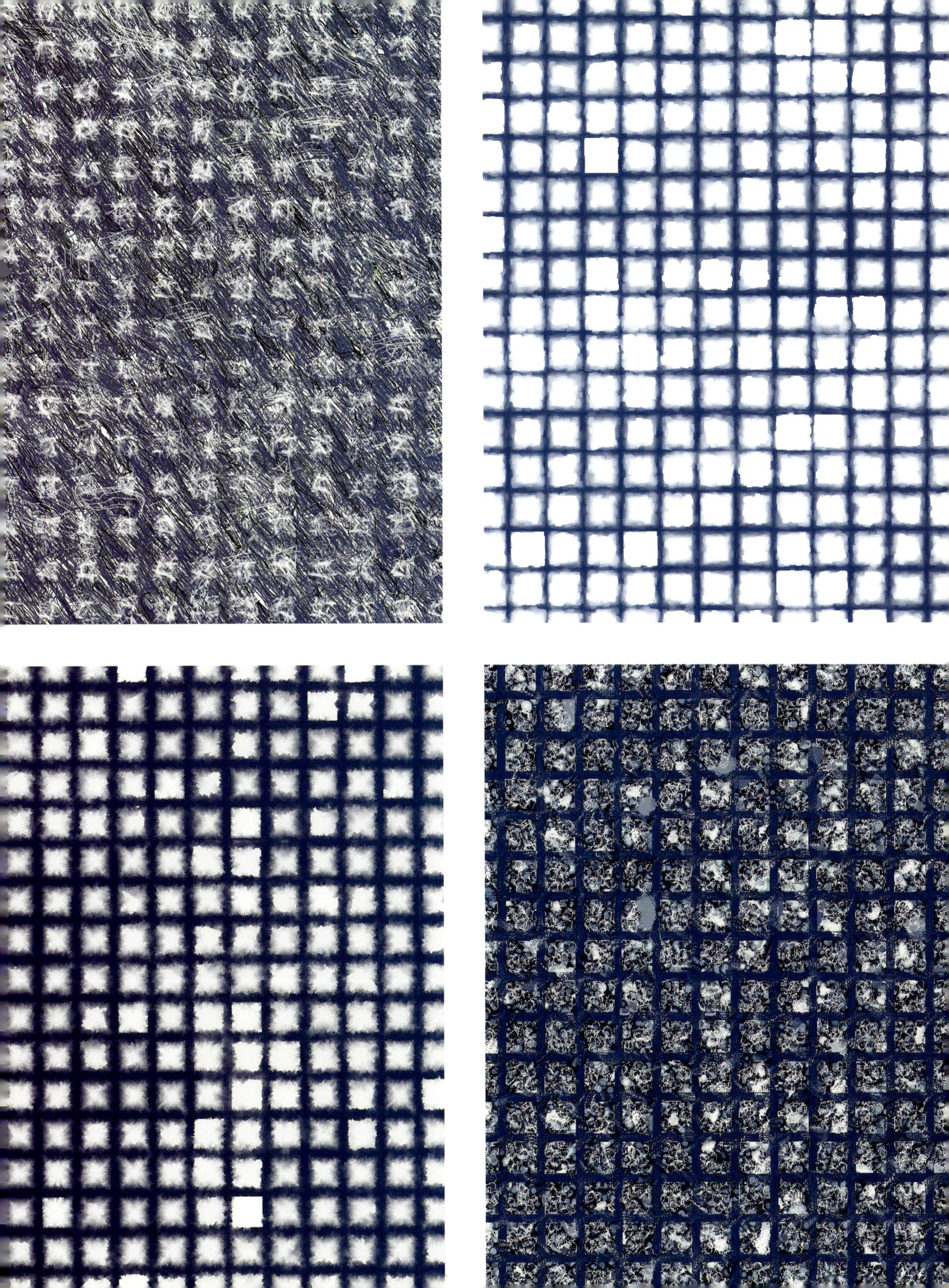

page 046

GGT0069
pattern size
48 cm x 60 cm
5670 x 7087 pixels
at 300 ppi in CMYK

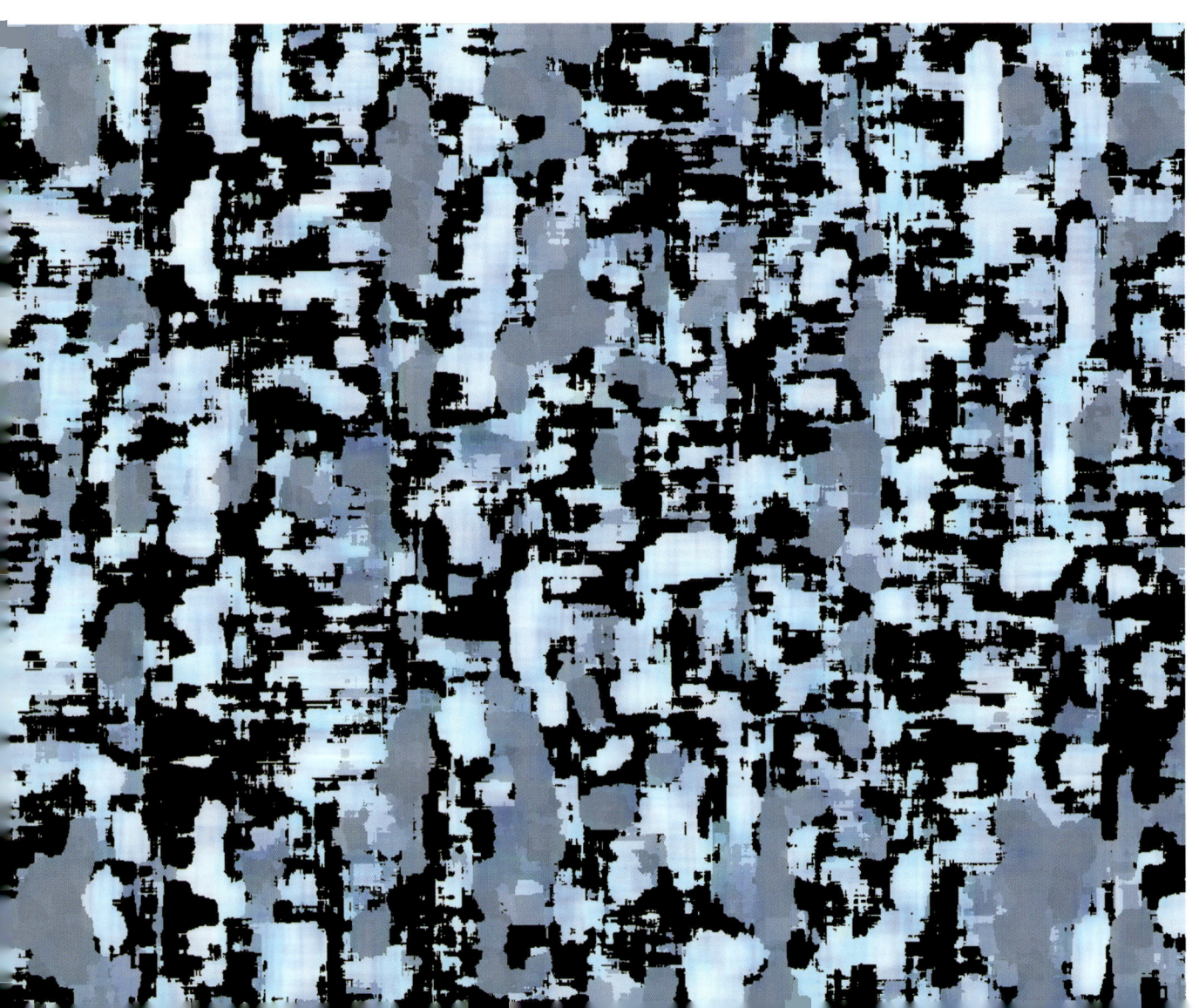

GGT0070
pattern size
45 cm x 60 cm
5315 x 7087 pixels
at 300 ppi in CMYK

page 047

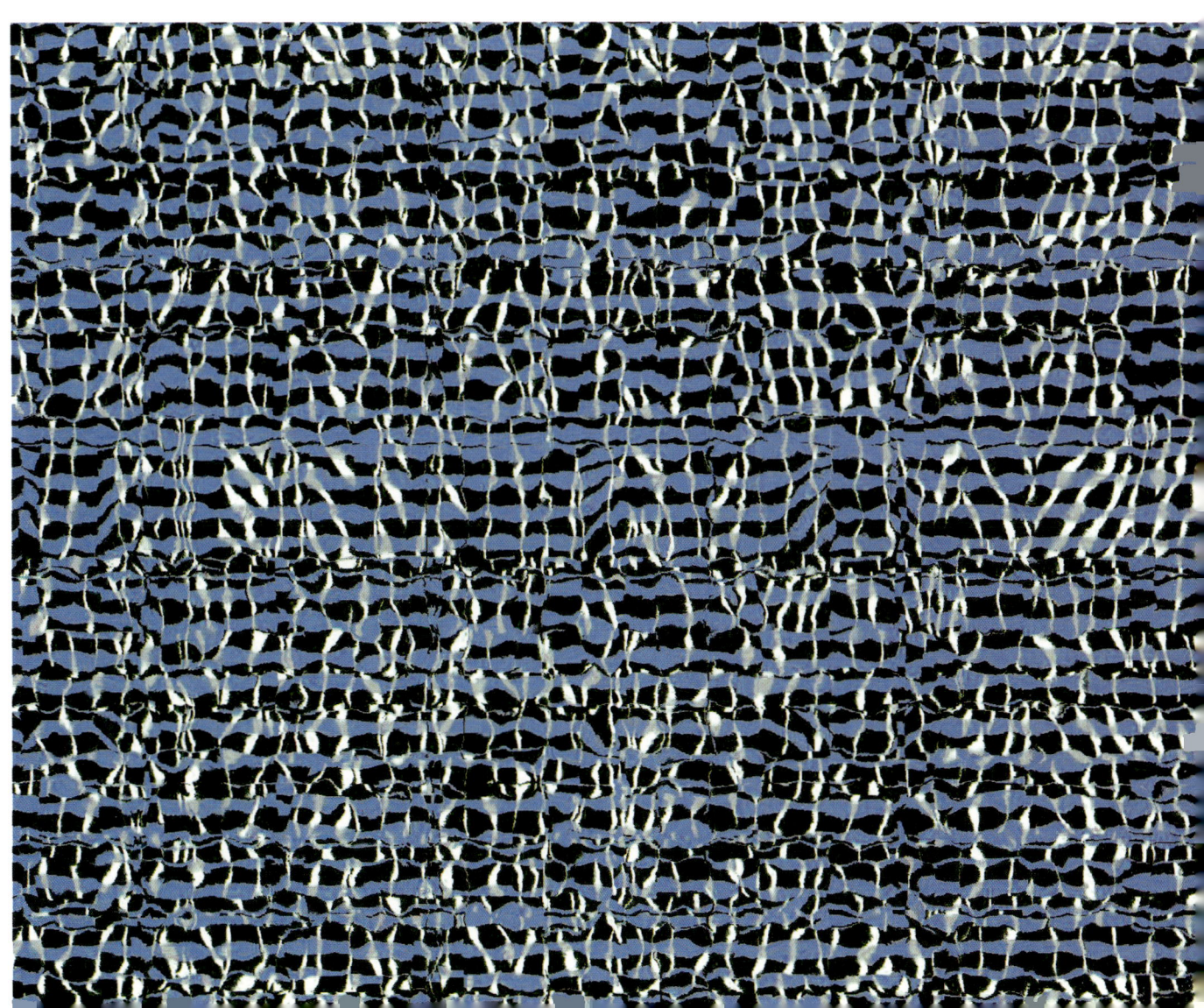

GGT0071
pattern size
60 cm x 60 cm
7087 x 7087 pixels
at 300 ppi in CMYK

GGT0072
pattern size
60 cm x 60 cm
7087 x 7087 pixels
at 300 ppi in CMYK

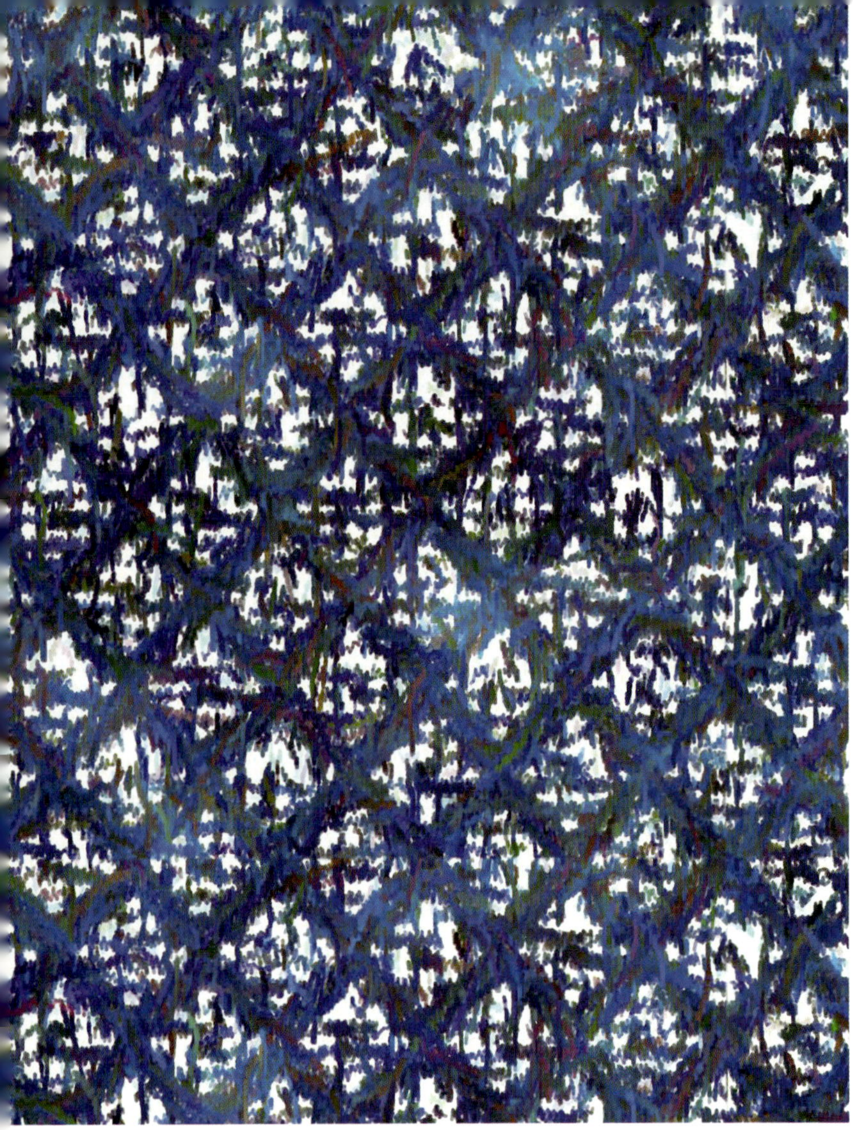

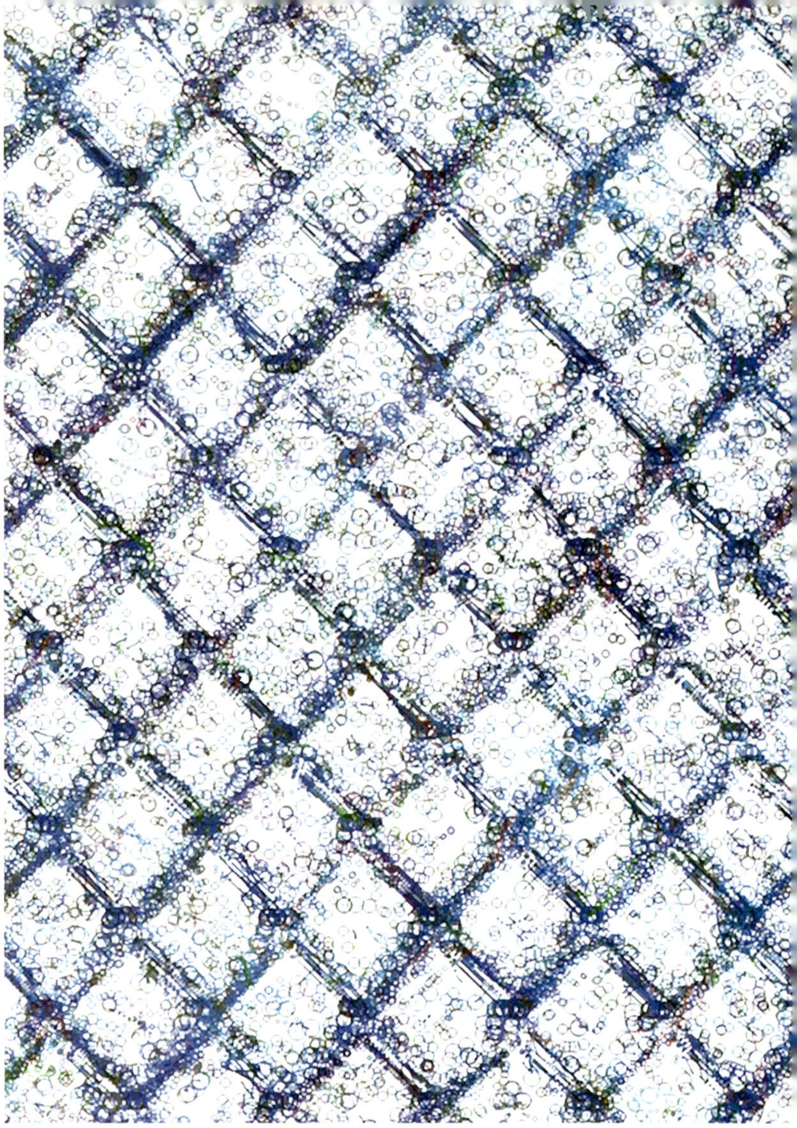

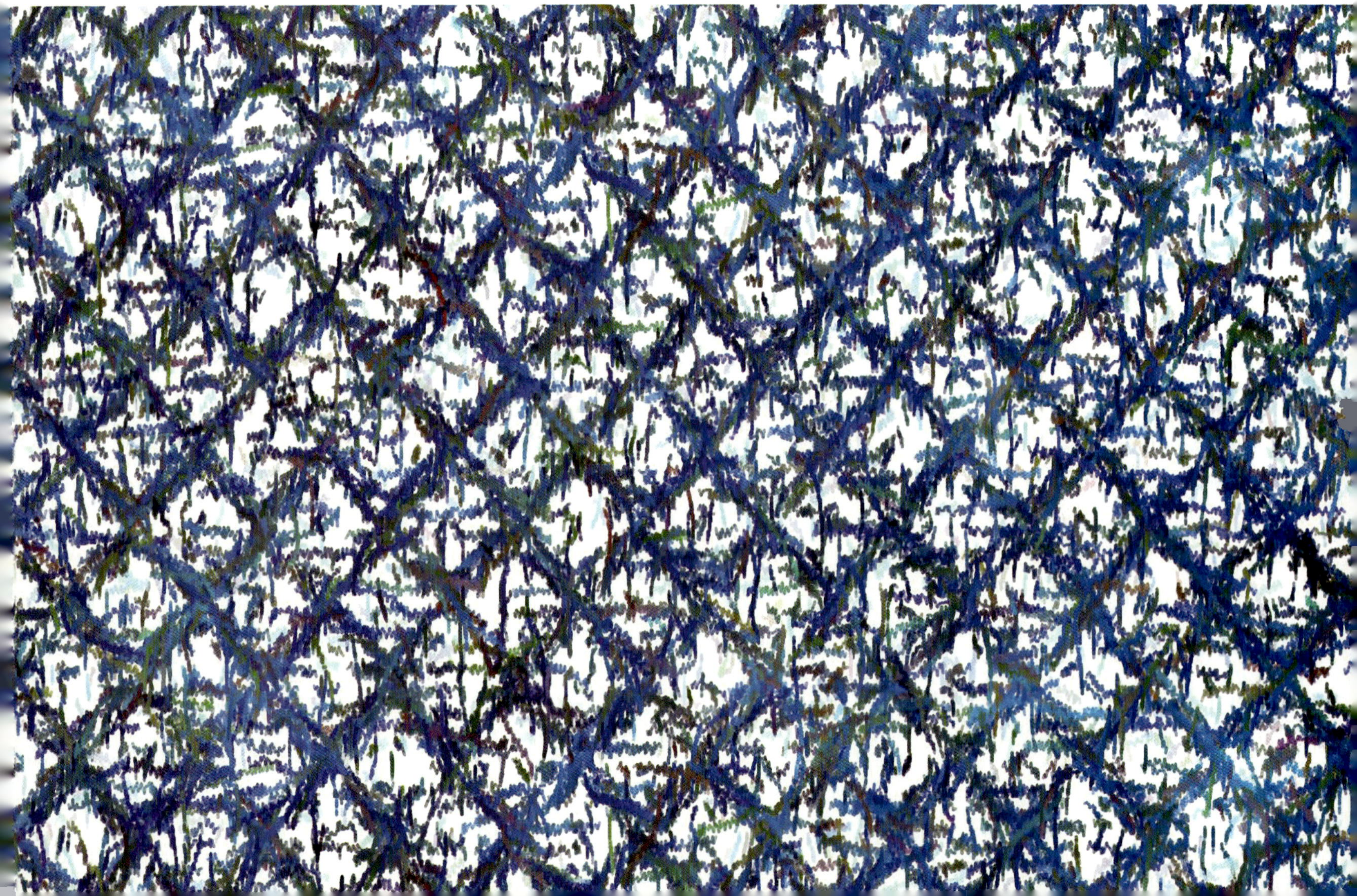

page 049

GGT0076
pattern size
60 cm x 60 cm
7087 x 7087 pixels
at 300 ppi in CMYK

GGT0077
pattern size
60 cm x 60 cm
7087 x 7087 pixels
at 300 ppi in CMYK

GGT0073
pattern size
60 cm x 45 cm
7087 x 5315 pixels
at 300 ppi in CMYK

GGT0074
pattern size
60 cm x 45 cm
7087 x 5315 pixels
at 300 ppi in CMYK

GGT0075
pattern size
50 cm x 45 cm
5906 x 5315 pixels
at 300 ppi in CMYK

< page 048

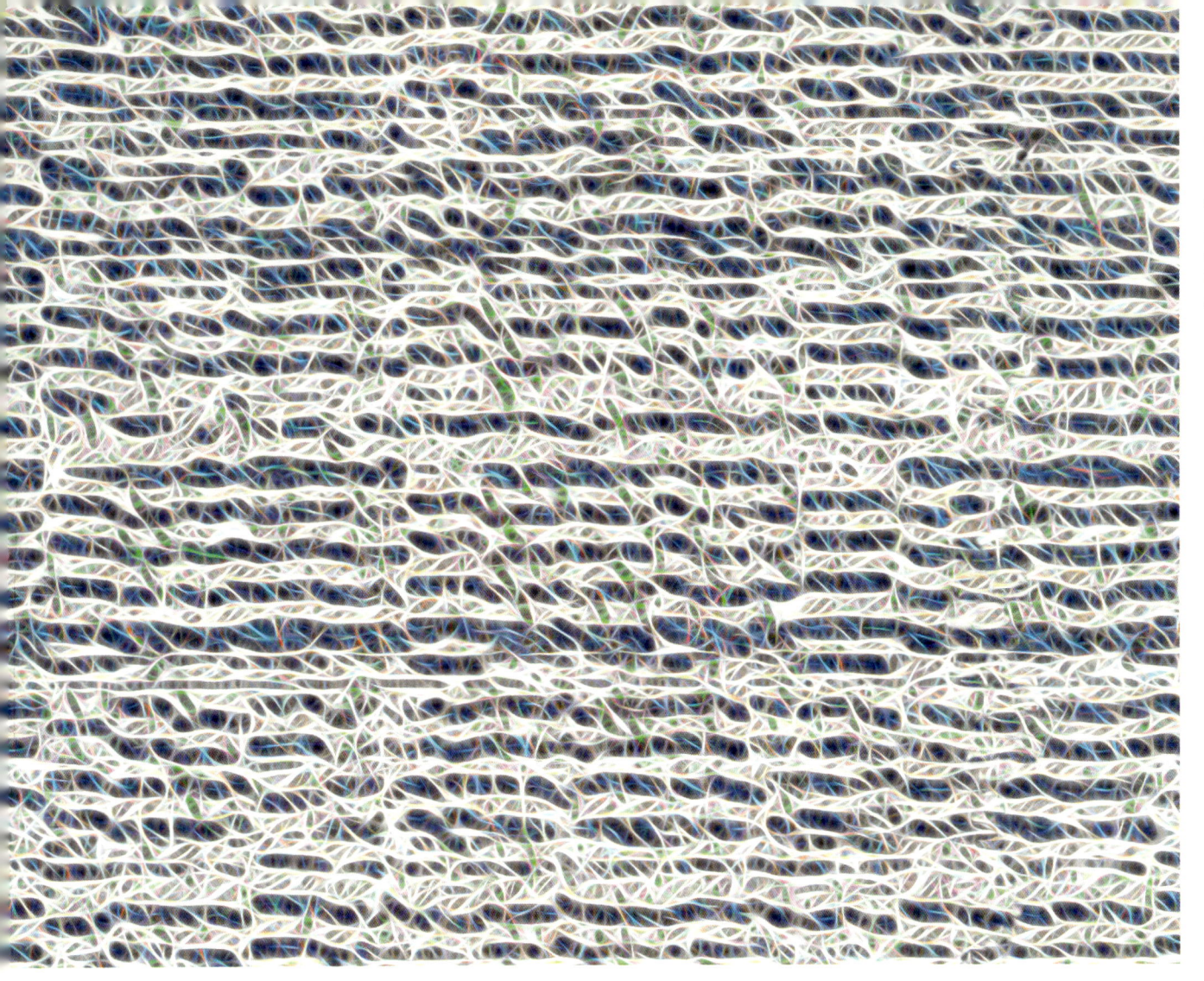

page 050

GGT0078
pattern size
60 cm x 60 cm
7087 x 7087 pixels
at 300 ppi in CMYK

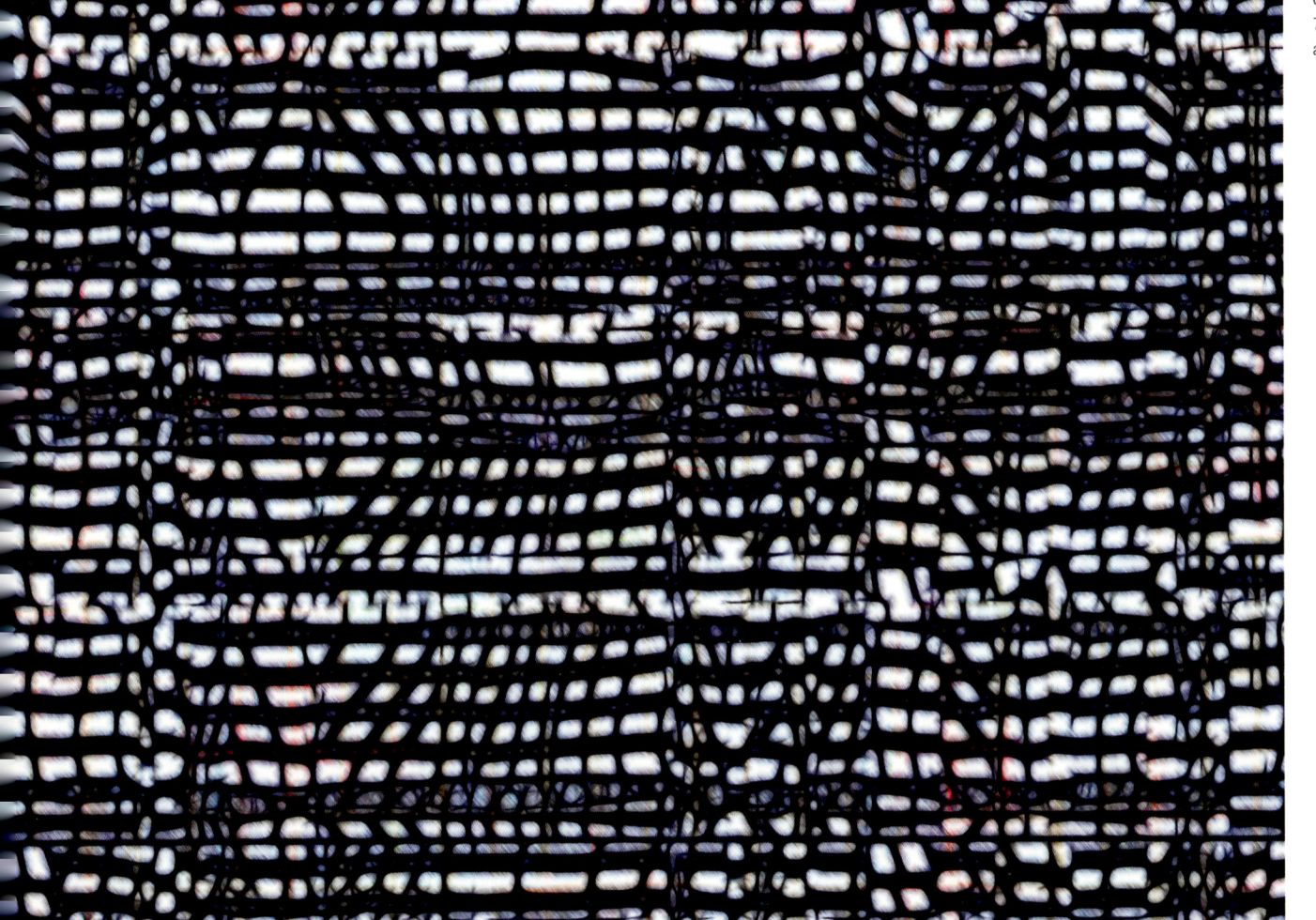

GGT0079
pattern size
60 cm x 60 cm
7087 x 7087 pixels
at 300 ppi in CMYK

GGT0080
pattern size
60 cm x 60 cm
7087 x 7087 pixels
at 300 ppi in CMYK

GGT0081
pattern size
60 cm x 60 cm
7087 x 7087 pixels
at 300 ppi in CMYK

GGT0082
pattern size
60 cm x 60 cm
7087 x 7087 pixels
at 300 ppi in CMYK

GGT0083
pattern size
60 cm x 60 cm
7087 x 7087 pixels
at 300 ppi in CMYK

page 051 >

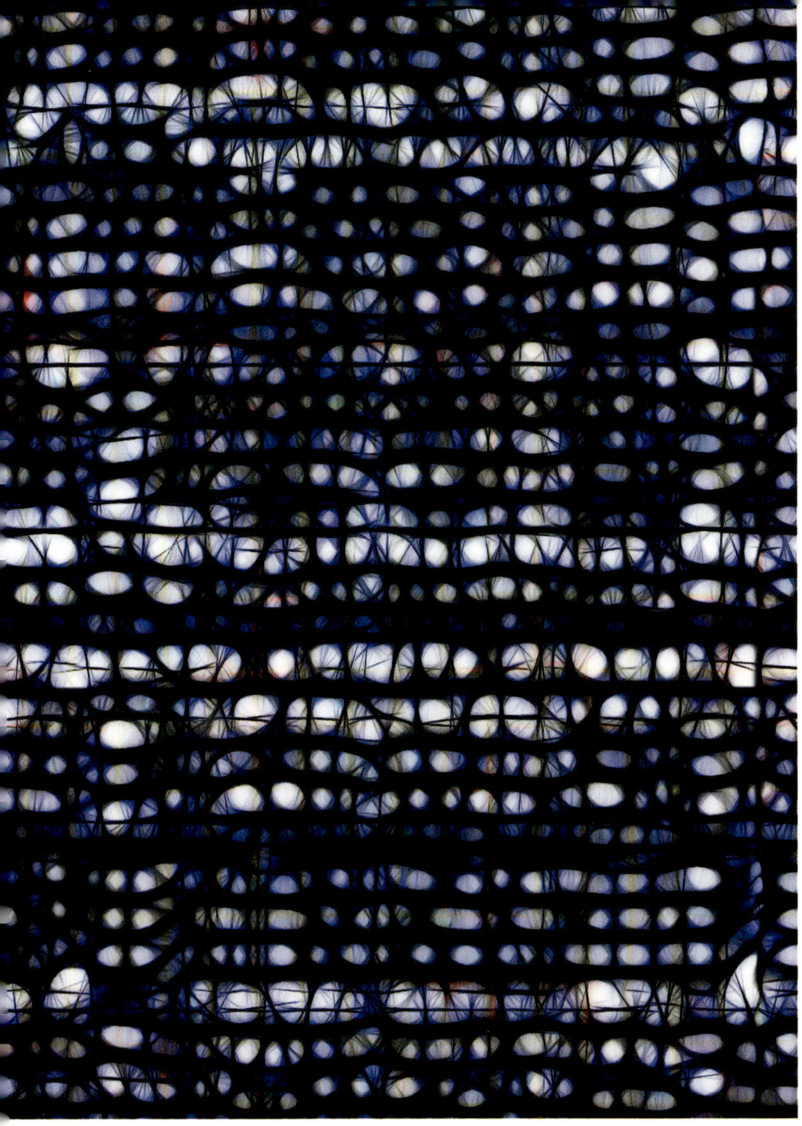
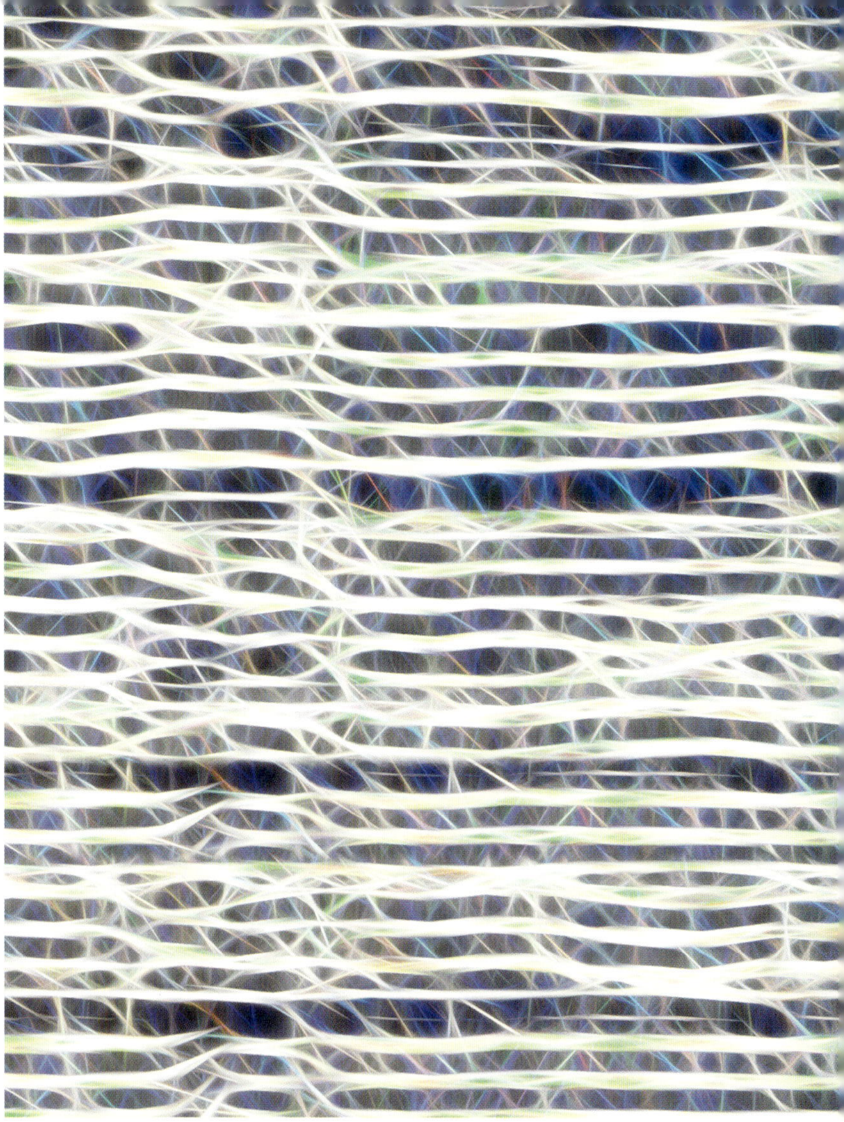
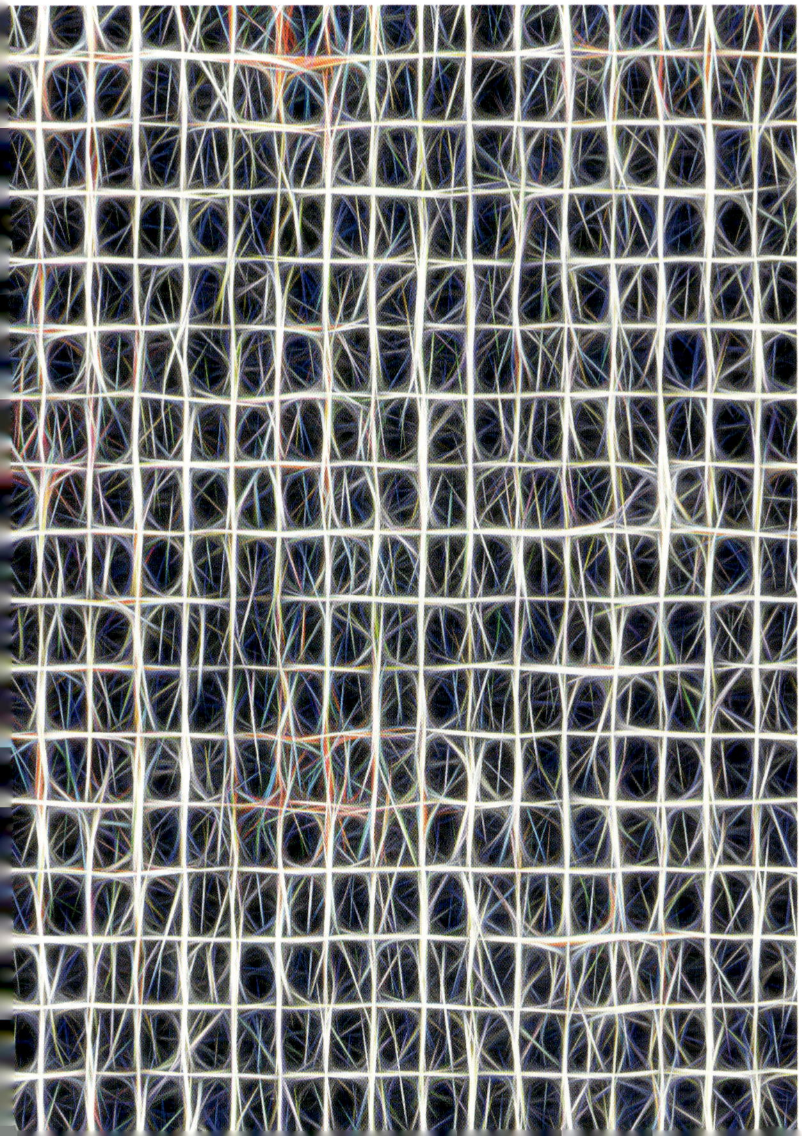
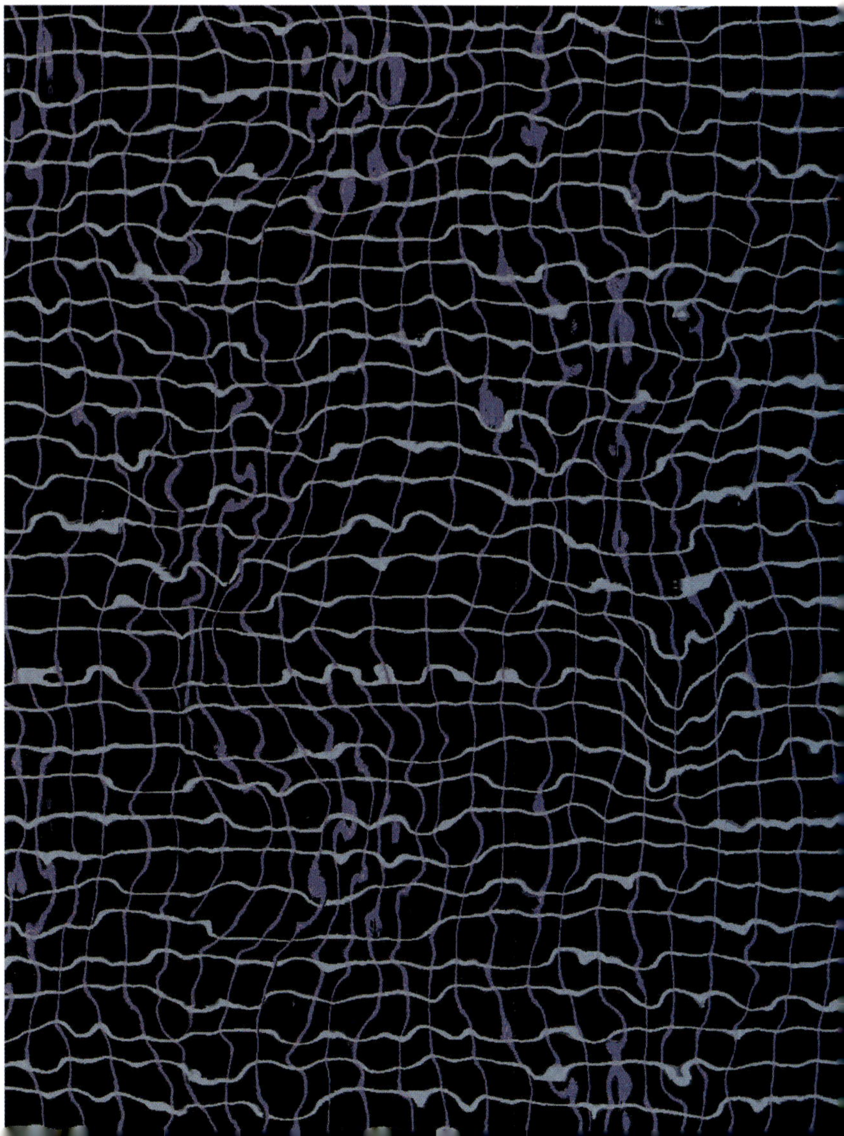

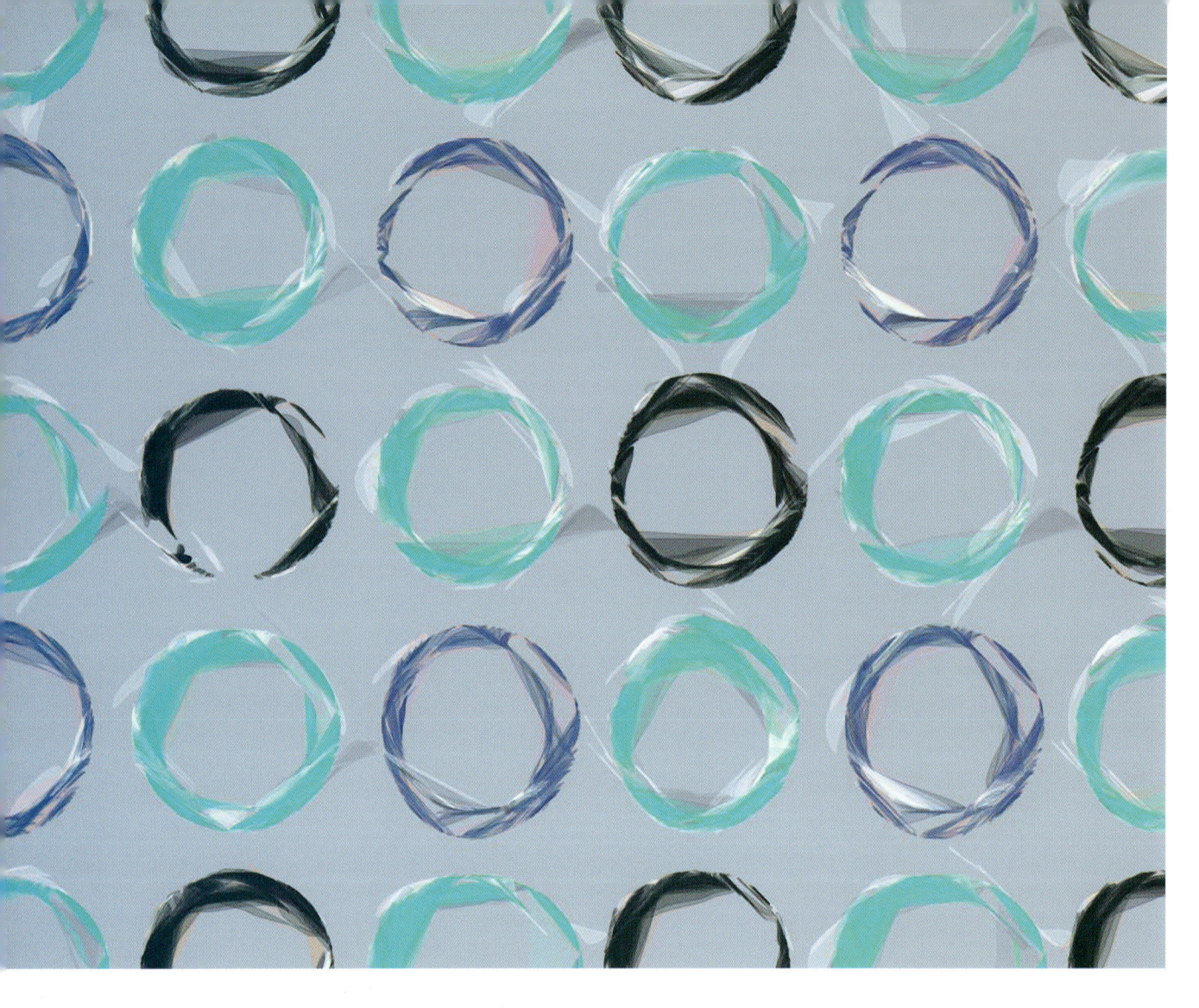

page 052

GGT0084
pattern size
45 cm x 60 cm
5315 x 7087 pixels
at 300 ppi in CMYK

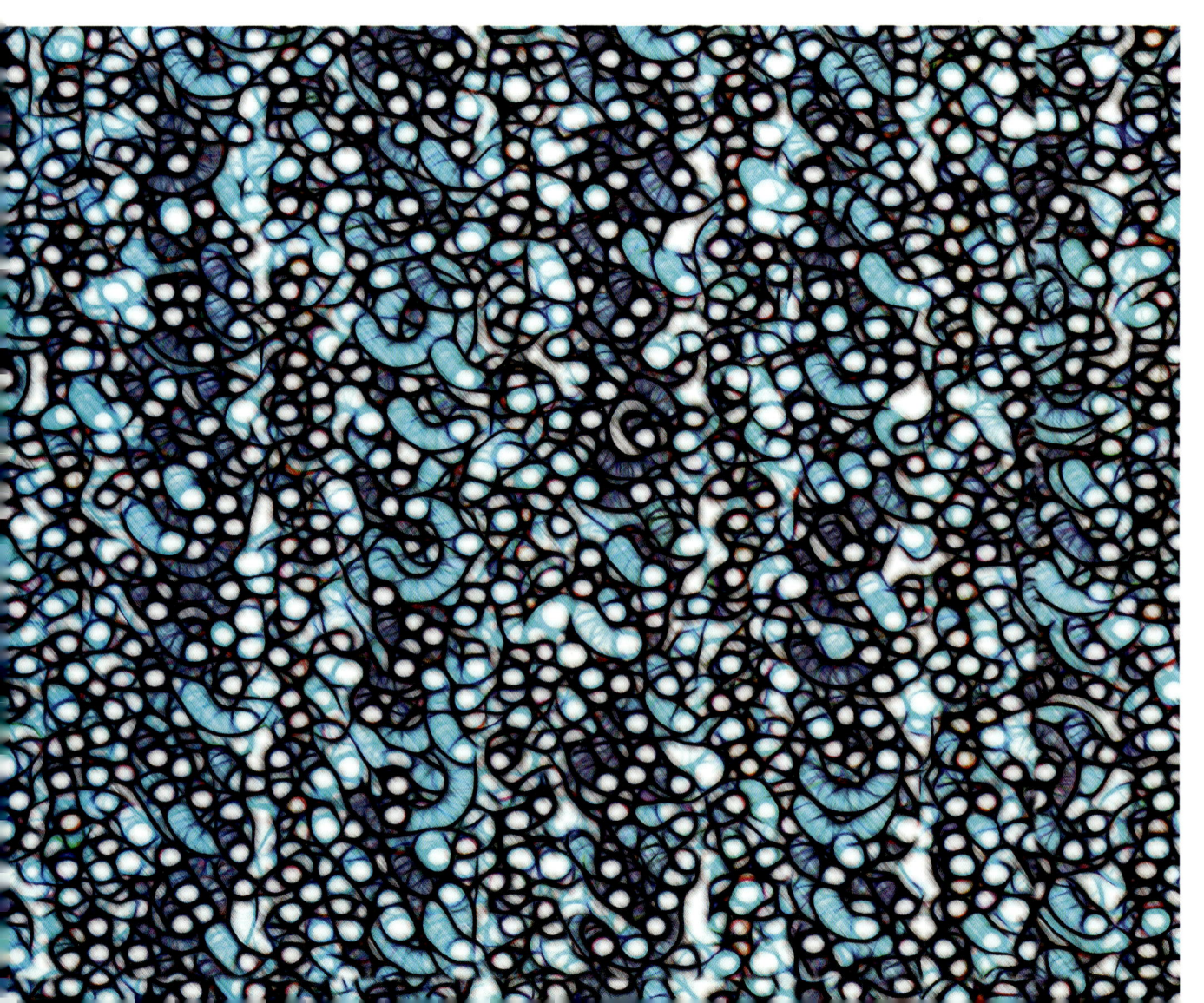

GGT0085
pattern size
45 cm x 60 cm
5315 x 7087 pixels
at 300 ppi in CMYK

page 053

GGT0086
pattern size
45 cm x 60 cm
5315 x 7087 pixels
at 300 ppi in CMYK

page 054

GGT0087
pattern size
50 cm x 50 cm
5906 x 5906 pixels
at 300 ppi in CMYK

page 055

GGT0088
pattern size
50 cm x 60 cm
5906 x 7087 pixels
at 300 ppi in CMYK

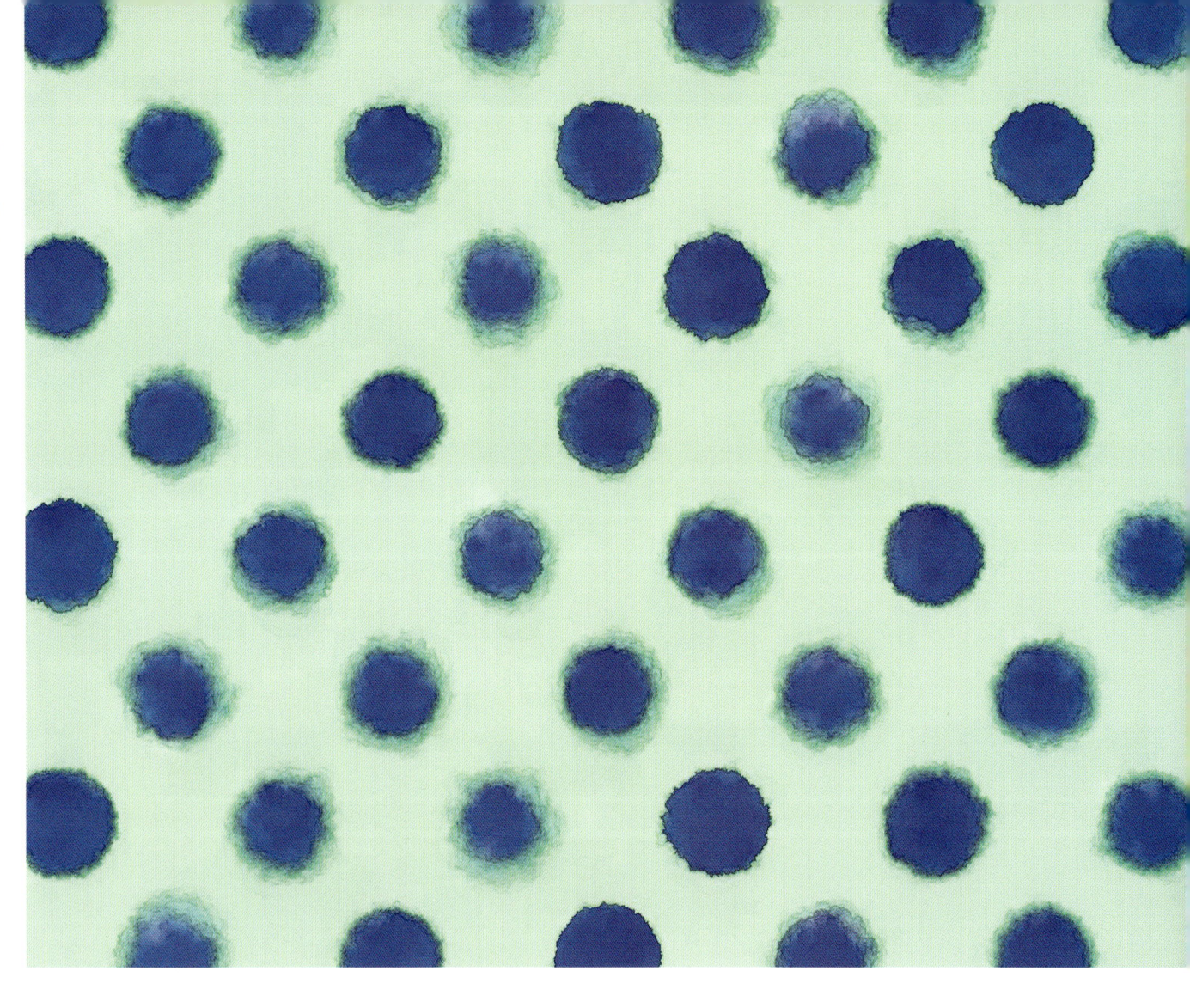

GGT0089
pattern size
50 cm x 60 cm
5906 x 7087 pixels
at 300 ppi in CMYK

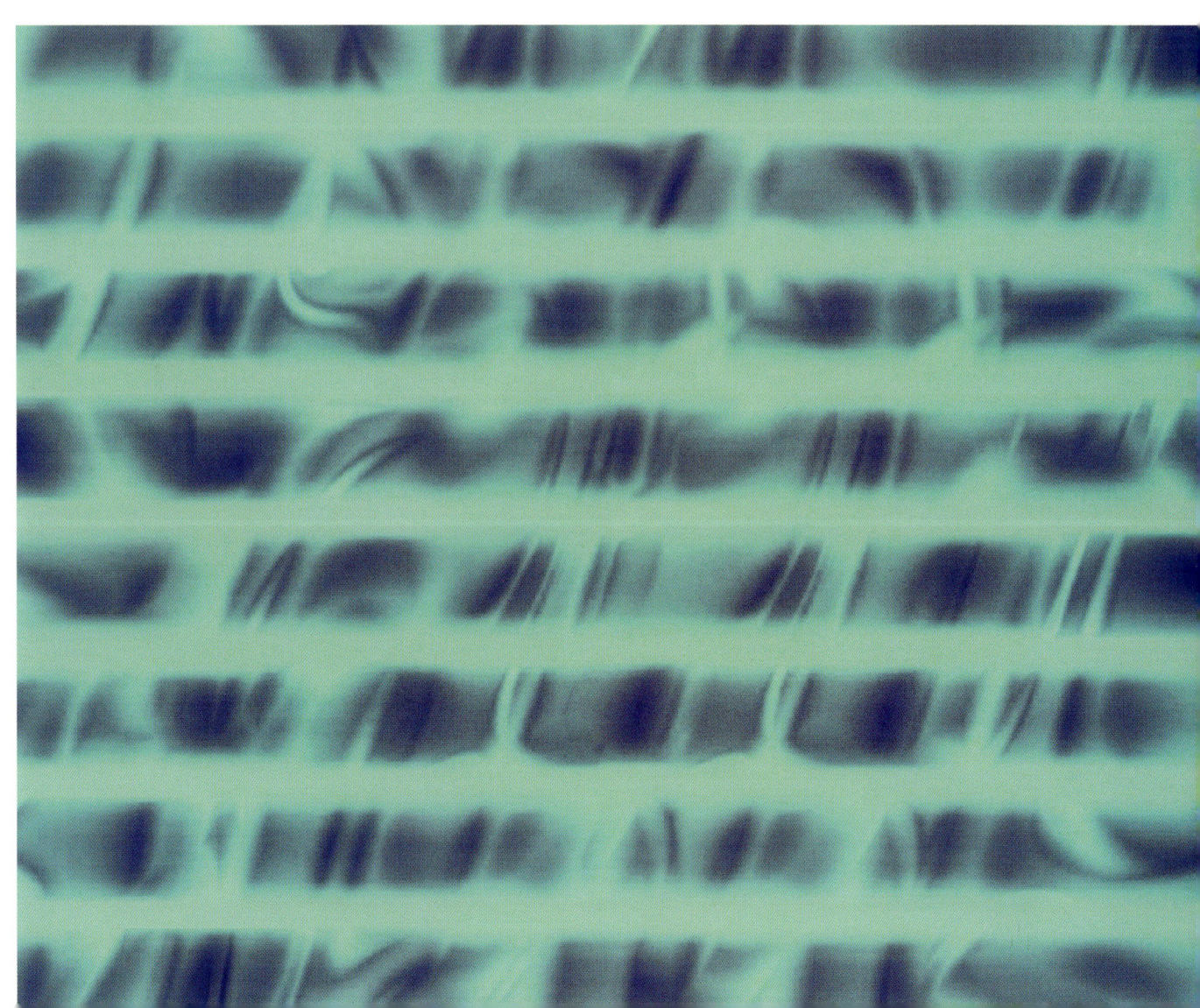

page 056

GGT0090
pattern size
50 cm x 65 cm
5906 x 7678 pixels
at 300 ppi in CMYK

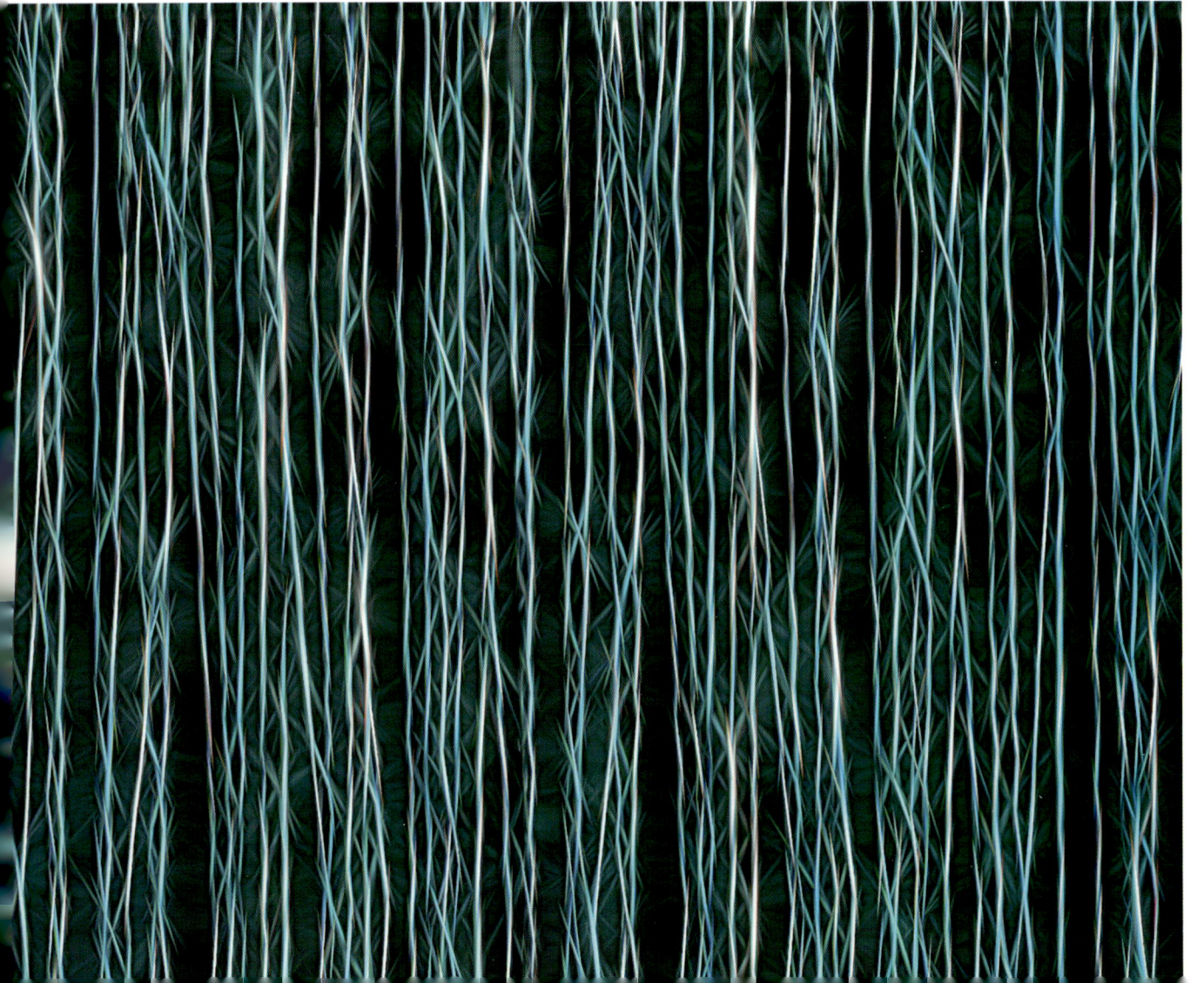

GGT0091
pattern size
50 cm x 60 cm
5906 x 7087 pixels
at 300 ppi in CMYK

page 057

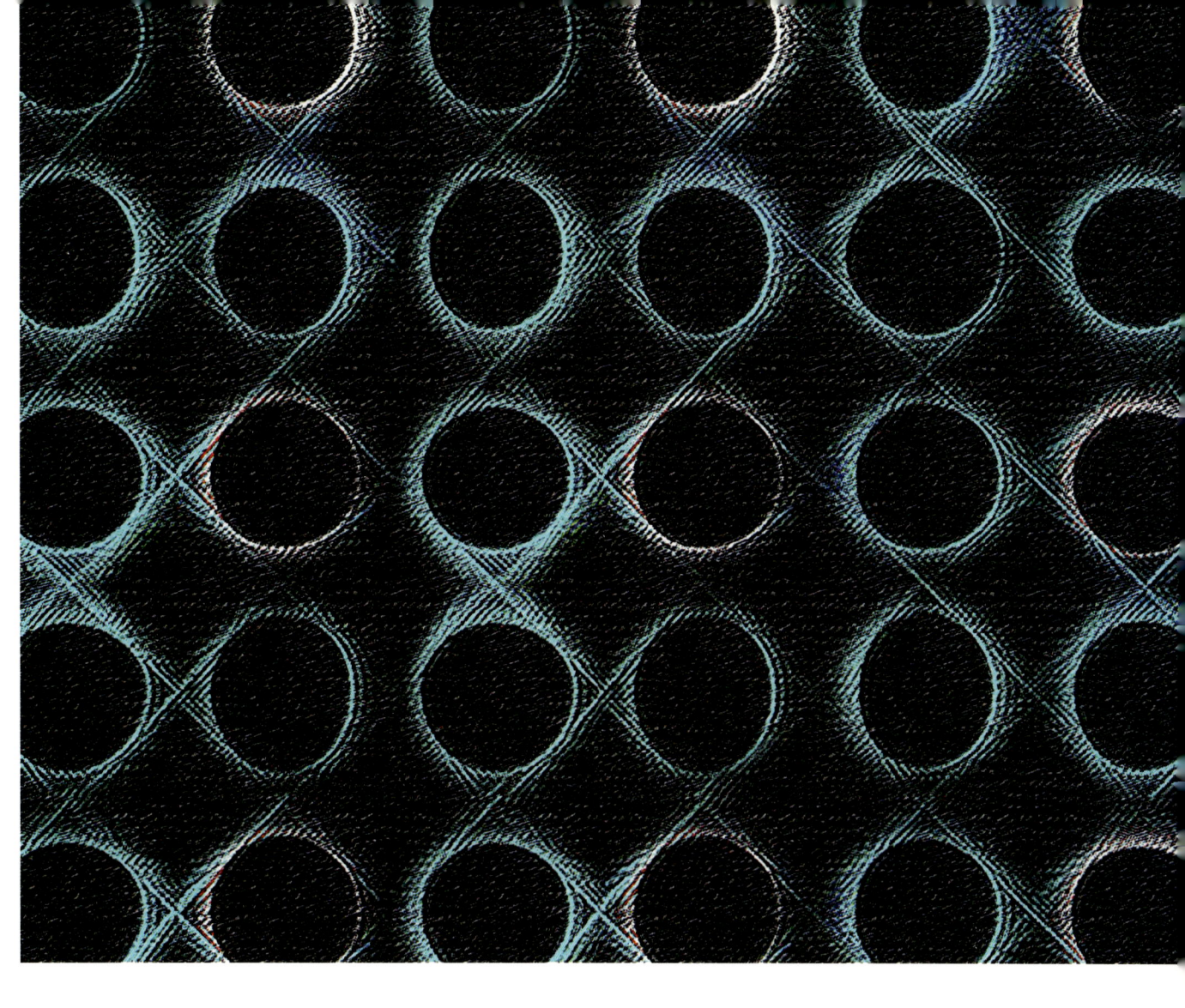

GGT0092
pattern size
45 cm x 60 cm
5315 x 7087 pixels
at 300 ppi in CMYK

GGT0093
pattern size
45 cm x 60 cm
5315 x 7087 pixels
at 300 ppi in CMYK

page 058

GGT0094
pattern size
50 cm x 50 cm
5906 x 5906 pixels
at 300 ppi in CMYK

page 059

GGT0095
pattern size
50 cm x 50 cm
5906 x 5906 pixels
at 300 ppi in CMYK

GGT0096
pattern size
50 cm x 55 cm
5906 x 6497 pixels
at 300 ppi in CMYK

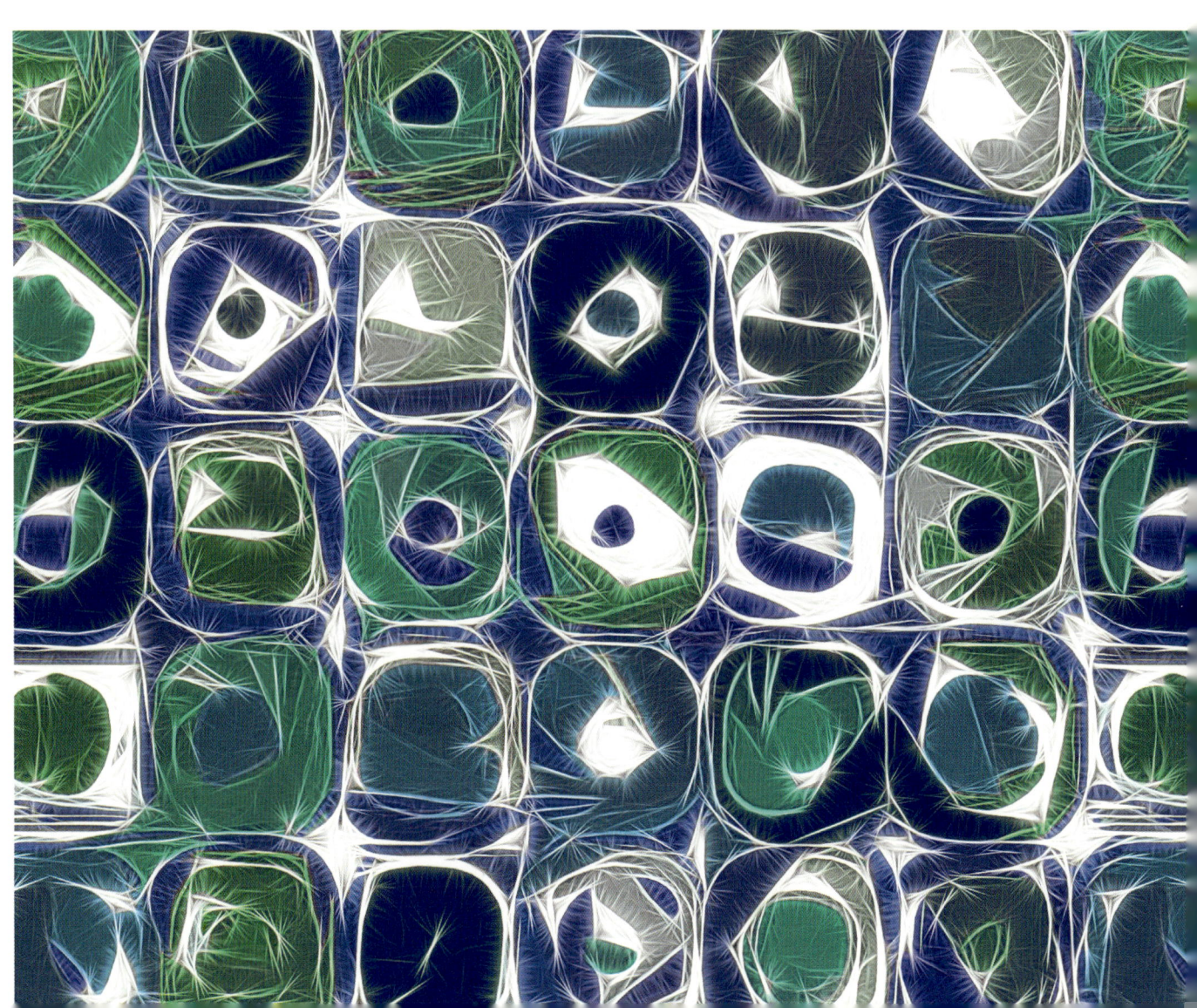

page 060

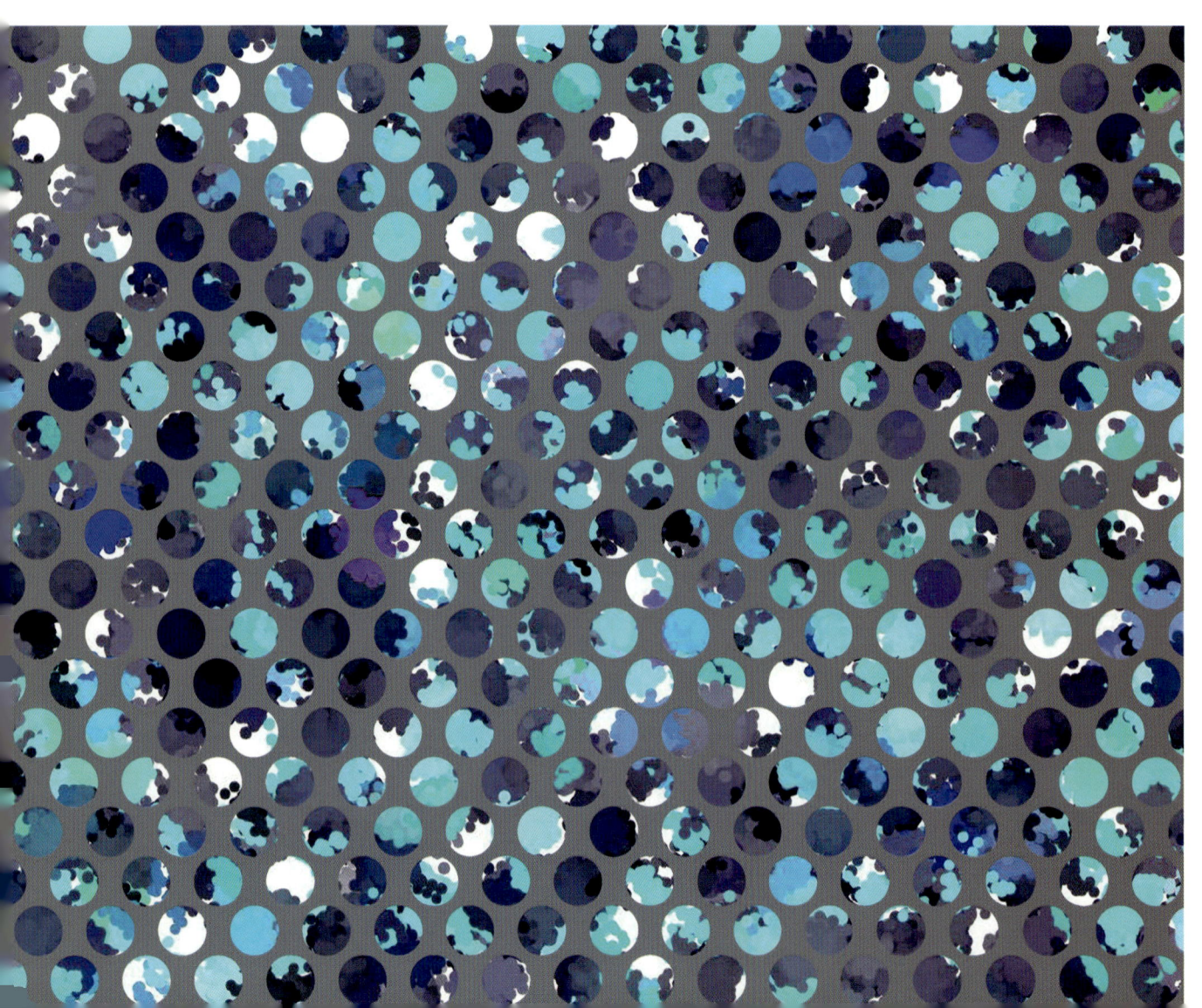

GGT0097
pattern size
50 cm x 60 cm
5906 x 7087 pixels
at 300 ppi in CMYK

GGT0098
pattern size
50 cm x 60 cm
5906 x 7087 pixels
at 300 ppi in CMYK

page 061

GGT0099
pattern size
50 cm x 60 cm
5906 x 7087 pixels
at 300 ppi in CMYK

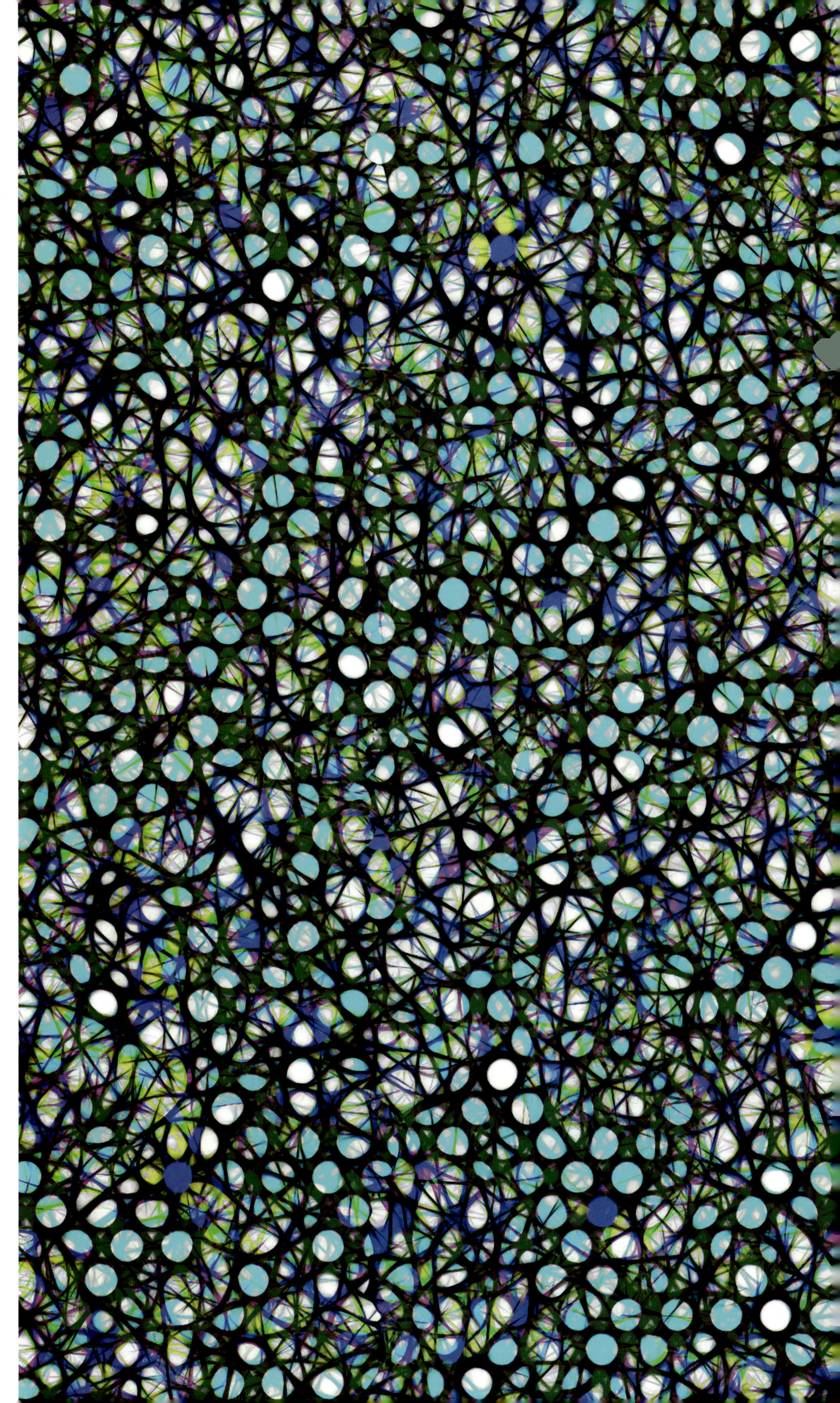

page 062

GGT0100
pattern size
40 cm x 40 cm
4725 x 4725 pixels
at 300 ppi in CMYK

GGT0101
pattern size
40 cm x 40 cm
4725 x 4725 pixels
at 300 ppi in CMYK

page 063

GGT0102
pattern size
60 cm x 75 cm
7087 x 8859 pixels
at 300 ppi in CMYK

GGT0103
pattern size
60 cm x 75 cm
7087 x 8859 pixels
at 300 ppi in CMYK

page 064

GGT0104
pattern size
45 cm x 60 cm
5315 x 7087 pixels
at 300 ppi in CMYK

GGT0105
pattern size
45 cm x 60 cm
5315 x 7087 pixels
at 300 ppi in CMYK

page 065

GGT0106
pattern size
60 cm x 70 cm
7087 x 8268 pixels
at 300 ppi in CMYK

page 066

GGT0107
pattern size
60 cm x 75 cm
7087 x 8859 pixels
at 300 ppi in CMYK

page 067

GGT0108
pattern size
80 cm x 60 cm
9449 x 7087 pixels
at 300 ppi in CMYK

GGT0109
pattern size
80 cm x 60 cm
9449 x 7087 pixels
at 300 ppi in CMYK

page 068

GGT0110
pattern size
45 cm x 60 cm
5315 x 7087 pixels
at 300 ppi in CMYK

page 069

GGT0111
pattern size
45 cm x 60 cm
5315 x 7087 pixels
at 300 ppi in CMYK

GGT0112
pattern size
45 cm x 60 cm
5315 x 7087 pixels
at 300 ppi in CMYK

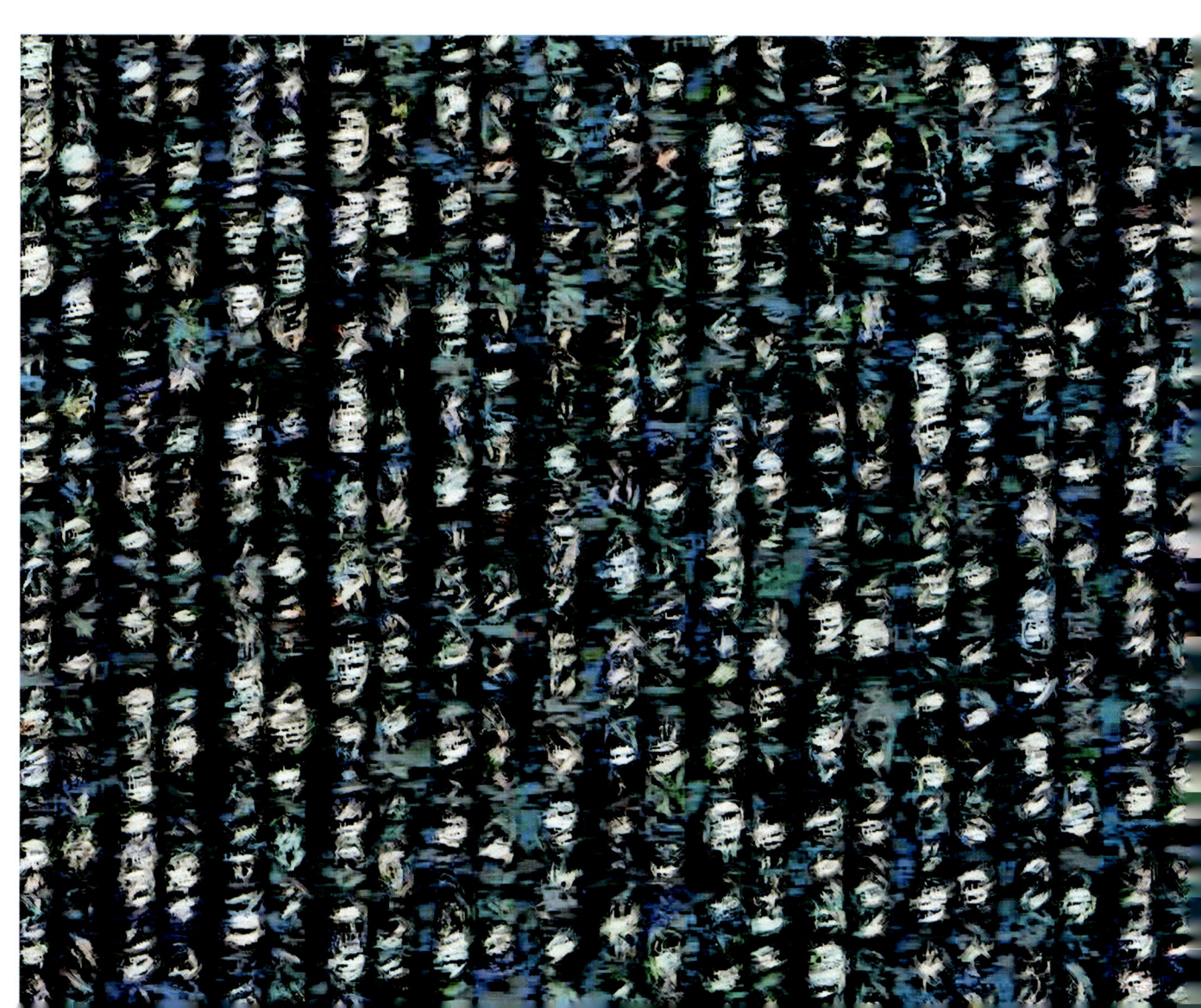

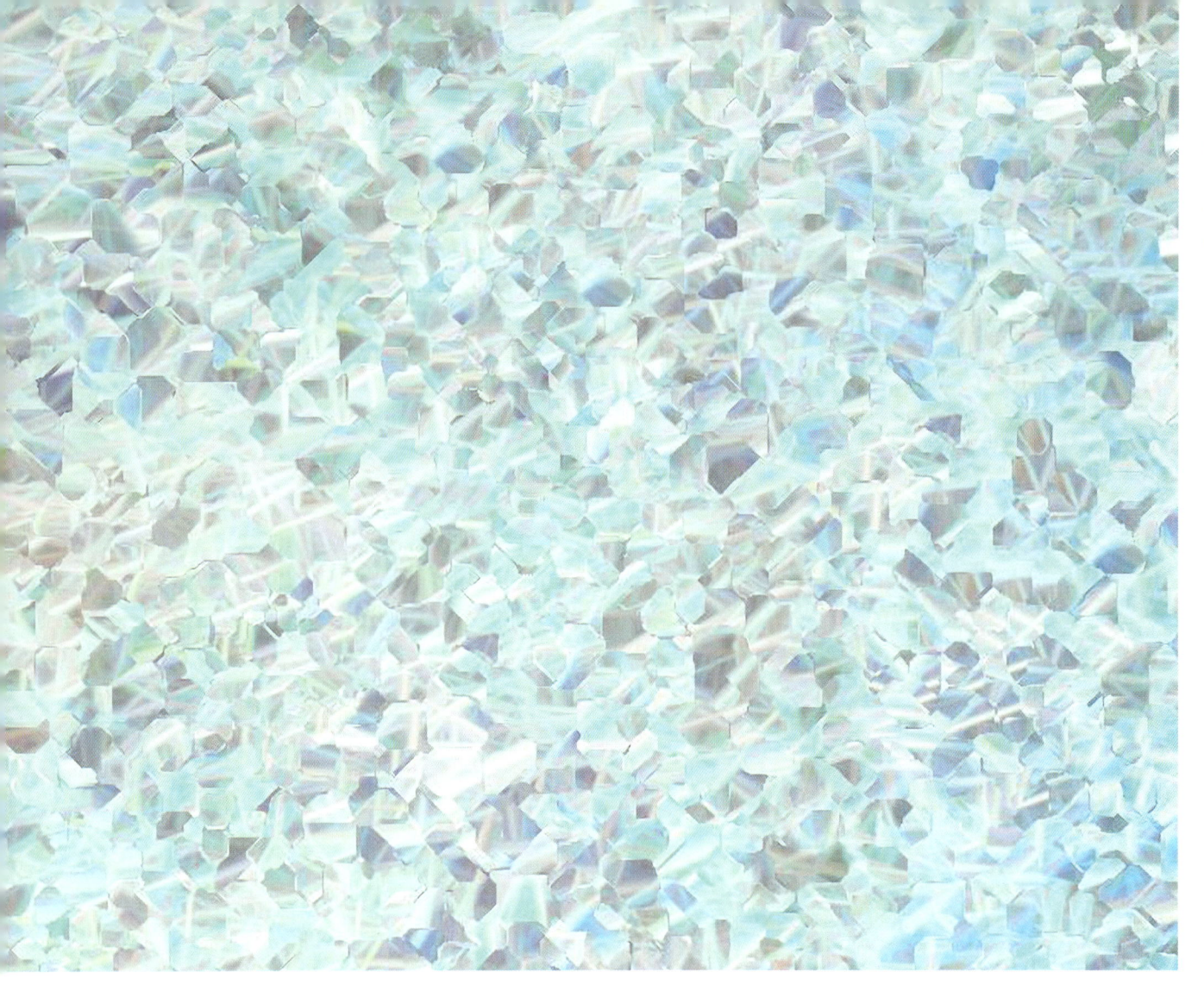

page 070

GGT0113
pattern size
45 cm x 60 cm
5315 x 7087 pixels
at 300 ppi in CMYK

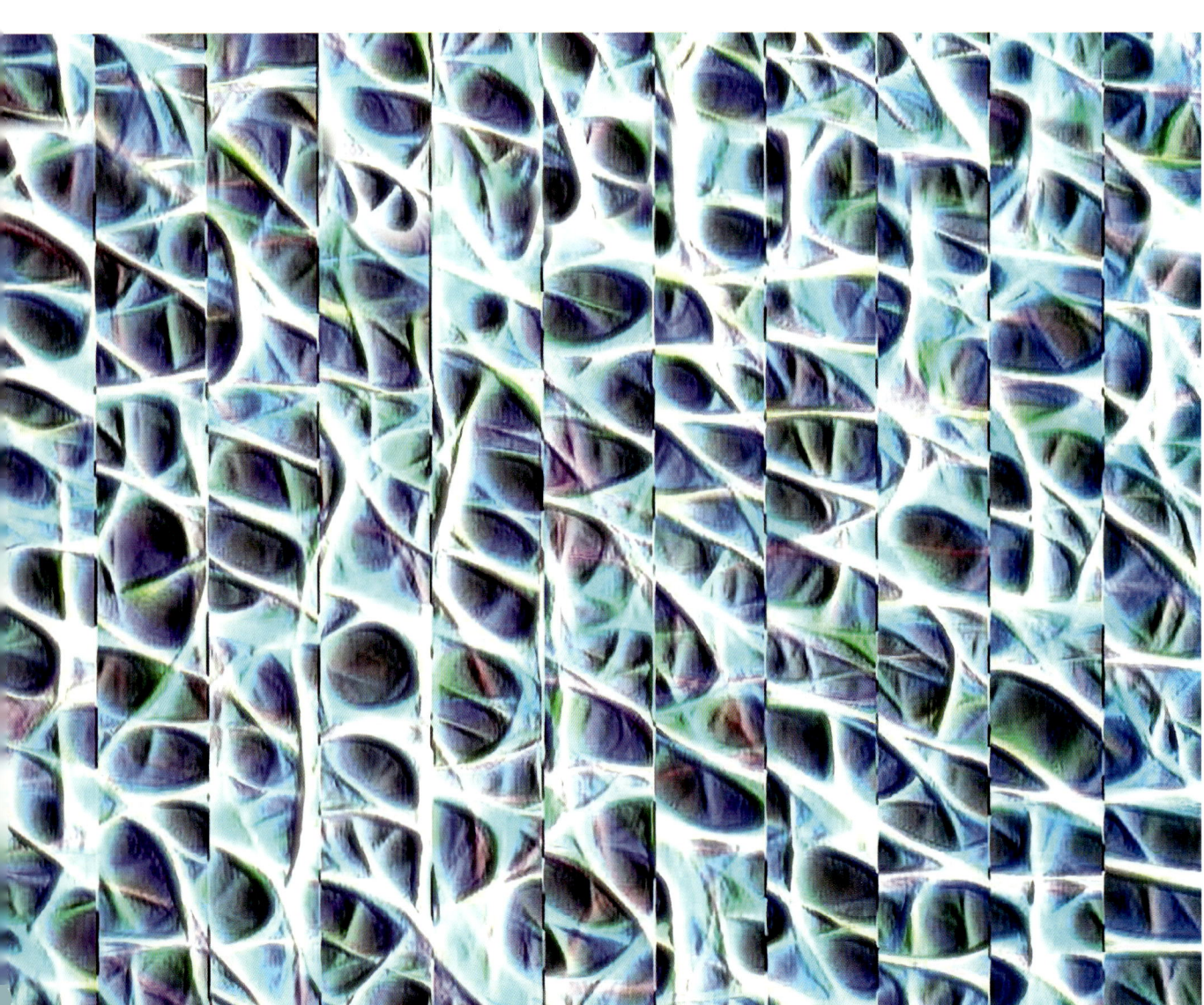

GGT0114
pattern size
45 cm x 60 cm
5315 x 7087 pixels
at 300 ppi in CMYK

page 071

GGT0115
pattern size
72 cm x 72 cm
8504 x 8504 pixels
at 300 ppi in CMYK

page 072

GGT0116
pattern size
60 cm x 60 cm
7087 x 7087 pixels
at 300 ppi in CMYK

page 073

GGT0117
pattern size
50 cm x 60 cm
5906 x 7087 pixels
at 300 ppi in CMYK

GGT0118
pattern size
50 cm x 50 cm
5906 x 5906 pixels
at 300 ppi in CMYK

page 074

GGT0119
pattern size
60 cm x 50 cm
7087 x 5906 pixels
at 300 ppi in CMYK

GGT0120
pattern size
70 cm x 70 cm
8268 x 8268 pixels
at 300 ppi in CMYK

page 075

GGT0121
pattern size
60 cm x 60 cm
7087 x 7087 pixels
at 300 ppi in CMYK

GGT0122
pattern size
50 cm x 50 cm
5906 x 5906 pixels
at 300 ppi in CMYK

page 076

GGT0123
pattern size
50 cm x 50 cm
5906 x 5906 pixels
at 300 ppi in CMYK

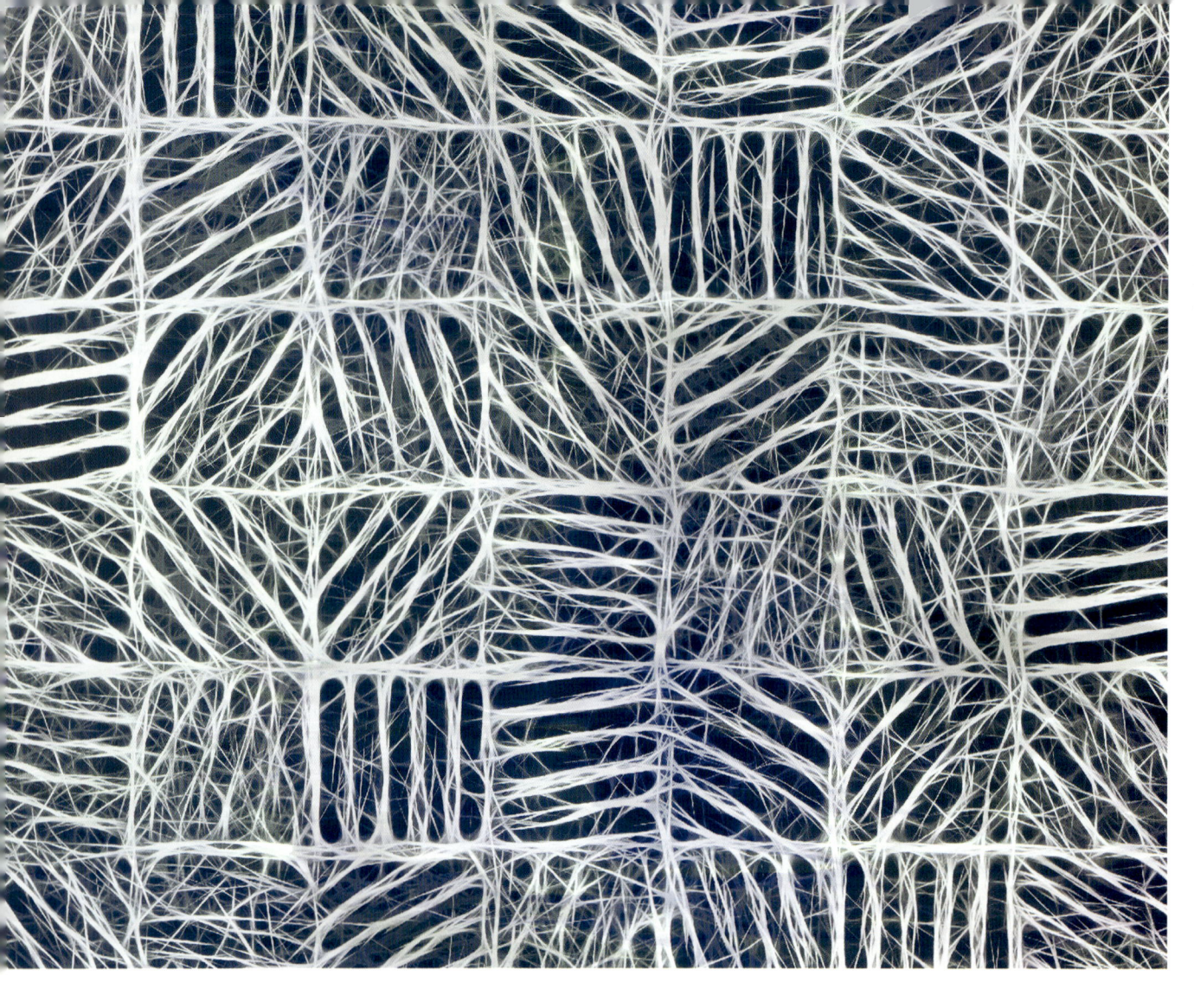

GGT0124
pattern size
50 cm x 70 cm
5906 x 8268 pixels
at 300 ppi in CMYK

page 077

GGT0125
pattern size
70 cm x 70 cm
8268 x 8268 pixels
at 300 ppi in CMYK

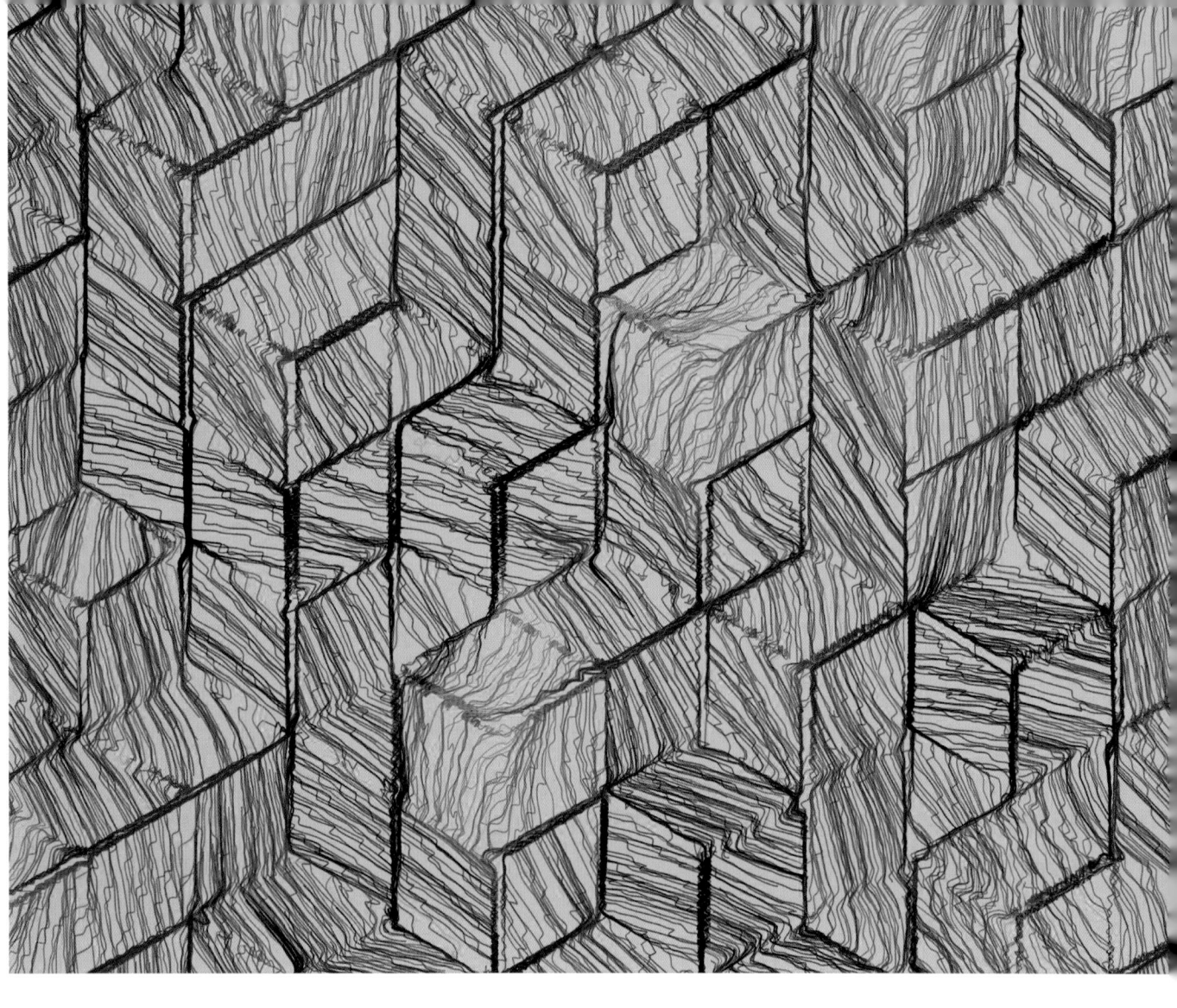

GGT0126
pattern size
70 cm x 70 cm
8268 x 8268 pixels
at 300 ppi in CMYK

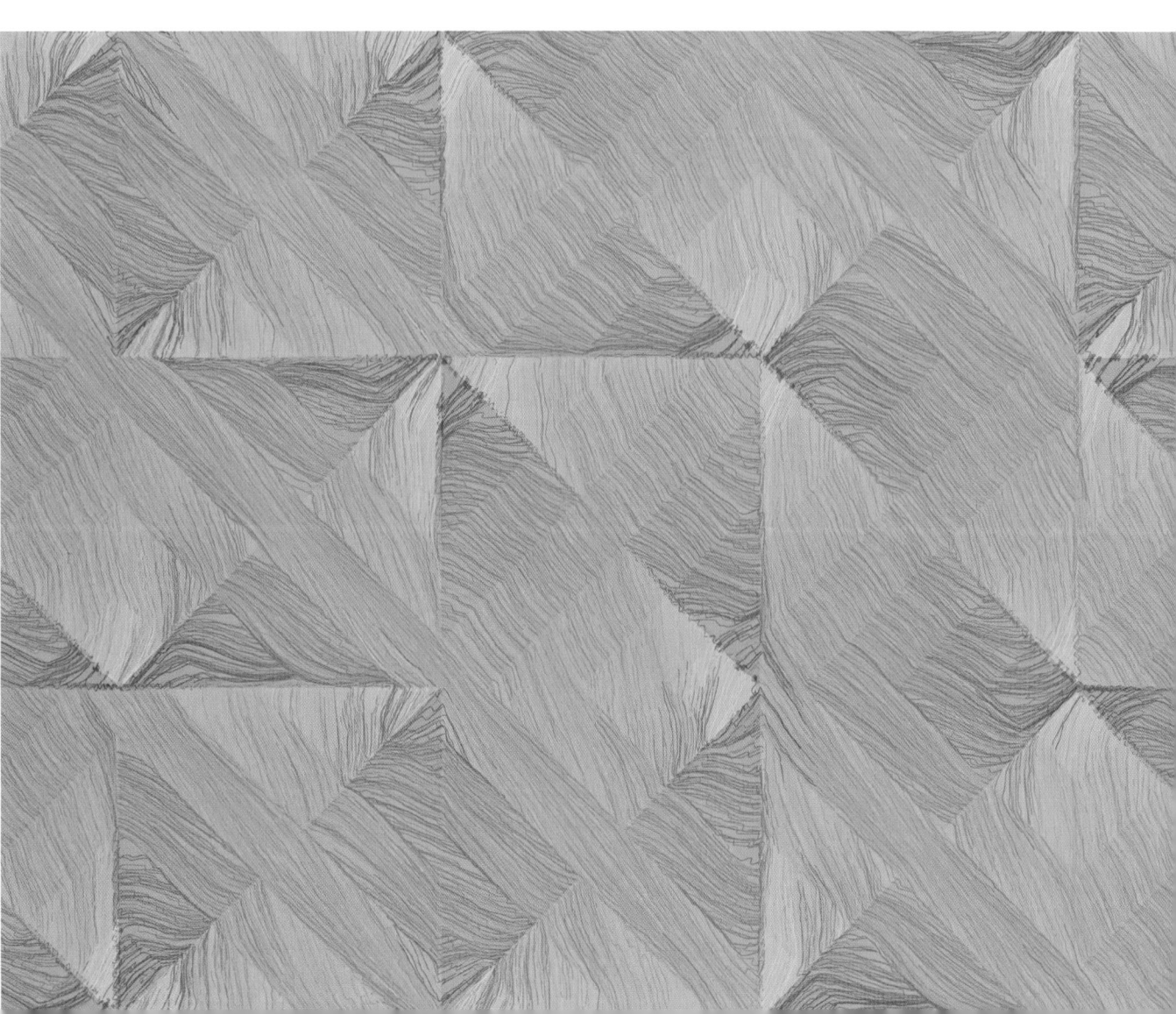

page 078

GGT0127
pattern size
42 cm x 50 cm
4961 x 5906 pixels
at 300 ppi in CMYK

page 079

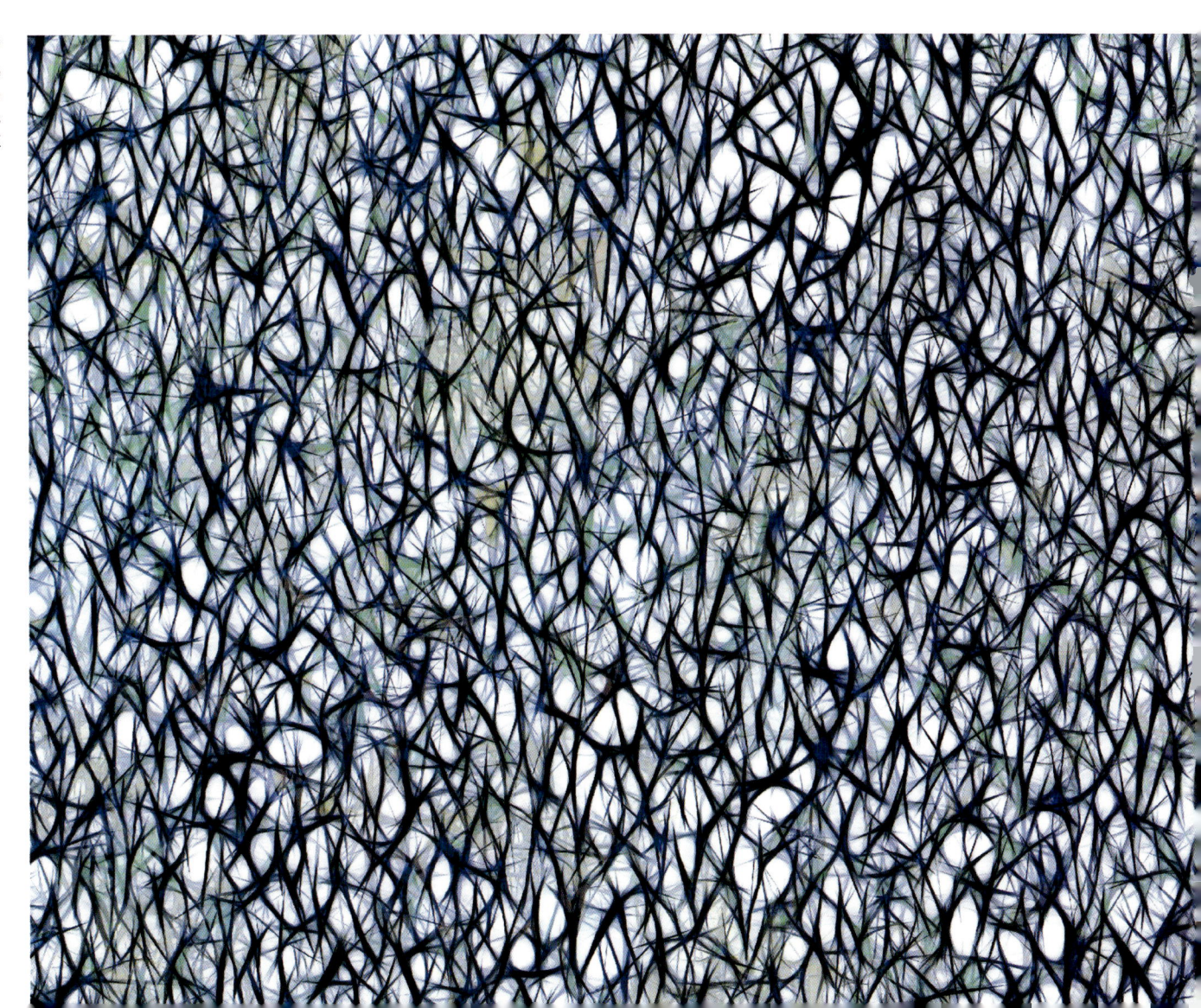

GGT0128
pattern size
50 cm x 60 cm
5906 x 7087 pixels
at 300 ppi in CMYK

GGT0129
pattern size
50 cm x 60 cm
5906 x 7087 pixels
at 300 ppi in CMYK

page 080

GGT0130

pattern size
52 cm x 60 cm
6142 x 7087 pixels
at 300 ppi in CMYK

GGT0131

pattern size
42 cm x 60 cm
4961 x 7087 pixels
at 300 ppi in CMYK

page 081

GGT0132
pattern size
65 cm x 60 cm
7677 x 7087 pixels
at 300 ppi in CMYK

page 082

GGT0133
pattern size
50 cm x 42 cm
5906 x 4961 pixels
at 300 ppi in CMYK

page 083

GGT0134
pattern size
52 cm x 60 cm
6142 x 7087 pixels
at 300 ppi in CMYK

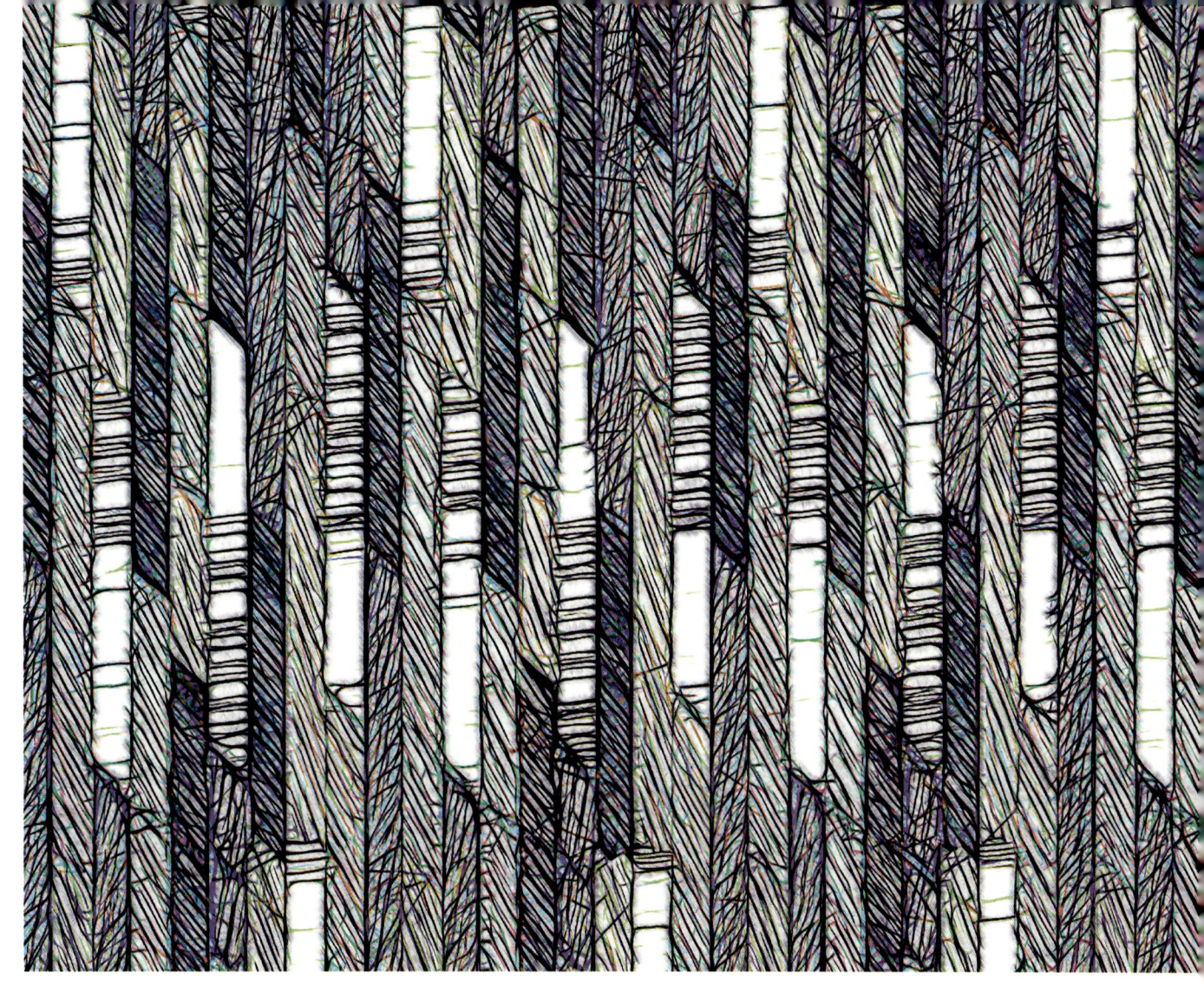

GGT0135
pattern size
60 cm x 42 cm
7087 x 4961 pixels
at 300 ppi in CMYK

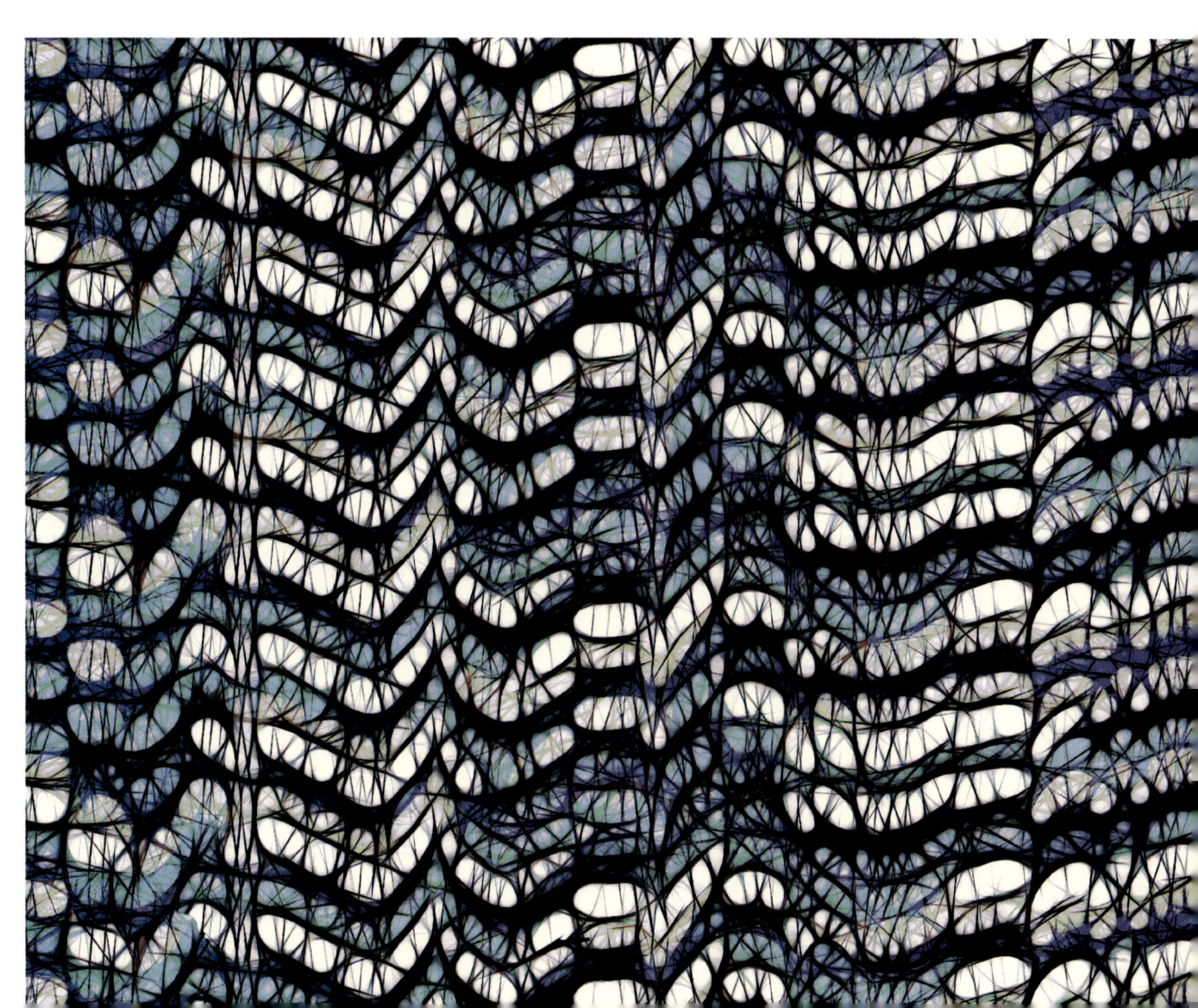

page 084

GGT0136
pattern size
42 cm x 60 cm
4961 x 7087 pixels
at 300 ppi in CMYK

page 085

GGT0137
pattern size
42 cm x 60 cm
4961 x 7087 pixels
at 300 ppi in CMYK

page 086

GGT0138
pattern size
50 cm x 60 cm
5906 x 7087 pixels
at 300 ppi in CMYK

page 087

GGT0139
pattern size
45 cm x 60 cm
5315 x 7087 pixels
at 300 ppi in CMYK

page 088

GGT0140
pattern size
70 cm x 62 cm
8268 x 7323 pixels
at 300 ppi in CMYK

GGT0141
pattern size
70 cm x 62 cm
8268 x 7323 pixels
at 300 ppi in CMYK

page 089

GGT0142
pattern size
70 cm x 62 cm
8268 x 7323 pixels
at 300 ppi in CMYK

page 090

GGT0143
pattern size
40 cm x 40 cm
4725 x 4725 pixels
at 300 ppi in CMYK

GGT0144
pattern size
40 cm x 40 cm
4725 x 4725 pixels
at 300 ppi in CMYK

page 091

GGT0145
pattern size
40 cm x 40 cm
4725 x 4725 pixels
at 300 ppi in CMYK

GGT0146
pattern size
40 cm x 40 cm
4725 x 4725 pixels
at 300 ppi in CMYK

page 092

GGT0147
pattern size
60 cm x 60 cm
7087 x 7087 pixels
at 300 ppi in CMYK

GGT0148
pattern size
70 cm x 63 cm
8268 x 7441 pixels
at 300 ppi in CMYK

page 093

GGT0149
pattern size
60 cm x 52 cm
7087 x 6142 pixels
at 300 ppi in CMYK

page 094

GGT0150
pattern size
55 cm x 60 cm
6496 x 7087 pixels
at 300 ppi in CMYK

page 095

GGT0151
pattern size
55 cm x 60 cm
6497 x 7087 pixels
at 300 ppi in CMYK

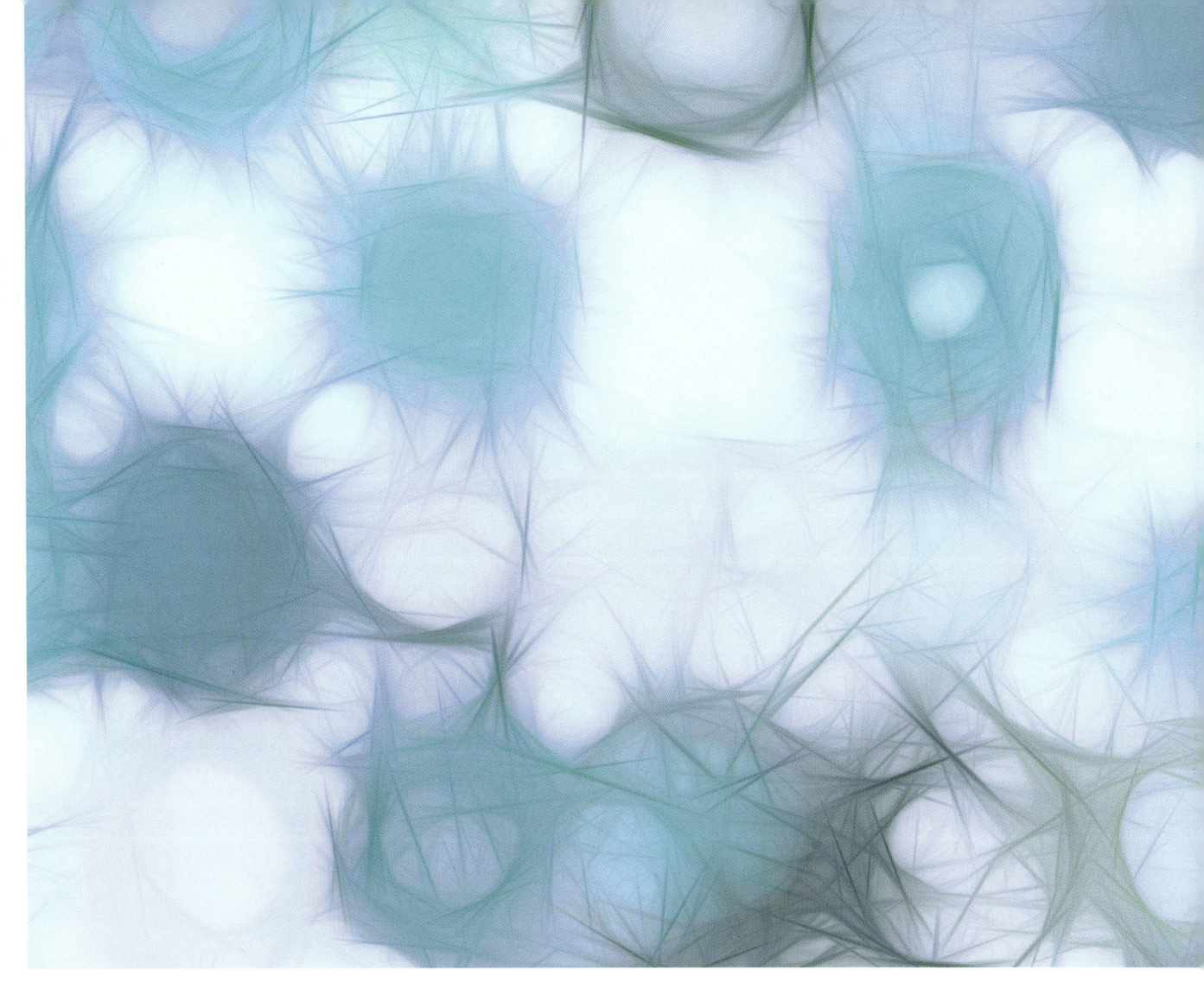

GGT0152
pattern size
55 cm x 60 cm
6497 x 7087 pixels
at 300 ppi in CMYK

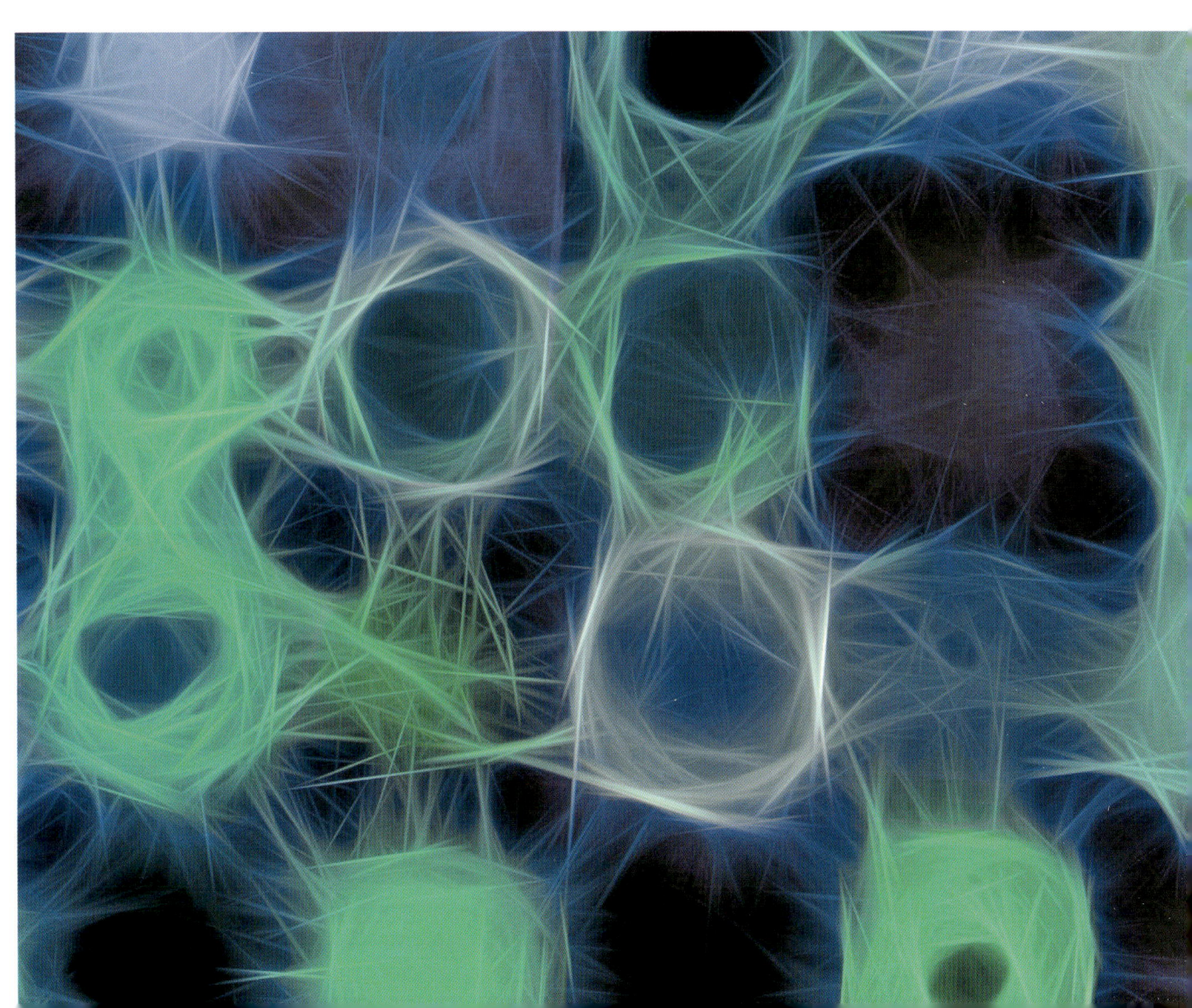

page 096

GGT0153
pattern size
60 cm x 56 cm
7087 x 6615 pixels
at 300 ppi in CMYK

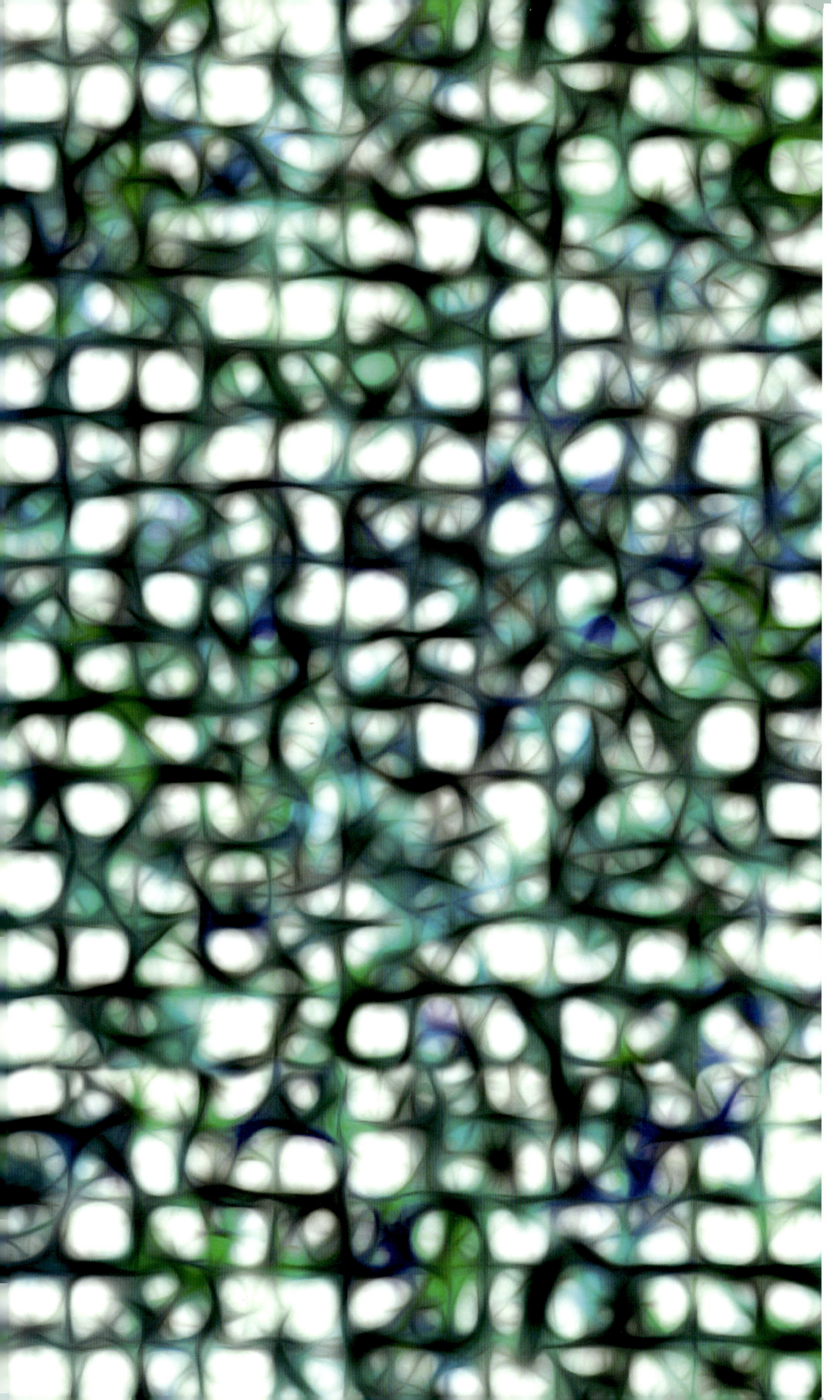

page 097

GGT0154
pattern size
50 cm x 60 cm
5906 x 7087 pixels
at 300 ppi in CMYK

GGT0155
pattern size
50 cm x 60 cm
5906 x 7087 pixels
at 300 ppi in CMYK

page 098

GGT0156
pattern size
35 cm x 40 cm
4134 x 4725 pixels
at 300 ppi in CMYK

GGT0157
pattern size
48 cm x 50 cm
5670 x 5906 pixels
at 300 ppi in CMYK

page 099

GGT0158
pattern size
35 cm x 40 cm
4134 x 4725 pixels
at 300 ppi in CMYK

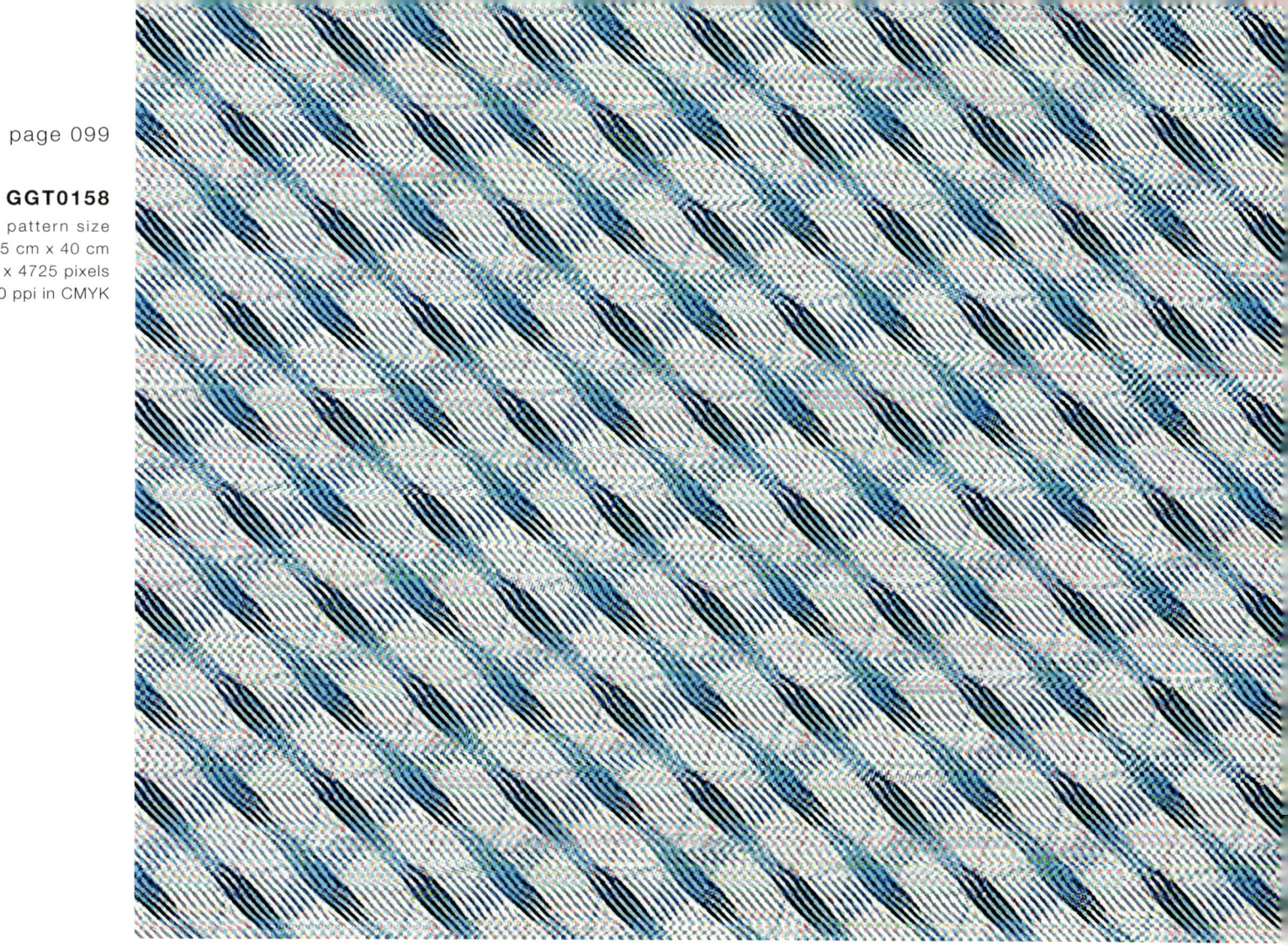

GGT0159
pattern size
44 cm x 50 cm
5197 x 5906 pixels
at 300 ppi in CMYK

page 100

GGT0160
pattern size
62 cm x 50 cm
7323 x 5906 pixels
at 300 ppi in CMYK

GGT0161
pattern size
62 cm x 50 cm
7323 x 5906 pixels
at 300 ppi in CMYK

page 101

GGT0162
pattern size
60 cm x 52 cm
7087 x 6142 pixels
at 300 ppi in CMYK

GGT0163
pattern size
60 cm x 48 cm
7087 x 5669 pixels
at 300 ppi in CMYK

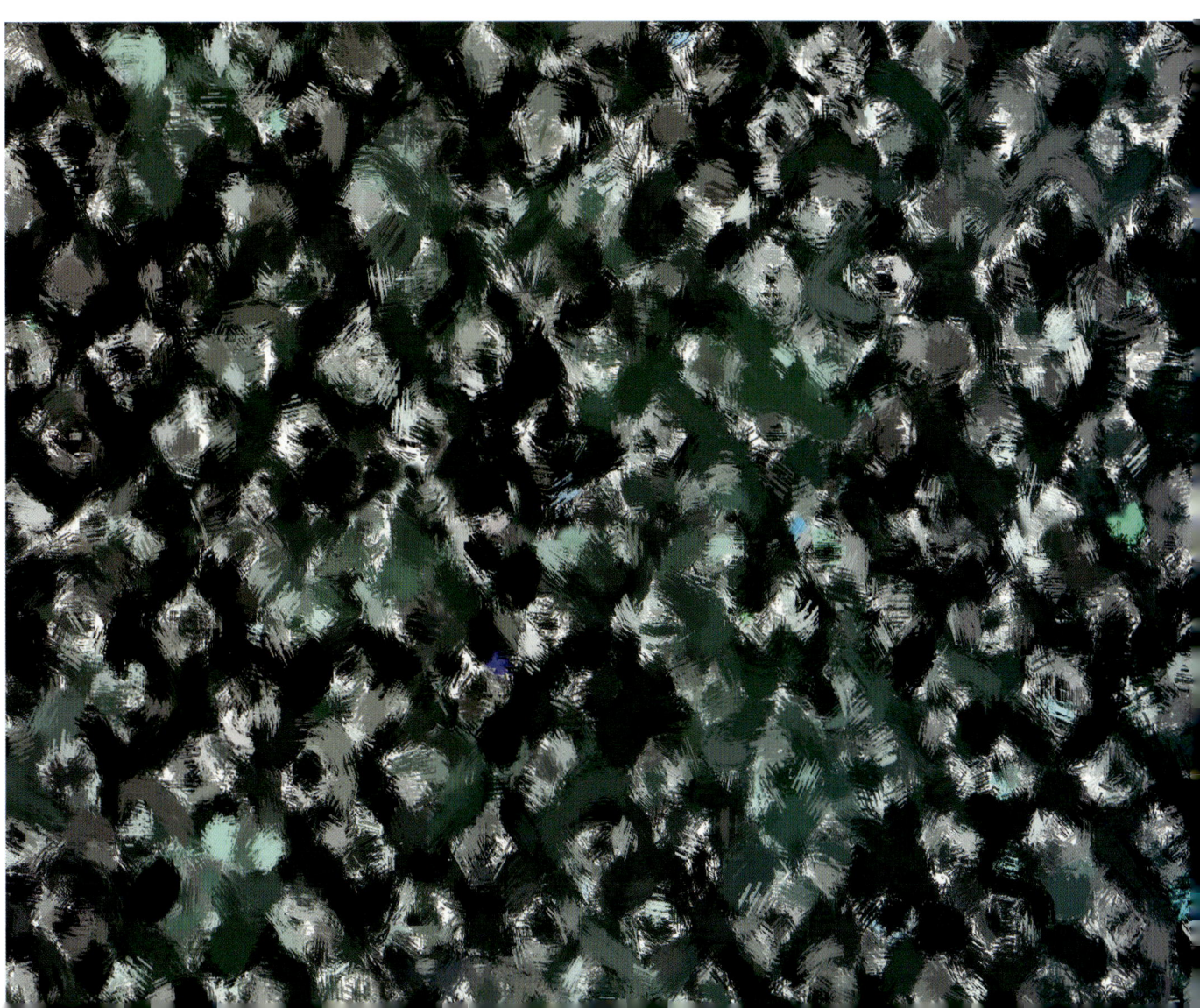

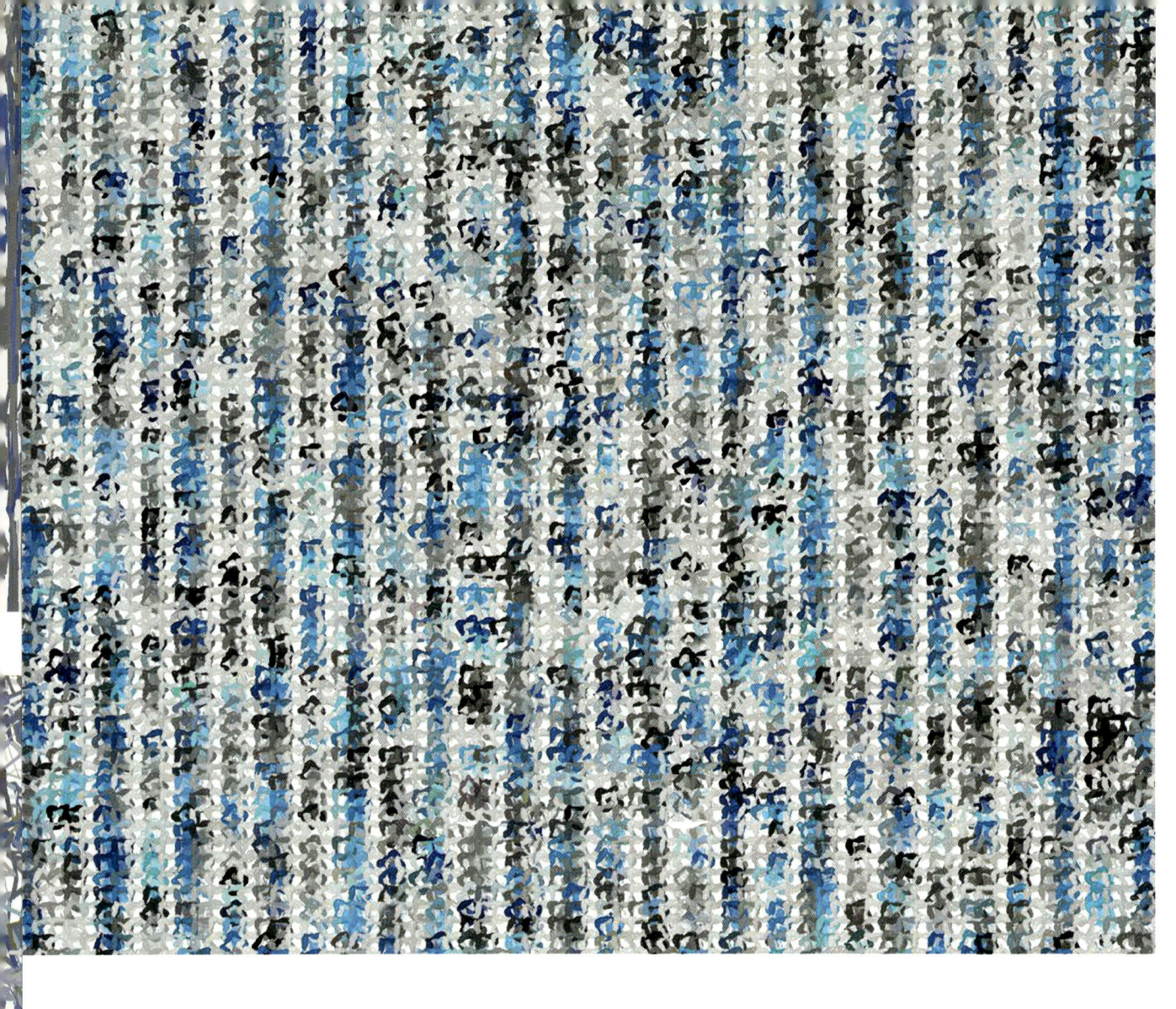

page 104

GGT0170

pattern size
36 cm x 50 cm
4252 x 5906 pixels
at 300 ppi in CMYK

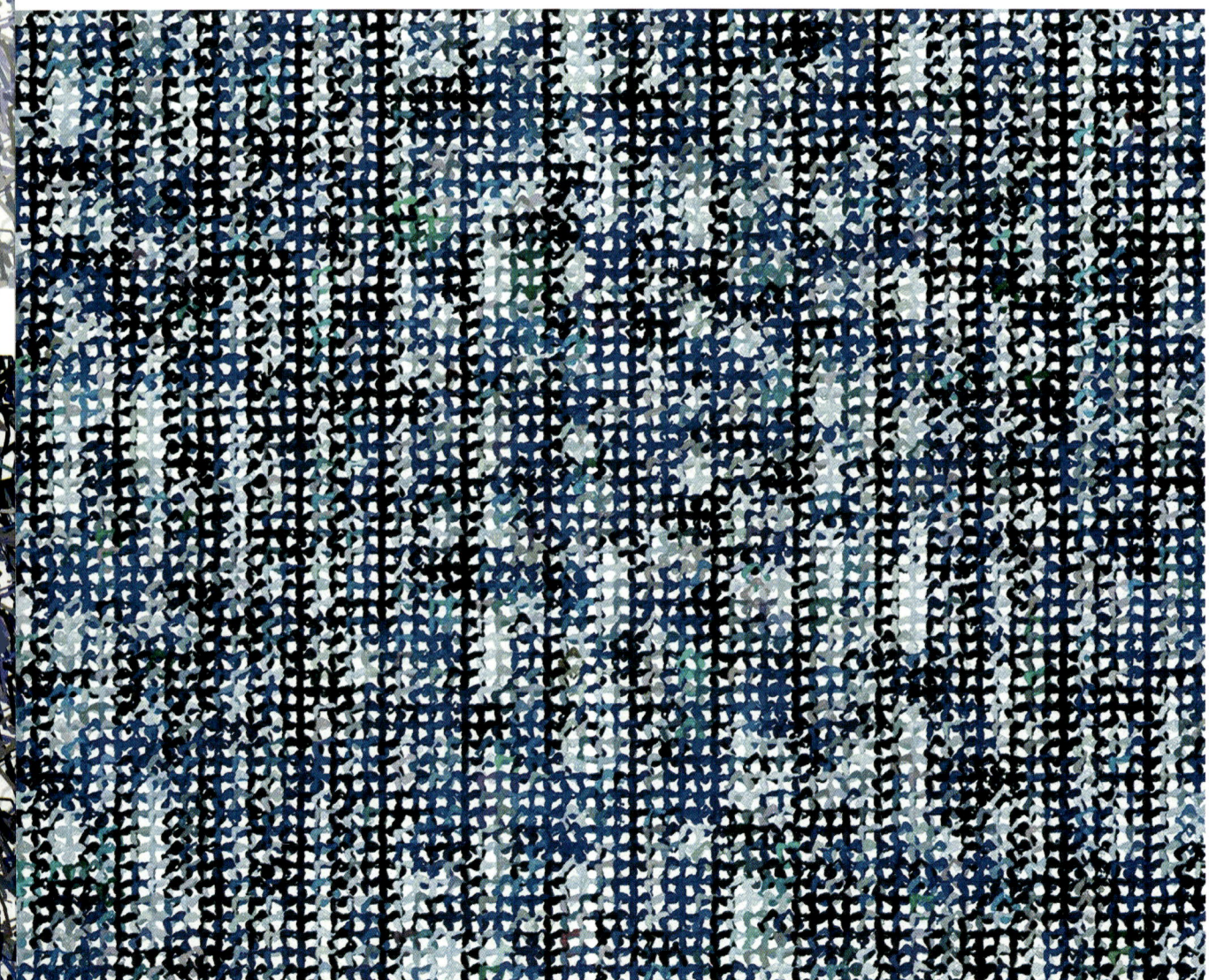

GGT0171

pattern size
36 cm x 50 cm
4252 x 5906 pixels
at 300 ppi in CMYK

page 101

GGT0162
pattern size
60 cm x 52 cm
7087 x 6142 pixels
at 300 ppi in CMYK

GGT0163
pattern size
60 cm x 48 cm
7087 x 5669 pixels
at 300 ppi in CMYK

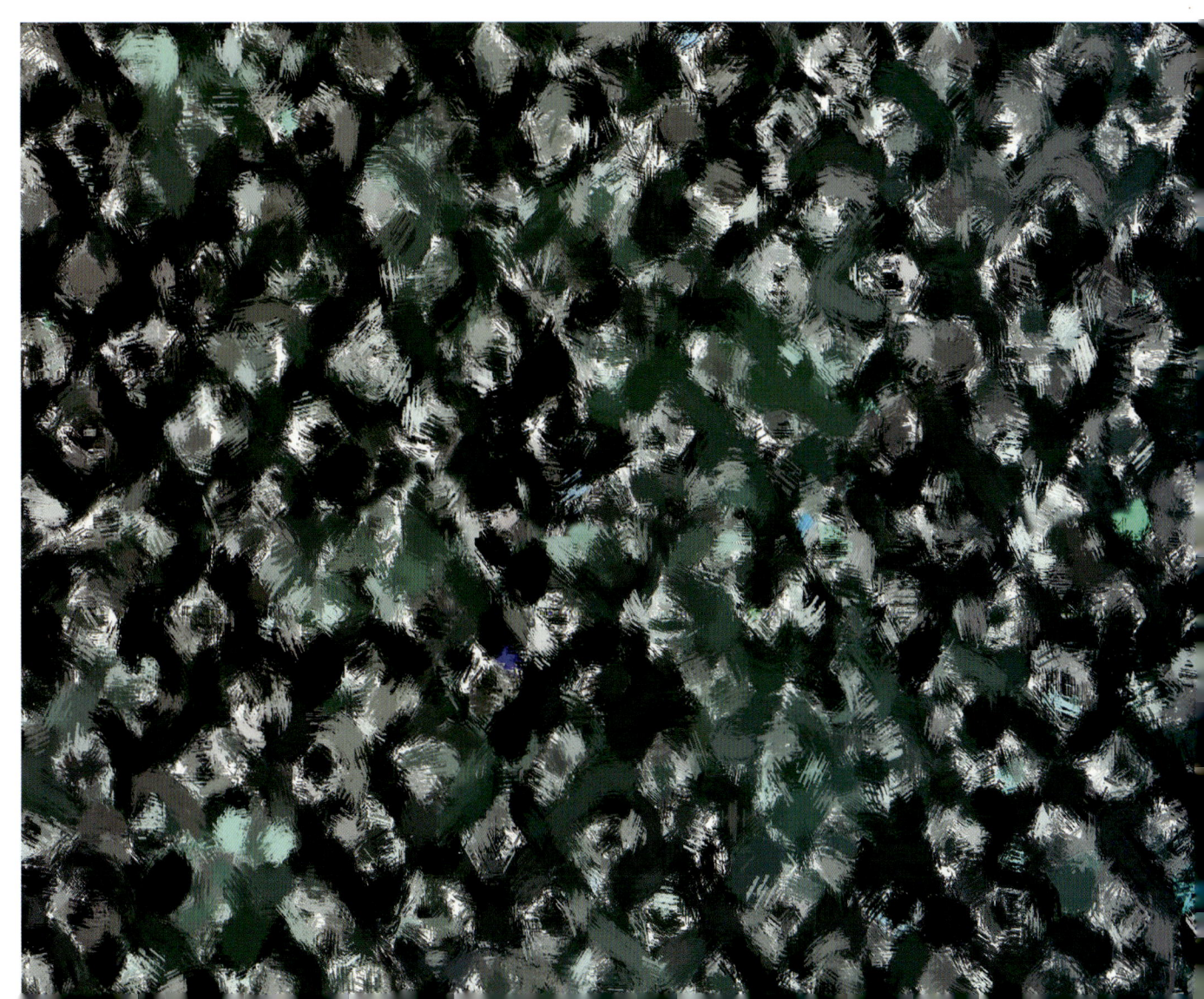

page 102

GGT0164
pattern size
60 cm x 42 cm
7087 x 4961 pixels
at 300 ppi in CMYK

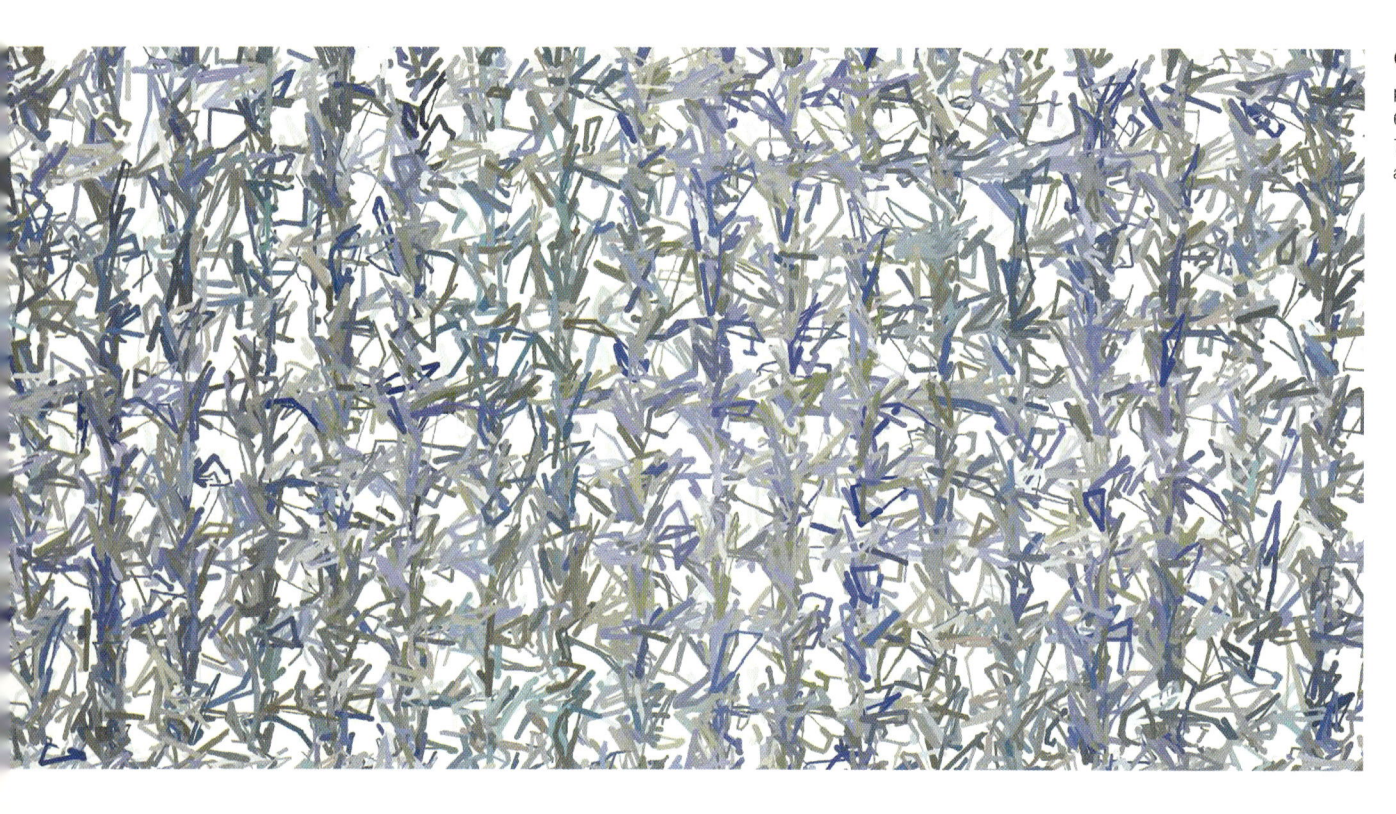

GGT0165
pattern size
60 cm x 42 cm
7087 x 4961 pixels
at 300 ppi in CMYK

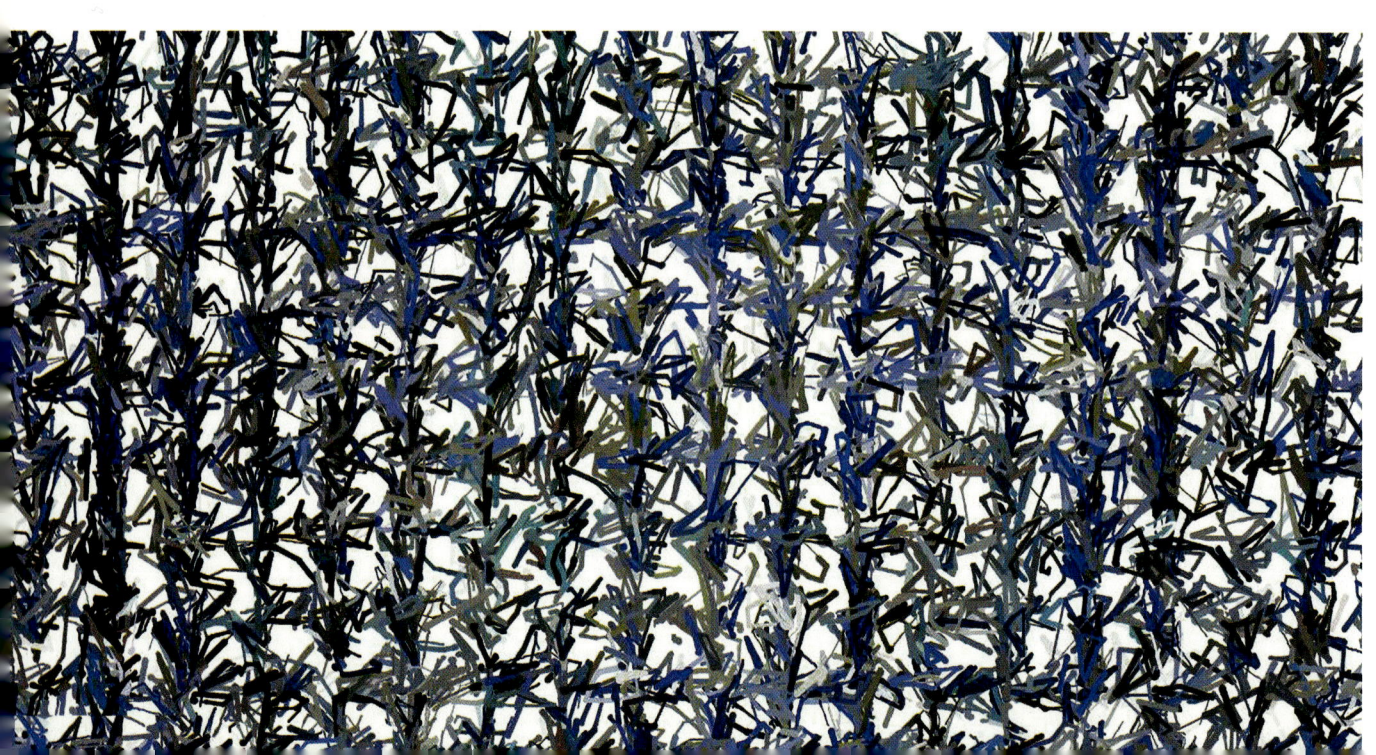

GGT0166
pattern size
60 cm x 42 cm
7087 x 4961 pixels
at 300 ppi in CMYK

page 103

GGT0167
pattern size
50 cm x 62 cm
5906 x 7323 pixels
at 300 ppi in CMYK

GGT0168
pattern size
50 cm x 62 cm
5906 x 7323 pixels
at 300 ppi in CMYK

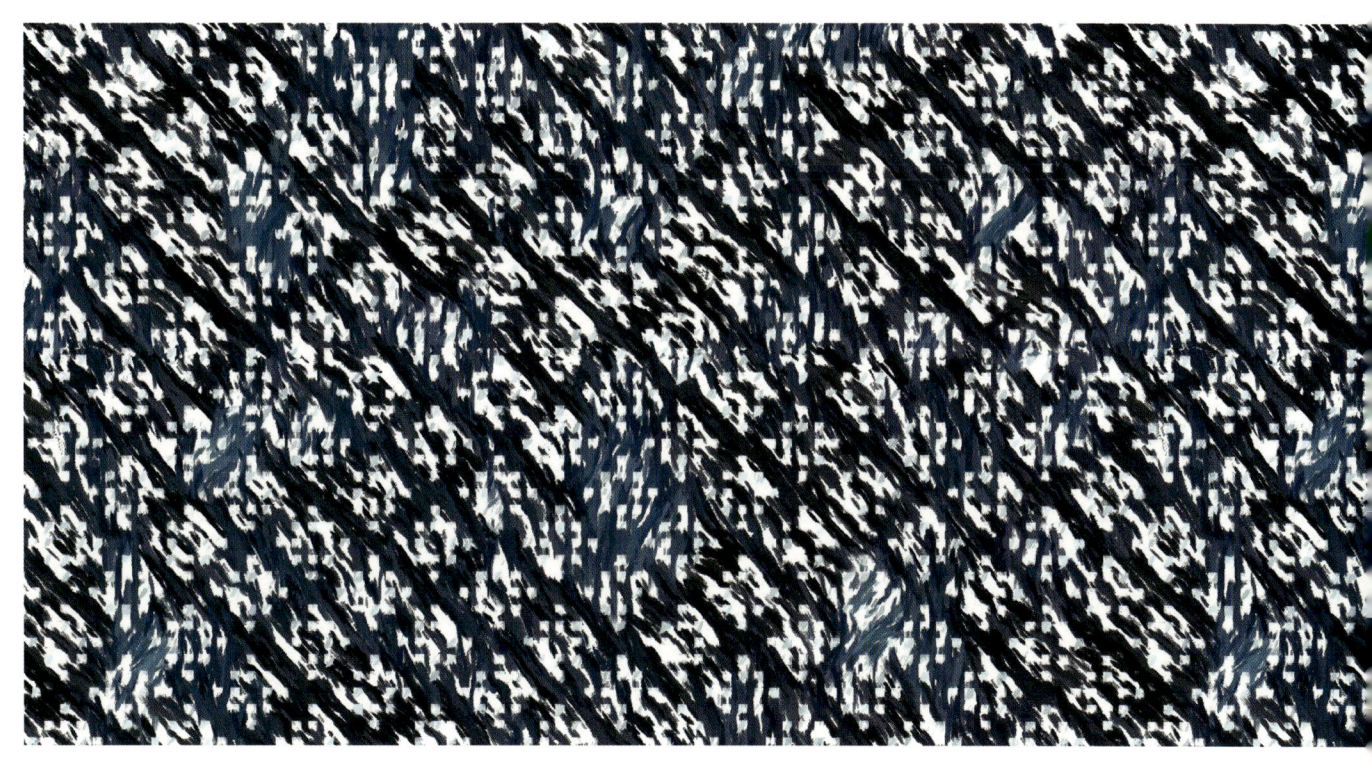

GGT0169
pattern size
50 cm x 62 cm
5906 x 7323 pixels
at 300 ppi in CMYK

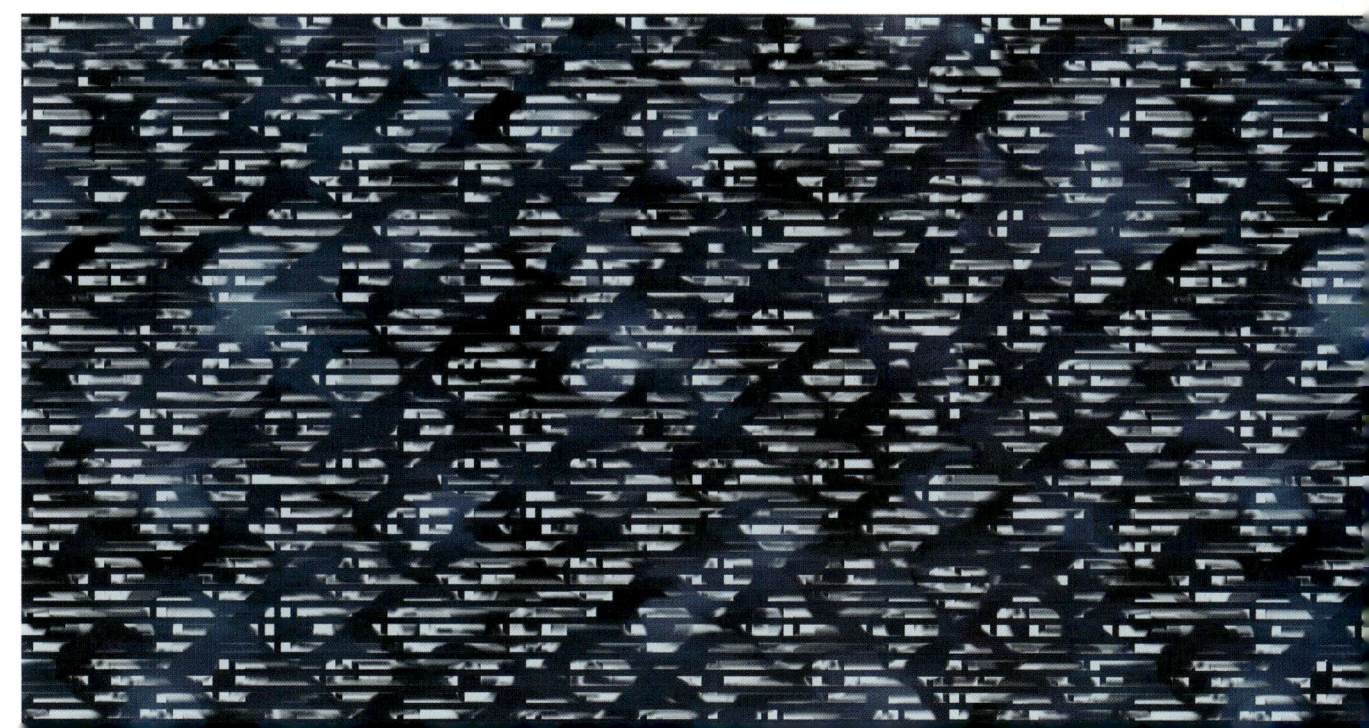

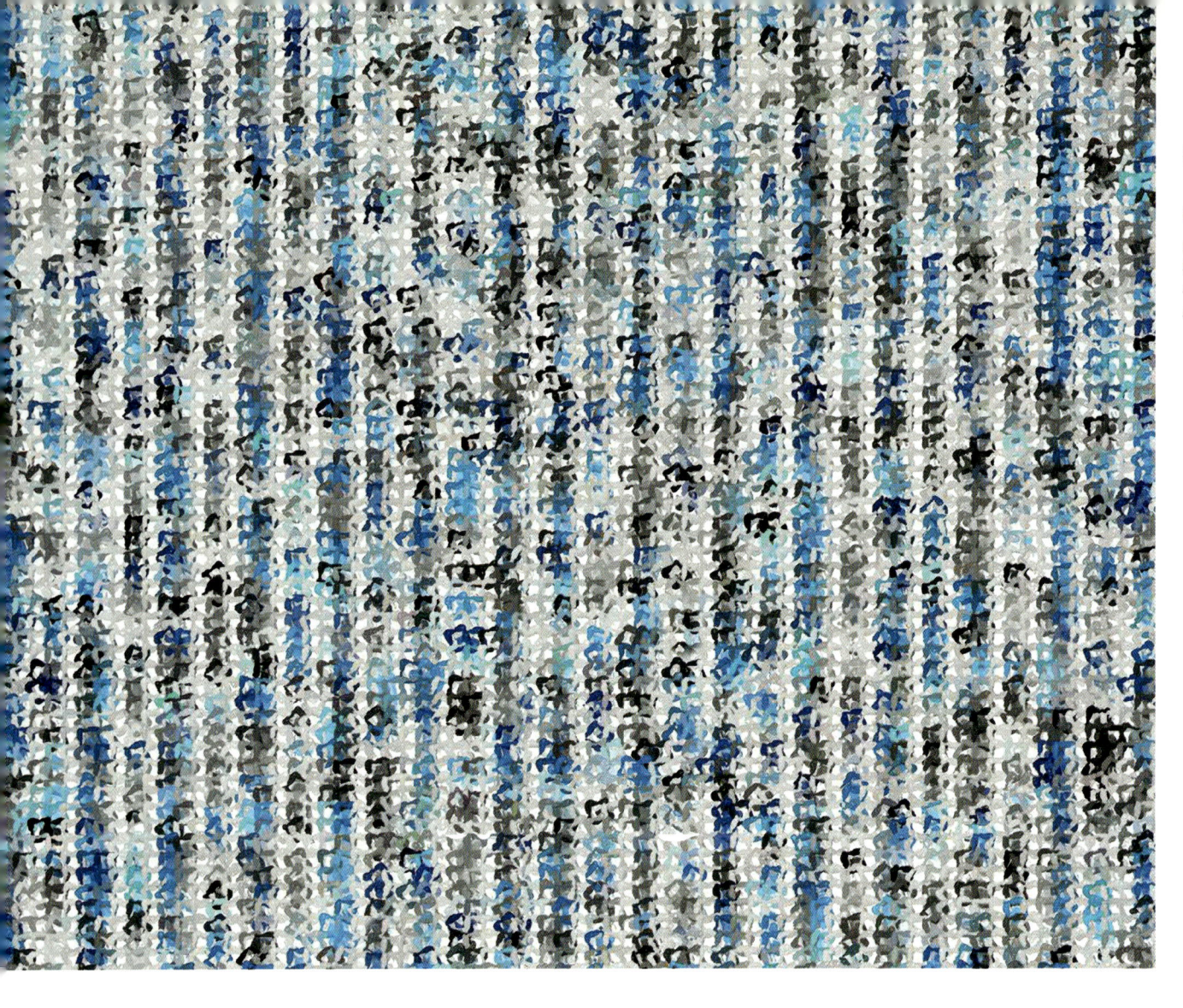

page 104

GGT0170
pattern size
36 cm x 50 cm
4252 x 5906 pixels
at 300 ppi in CMYK

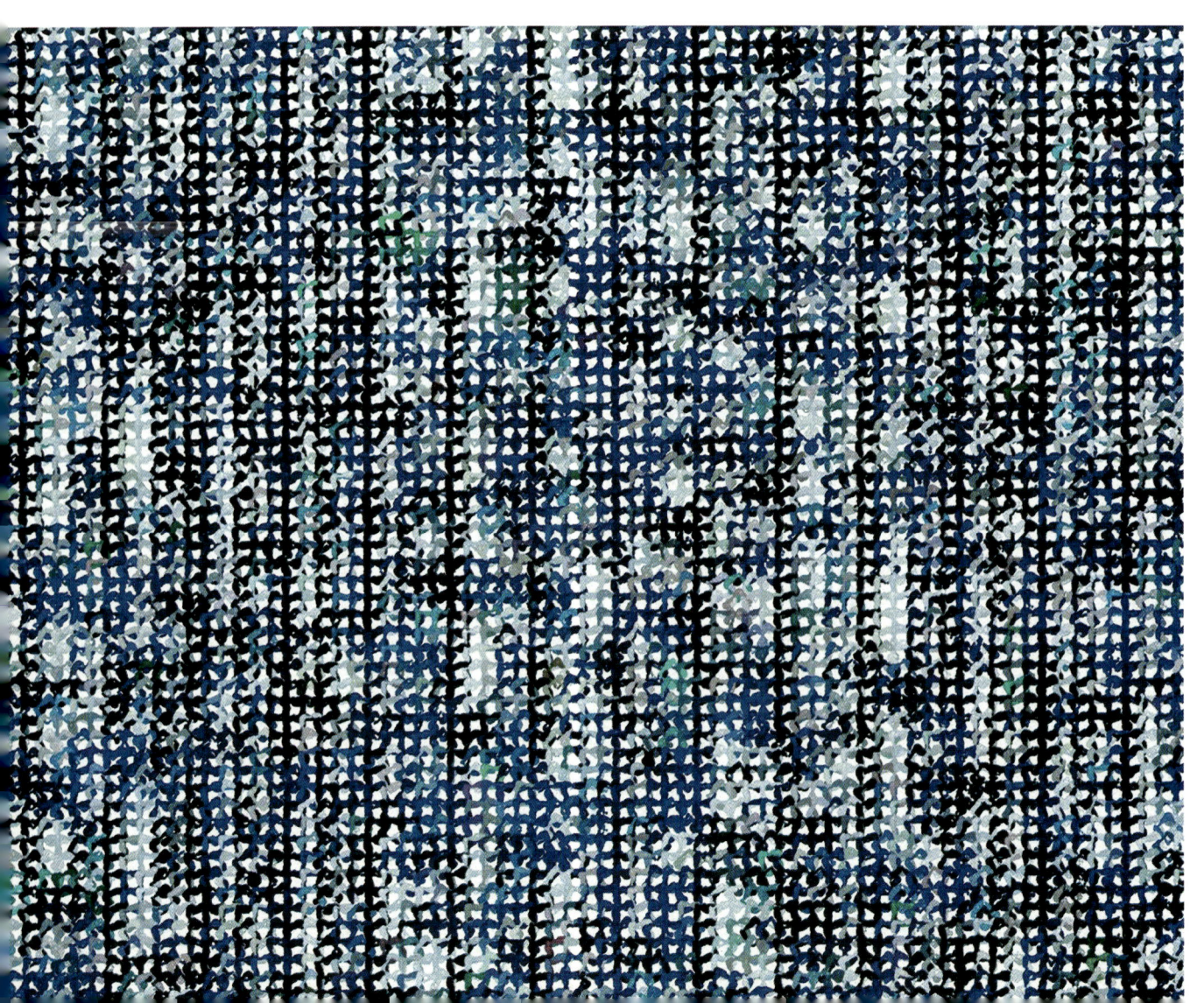

GGT0171
pattern size
36 cm x 50 cm
4252 x 5906 pixels
at 300 ppi in CMYK

page 105

GGT0172
pattern size
50 cm x 50 cm
5906 x 5906 pixels
at 300 ppi in CMYK

GGT0173
pattern size
70 cm x 70 cm
8268 x 8268 pixels
at 300 ppi in CMYK

page 106

GGT0174
pattern size
50 cm x 60 cm
5906 x 7087 pixels
at 300 ppi in CMYK

GGT0175
pattern size
50 cm x 60 cm
5906 x 7087 pixels
at 300 ppi in CMYK

page 107

GGT0176
pattern size
60 cm x 45 cm
7087 x 5315 pixels
at 300 ppi in CMYK

page 108

GGT0177
pattern size
60 cm x 40 cm
7087 x 4724 pixels
at 300 ppi in CMYK

GGT0178
pattern size
60 cm x 40 cm
7087 x 4724 pixels
at 300 ppi in CMYK

page 109

GGT0179
pattern size
60 cm x 40 cm
7087 x 4724 pixels
at 300 ppi in CMYK

page 110

GGT0180
pattern size
60 cm x 43 cm
7087 x 5079 pixels
at 300 ppi in CMYK

GGT0181
pattern size
60 cm x 43 cm
7087 x 5079 pixels
at 300 ppi in CMYK

GGT0182
pattern size
60 cm x 43 cm
7087 x 5079 pixels
at 300 ppi in CMYK

GGT0183
pattern size
60 cm x 43 cm
7087 x 5079 pixels
at 300 ppi in CMYK

GGT0184
pattern size
60 cm x 40 cm
7087 x 4724 pixels
at 300 ppi in CMYK

GGT0185
pattern size
60 cm x 40 cm
7087 x 4724 pixels
at 300 ppi in CMYK

page 111 >

page 112

GGT0186
pattern size
50 cm x 45 cm
5906 x 5315 pixels
at 300 ppi in CMYK

page 113

GGT0187
pattern size
45 cm x 60 cm
5315 x 7087 pixels
at 300 ppi in CMYK

GGT0188
pattern size
60 cm x 48 cm
7087 x 5669 pixels
at 300 ppi in CMYK

page 114

GGT0189
pattern size
52 cm x 40 cm
6142 x 4724 pixels
at 300 ppi in CMYK

GGT0190
pattern size
60 cm x 40 cm
7087 x 4724 pixels
at 300 ppi in CMYK

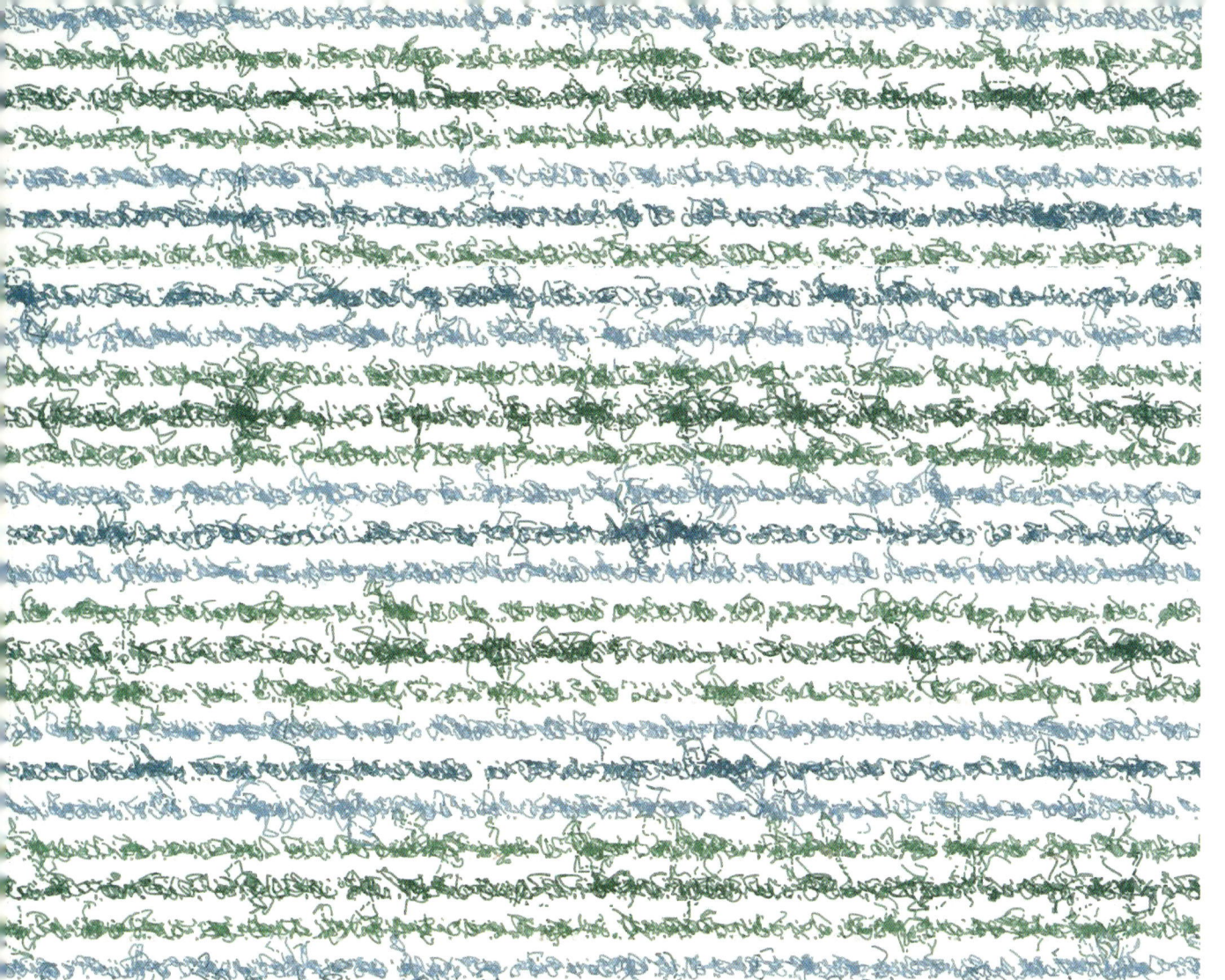

GGT0191
pattern size
45 cm x 42 cm
5315 x 4961 pixels
at 300 ppi in CMYK

GGT0192
pattern size
50 cm x 40 cm
5906 x 4724 pixels
at 300 ppi in CMYK

GGT0193
pattern size
40 cm x 45 cm
4724 x 5315 pixels
at 300 ppi in CMYK

GGT0194
pattern size
40 cm x 45 cm
4724 x 5315 pixels
at 300 ppi in CMYK

page 115 >

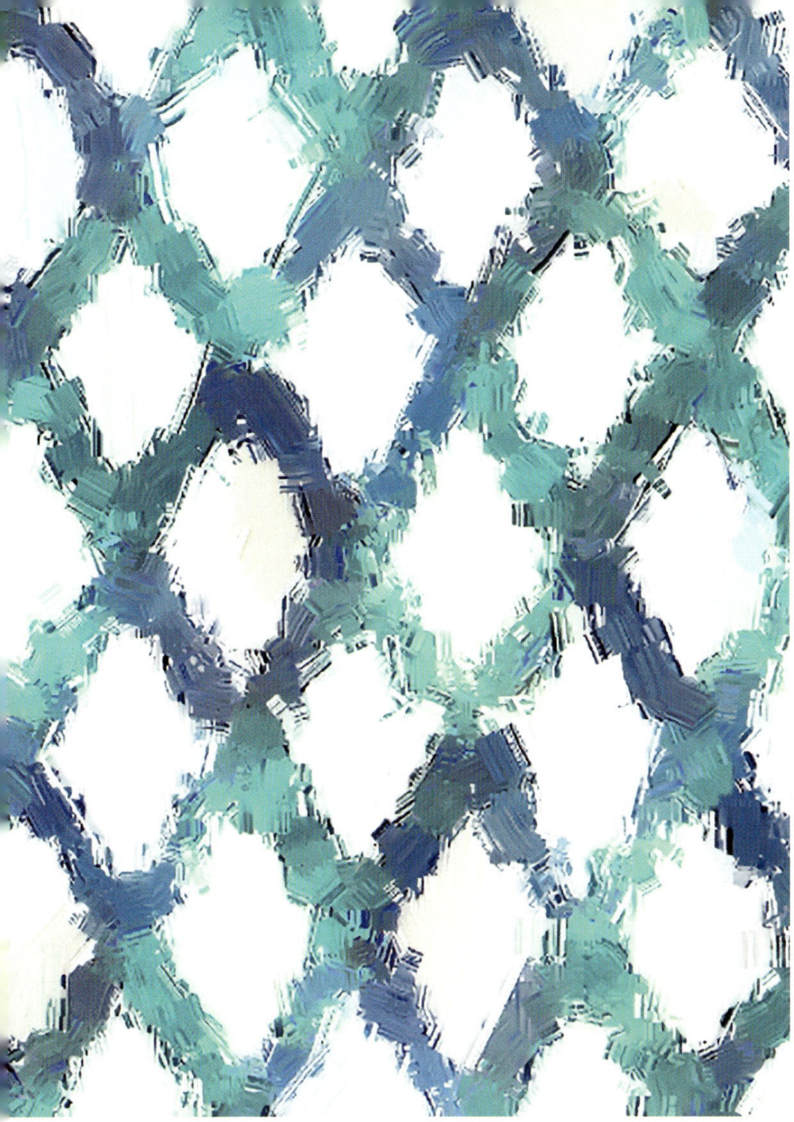
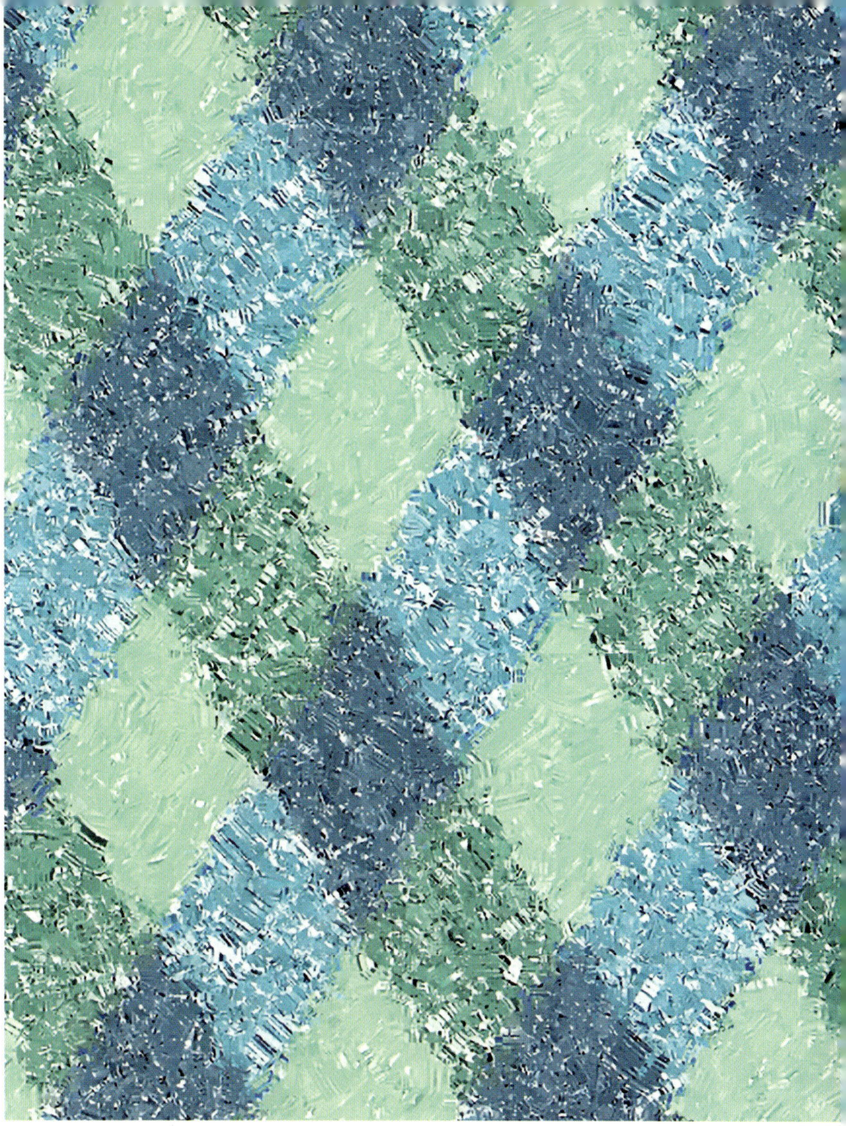
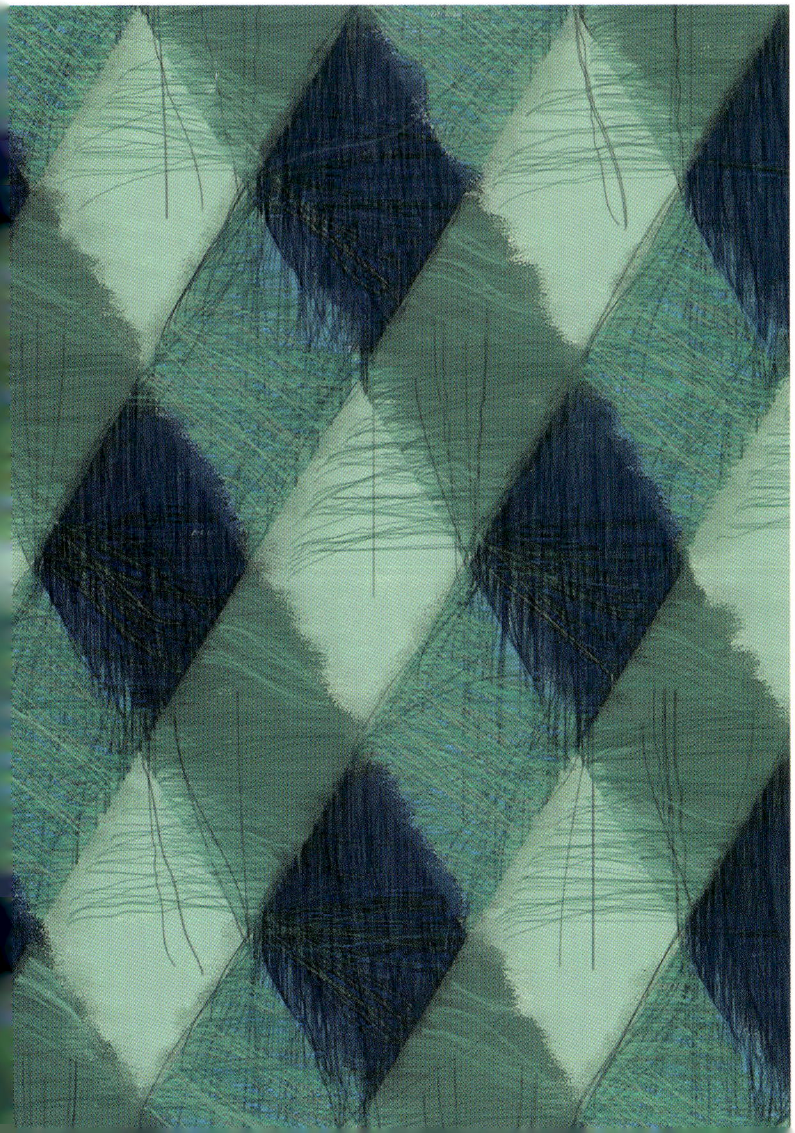
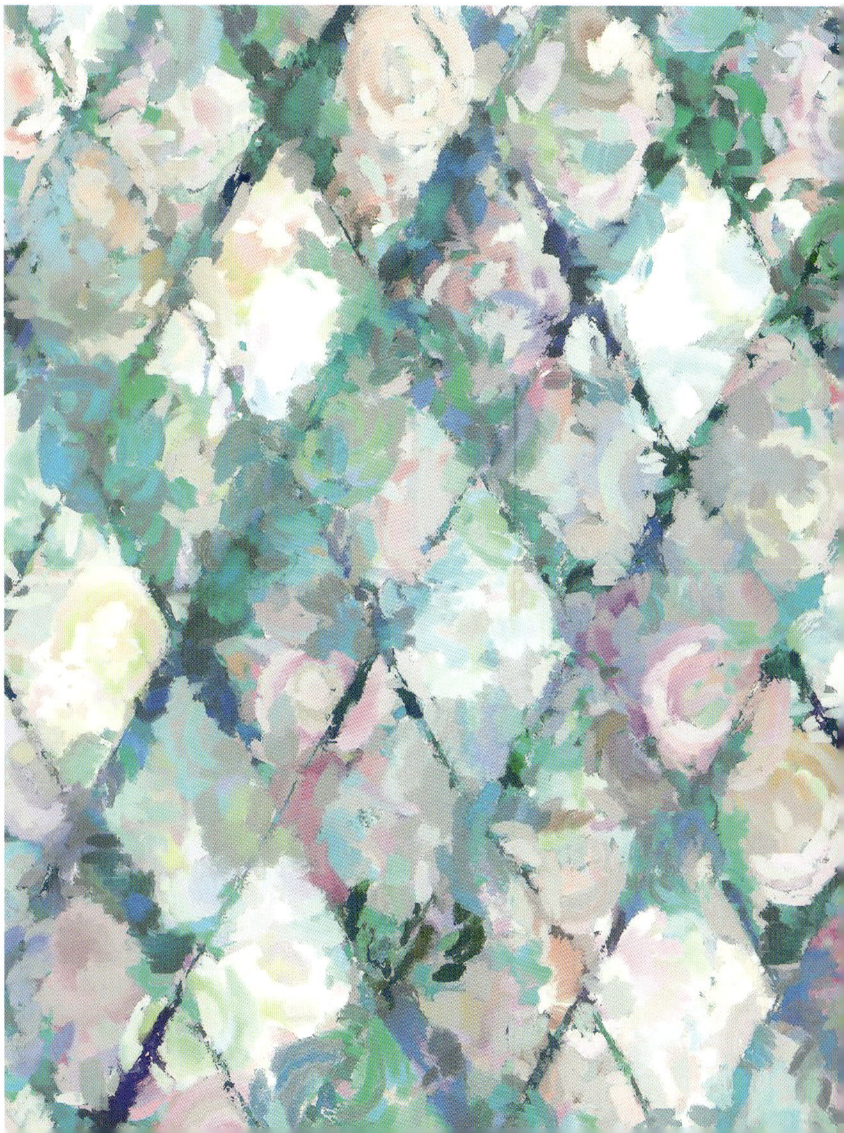

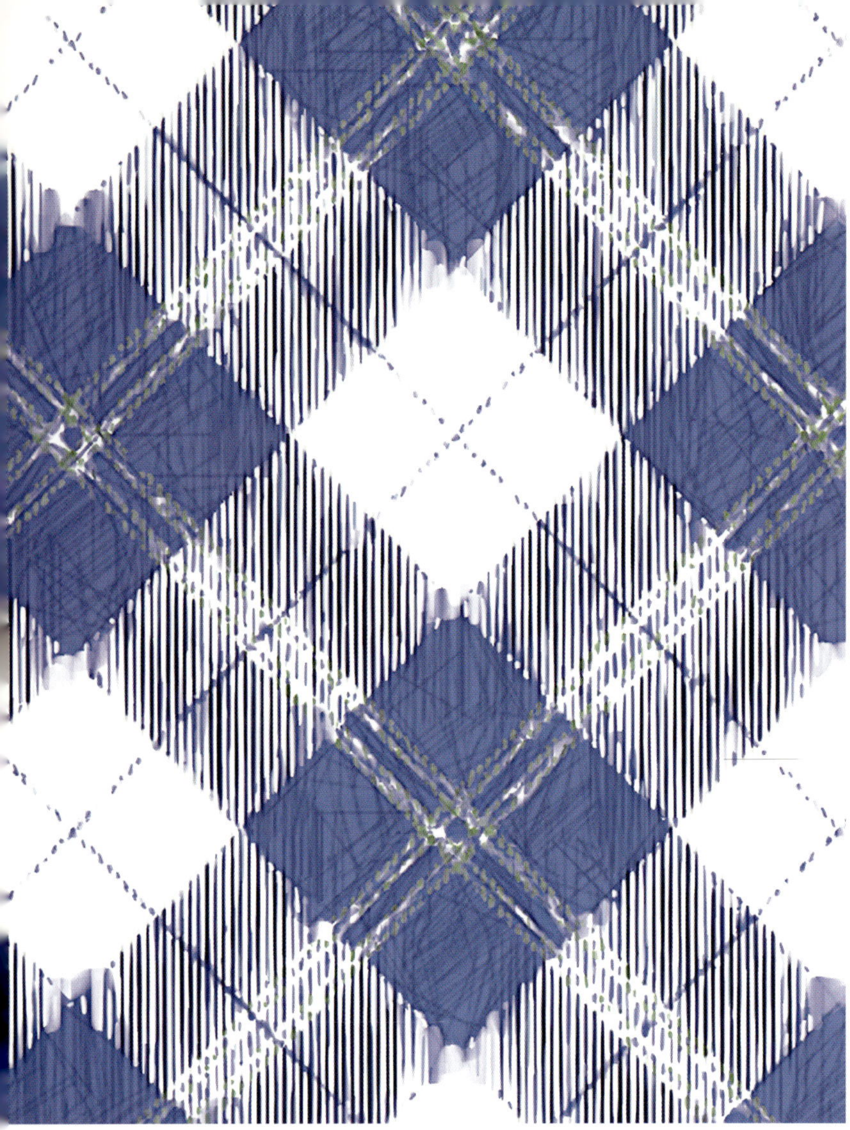
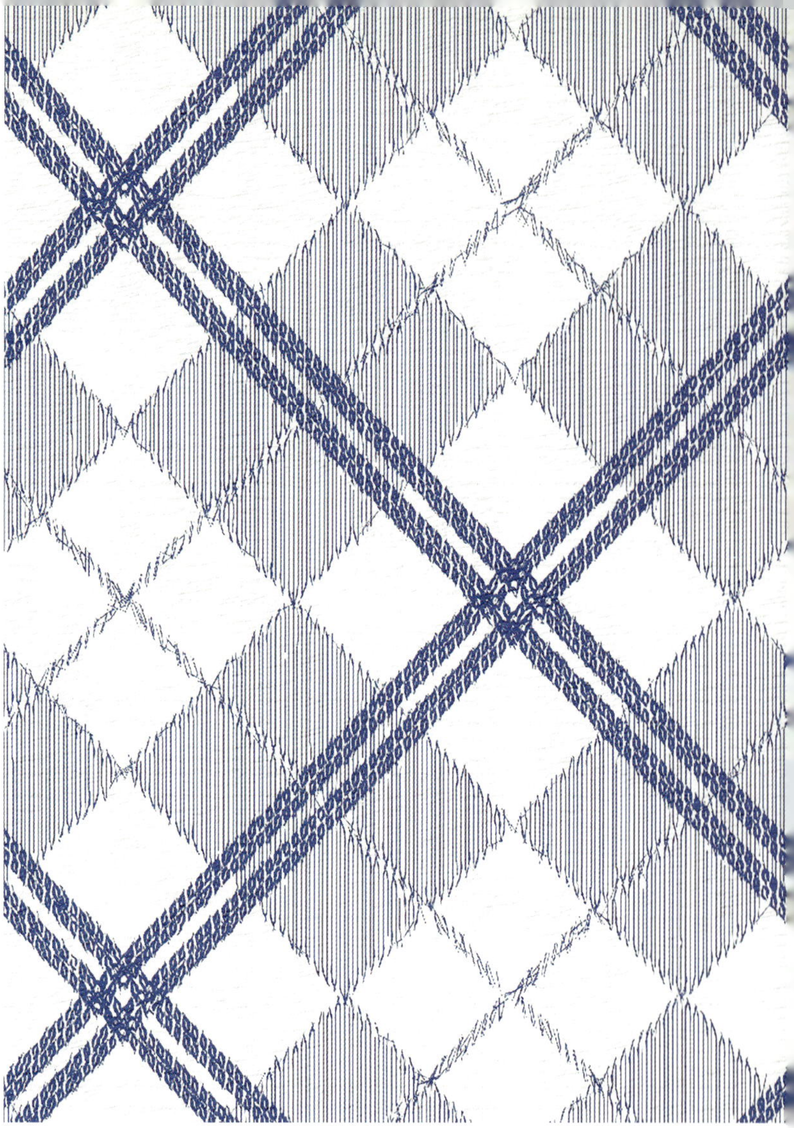
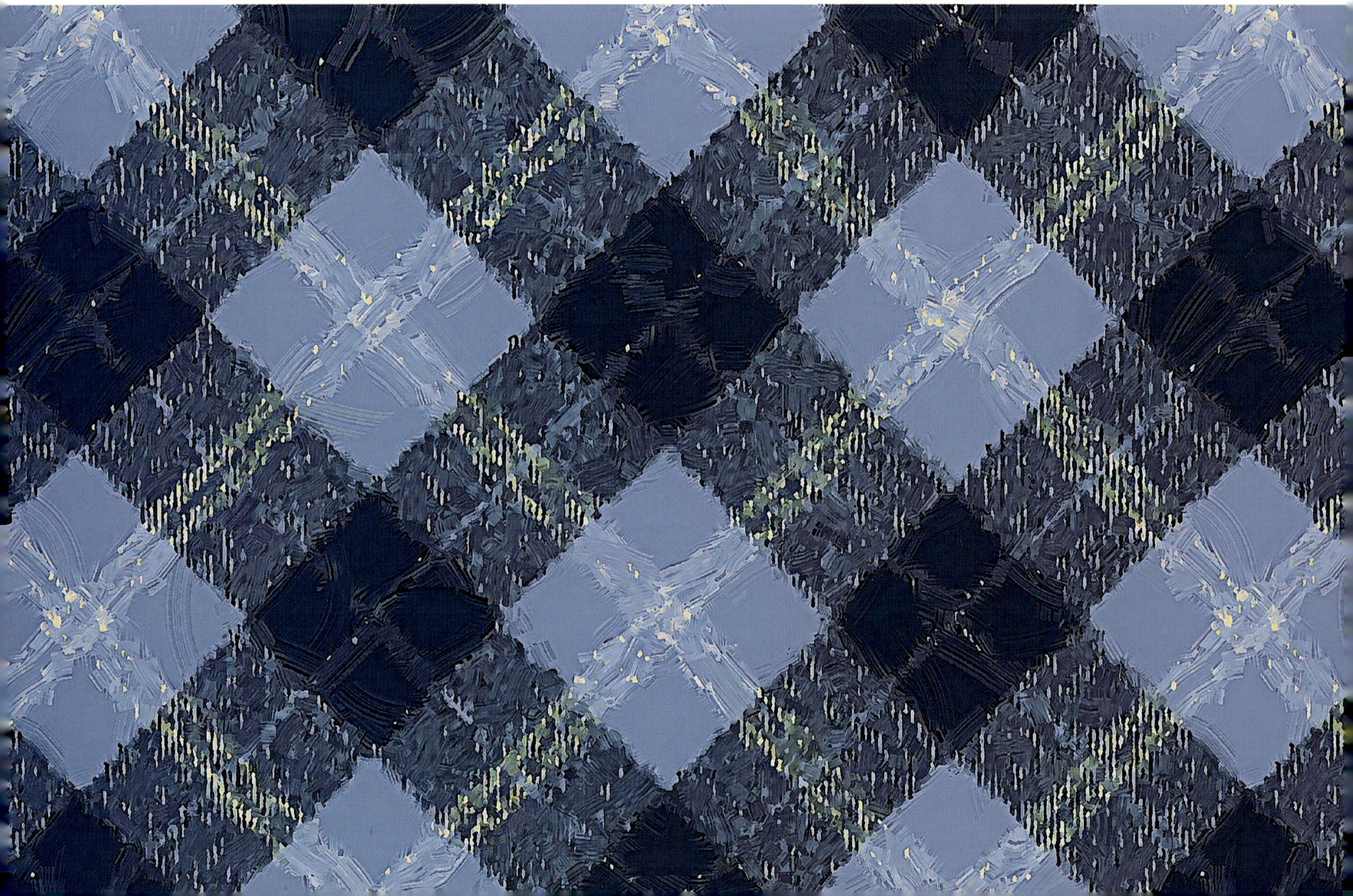

page 117

GGT0198
pattern size
50 cm x 50 cm
5906 x 5906 pixels
at 300 ppi in CMYK

GGT0195
pattern size
50 cm x 50 cm
5906 x 5906 pixels
at 300 ppi in CMYK

GGT0196
pattern size
50 cm x 50 cm
5906 x 5906 pixels
at 300 ppi in CMYK

GGT0197
pattern size
50 cm x 50 cm
5906 x 5906 pixels
at 300 ppi in CMYK

< page 116

page 118

GGT0199
pattern size
45 cm x 60 cm
5315 x 7087 pixels
at 300 ppi in CMYK

GGT0200
pattern size
50 cm x 50 cm
5906 x 5906 pixels
at 300 ppi in CMYK

page 119

GGT0201
pattern size
50 cm x 50 cm
5906 x 5906 pixels
at 300 ppi in CMYK

GGT0202
pattern size
50 cm x 50 cm
5906 x 5906 pixels
at 300 ppi in CMYK

page 120

GGT0203

pattern size
50 cm x 60 cm
5906 x 7087 pixels
at 300 ppi in CMYK

page 121

GGT0204
pattern size
56 cm x 70 cm
6614 x 8268 pixels
at 300 ppi in CMYK

GGT0205
pattern size
50 cm x 50 cm
5906 x 5906 pixels
at 300 ppi in CMYK

page 122

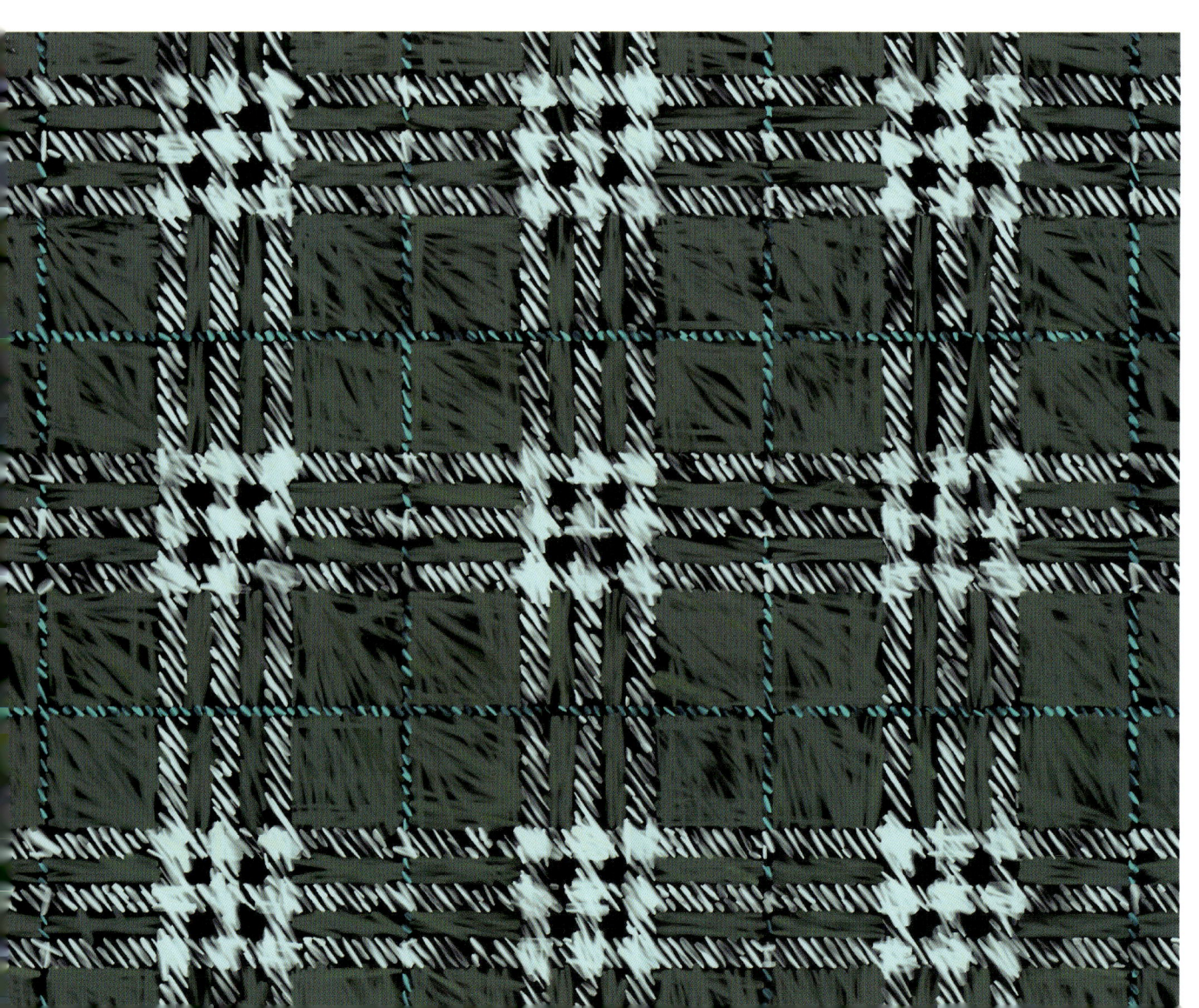

GGT0206
pattern size
50 cm x 50 cm
5906 x 5906 pixels
at 300 ppi in CMYK

GGT0207
pattern size
50 cm x 50 cm
5906 x 5906 pixels
at 300 ppi in CMYK

page 123

GGT0208
pattern size
50 cm x 50 cm
5906 x 5906 pixels
at 300 ppi in CMYK

GGT0209
pattern size
50 cm x 62 cm
5906 x 7323 pixels
at 300 ppi in CMYK

page 124

GGT0210
pattern size
50 cm x 50 cm
5906 x 5906 pixels
at 300 ppi in CMYK

GGT0211
pattern size
50 cm x 50 cm
5906 x 5906 pixels
at 300 ppi in CMYK

GGT0212
pattern size
50 cm x 50 cm
5906 x 5906 pixels
at 300 ppi in CMYK

GGT0213
pattern size
50 cm x 50 cm
5906 x 5906 pixels
at 300 ppi in CMYK

page 125 >

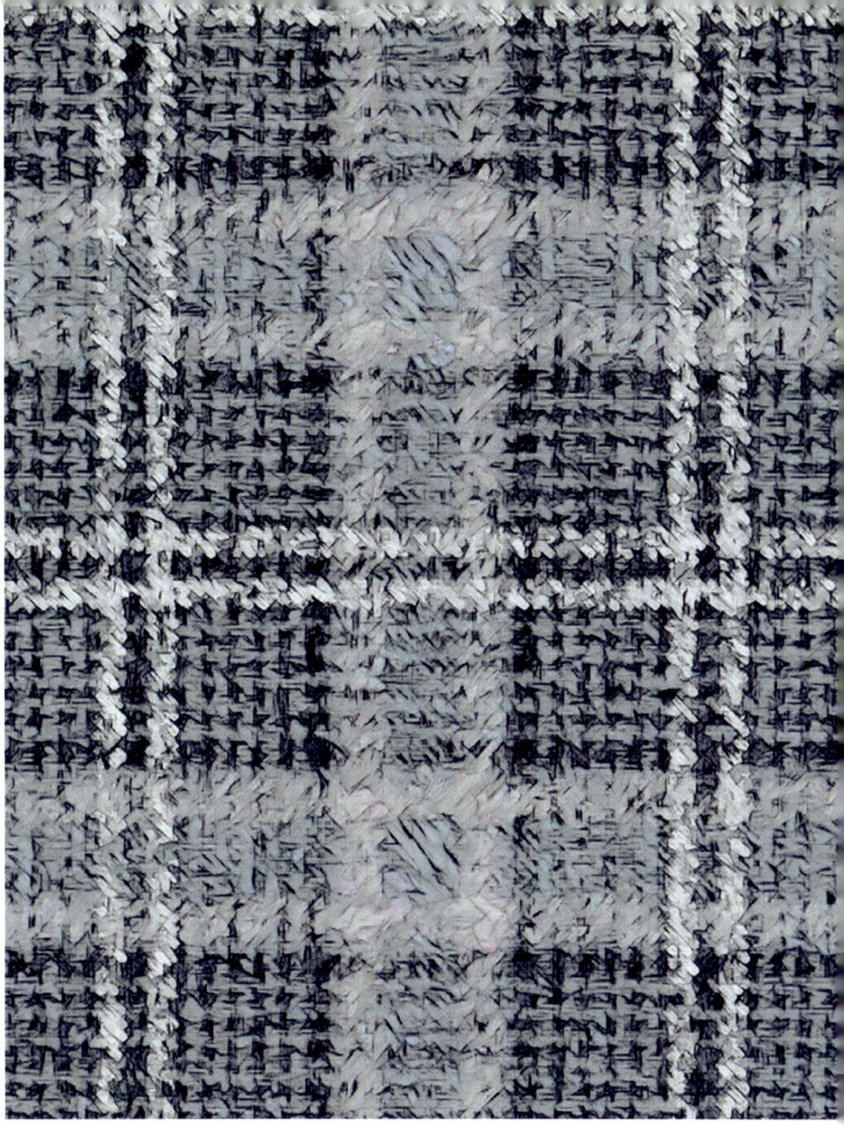
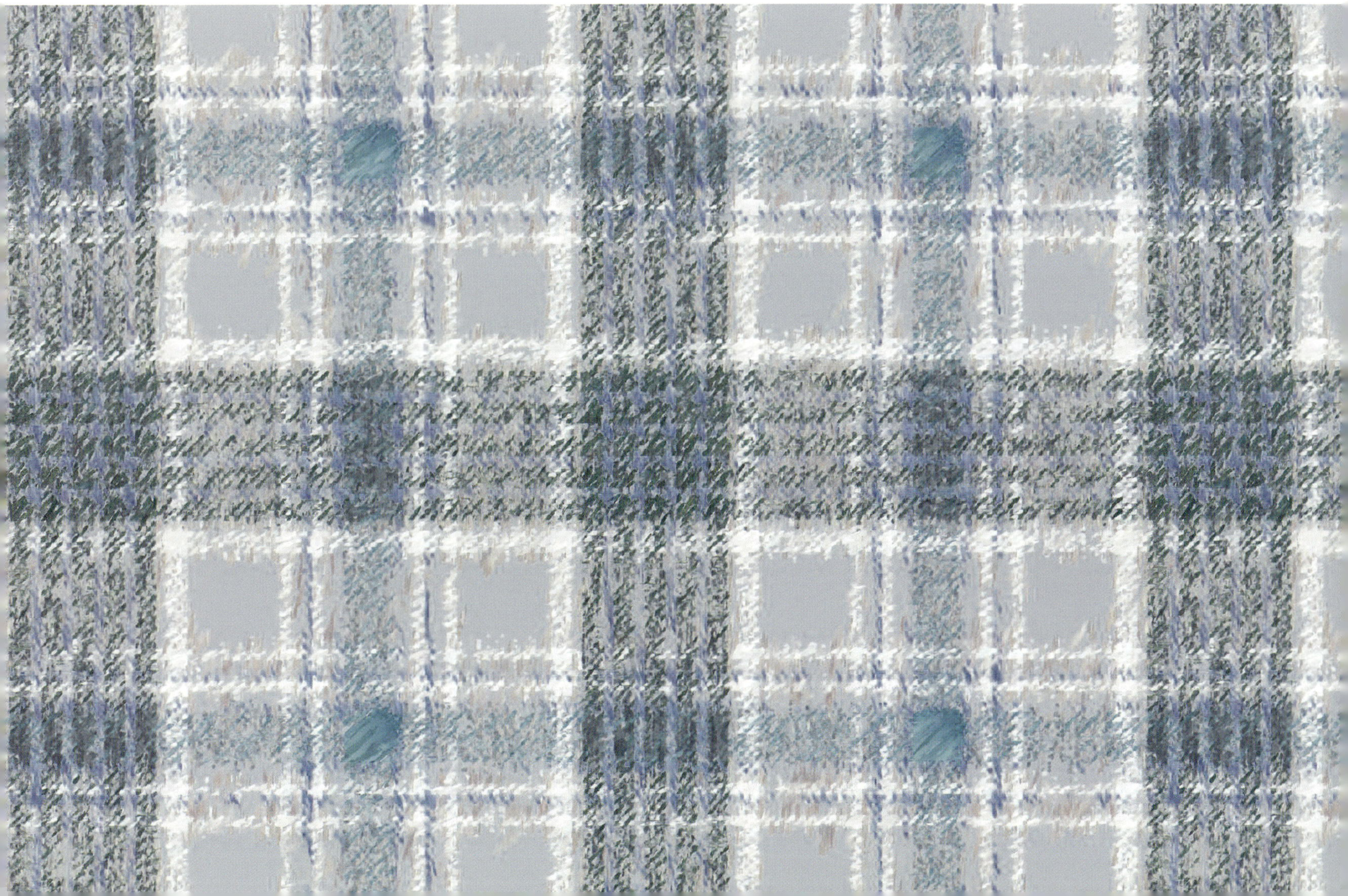

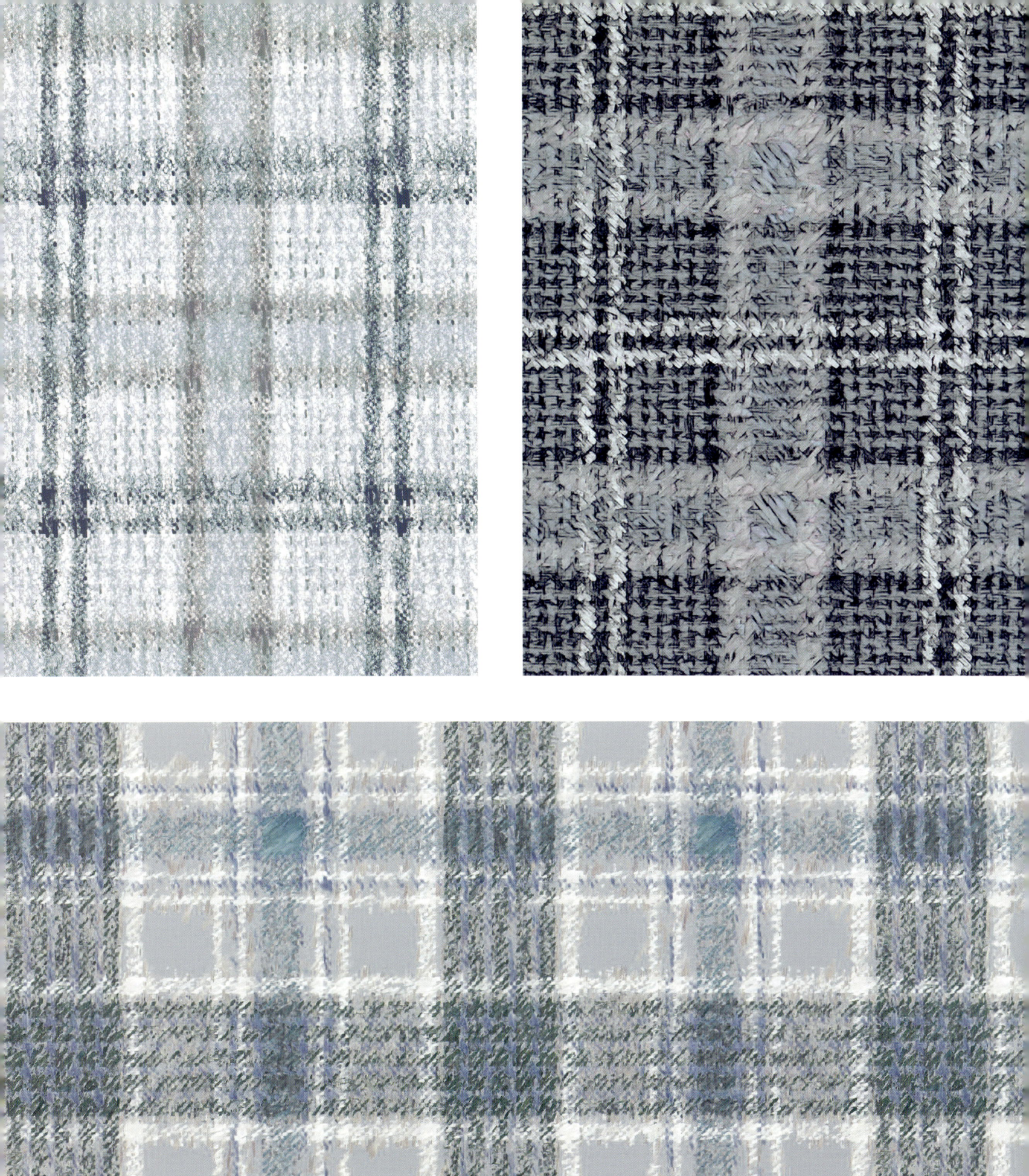

page 126

GGT0214

pattern size
70 cm x 70 cm
8268 x 8268 pixels
at 300 ppi in CMYK

GGT0215

pattern size
50 cm x 50 cm
5906 x 5906 pixels
at 300 ppi in CMYK

page 127

GGT0216
pattern size
50 cm x 50 cm
5906 x 5906 pixels
at 300 ppi in CMYK

GGT0217
pattern size
50 cm x 62 cm
5906 x 7323 pixels
at 300 ppi in CMYK

page 128

GGT0218
pattern size
48 cm x 60 cm
5670 x 7087 pixels
at 300 ppi in CMYK

GGT0219
pattern size
50 cm x 50 cm
5906 x 5906 pixels
at 300 ppi in CMYK

GGT0220
pattern size
50 cm x 50 cm
5906 x 5906 pixels
at 300 ppi in CMYK

GGT0221
pattern size
50 cm x 50 cm
5906 x 5906 pixels
at 300 ppi in CMYK

page 129 >

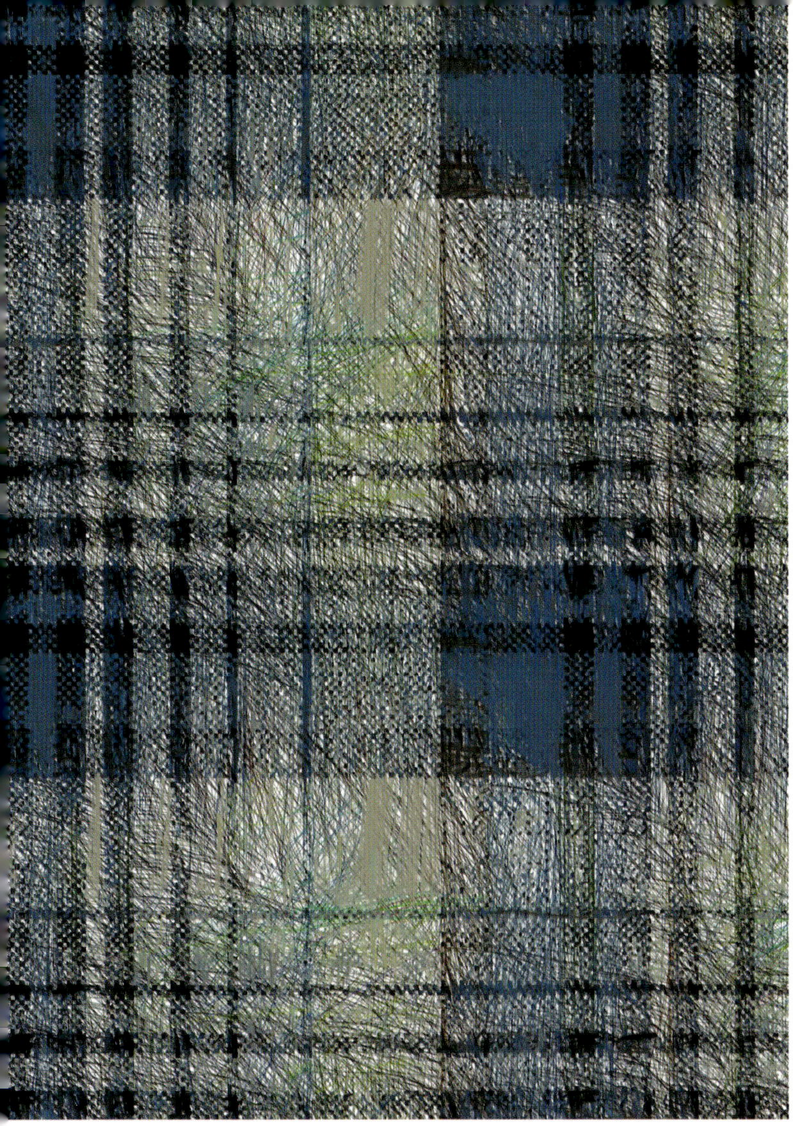

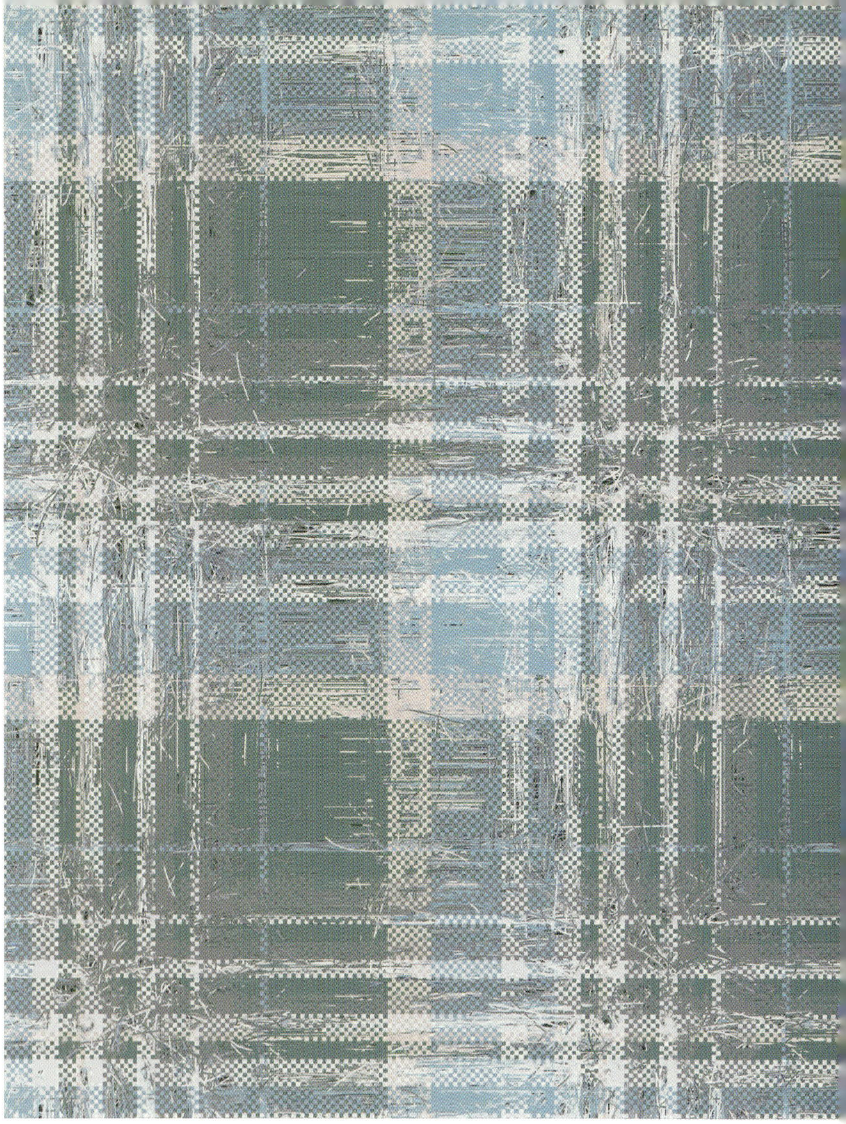

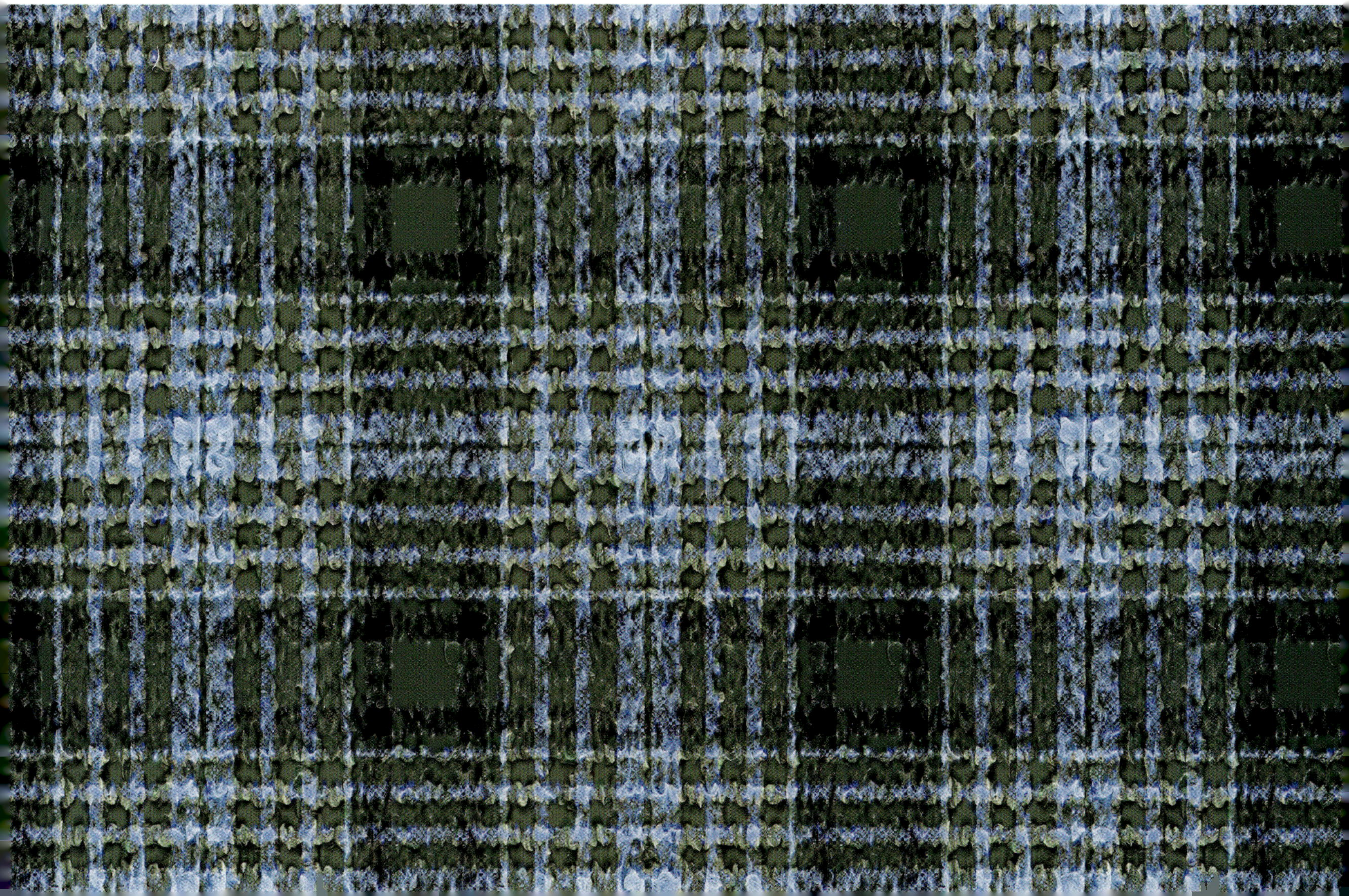

page 130

GGT0222
pattern size
70 cm x 70 cm
8268 x 8268 pixels
at 300 ppi in CMYK

GGT0223
pattern size
60 cm x 80 cm
7087 x 9449 pixels
at 300 ppi in CMYK

page 131

GGT0224
pattern size
50 cm x 50 cm
5906 x 5906 pixels
at 300 ppi in CMYK

GGT0225
pattern size
50 cm x 50 cm
5906 x 5906 pixels
at 300 ppi in CMYK

page 132

GGT0226
pattern size
70 cm x 70 cm
8268 x 8268 pixels
at 300 ppi in CMYK

GGT0227
pattern size
70 cm x 70 cm
8268 x 8268 pixels
at 300 ppi in CMYK

page 133

GGT0228
pattern size
50 cm x 50 cm
5906 x 5906 pixels
at 300 ppi in CMYK

GGT0229
pattern size
50 cm x 50 cm
5906 x 5906 pixels
at 300 ppi in CMYK

page 134

GGT0230
pattern size
60 cm x 60 cm
7087 x 7087 pixels
at 300 ppi in CMYK

GGT0231
pattern size
50 cm x 45 cm
5906 x 5315 pixels
at 300 ppi in CMYK

page 135

GGT0232
pattern size
45 cm x 60 cm
5315 x 7087 pixels
at 300 ppi in CMYK

page 136

GGT0233
pattern size
70 cm x 70 cm
8268 x 8268 pixels
at 300 ppi in CMYK

page 137

GGT0234
pattern size
60 cm x 50 cm
7087 x 5906 pixels
at 300 ppi in CMYK

GGT0235
pattern size
60 cm x 40 cm
7087 x 4725 pixels
at 300 ppi in CMYK

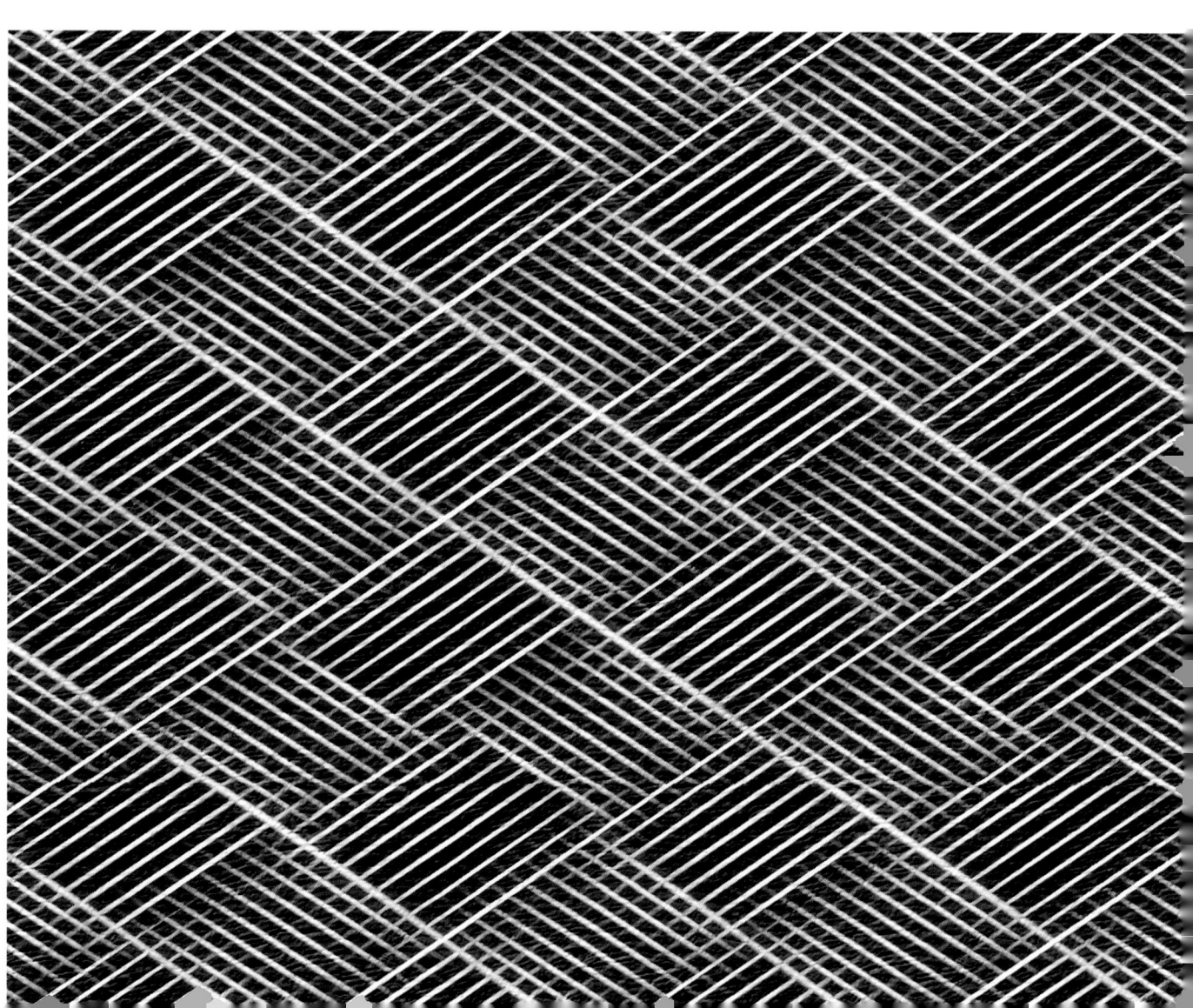

page 138

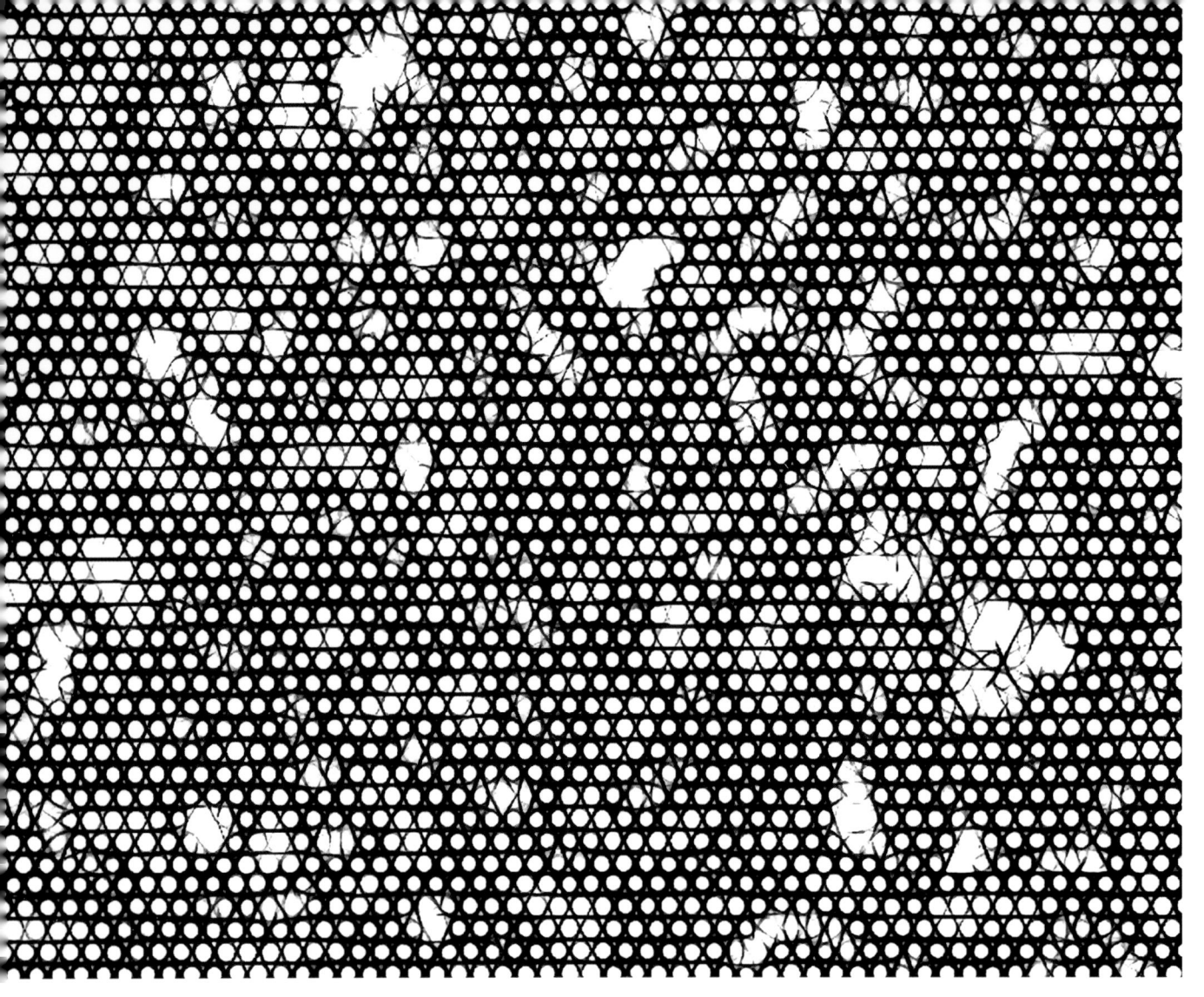

GGT0236
pattern size
50 cm x 50 cm
5906 x 5906 pixels
at 300 ppi in CMYK

GGT0237
pattern size
50 cm x 50 cm
5906 x 5906 pixels
at 300 ppi in CMYK

page 139

GGT0238
pattern size
60 cm x 60 cm
7087 x 7087 pixels
at 300 ppi in CMYK

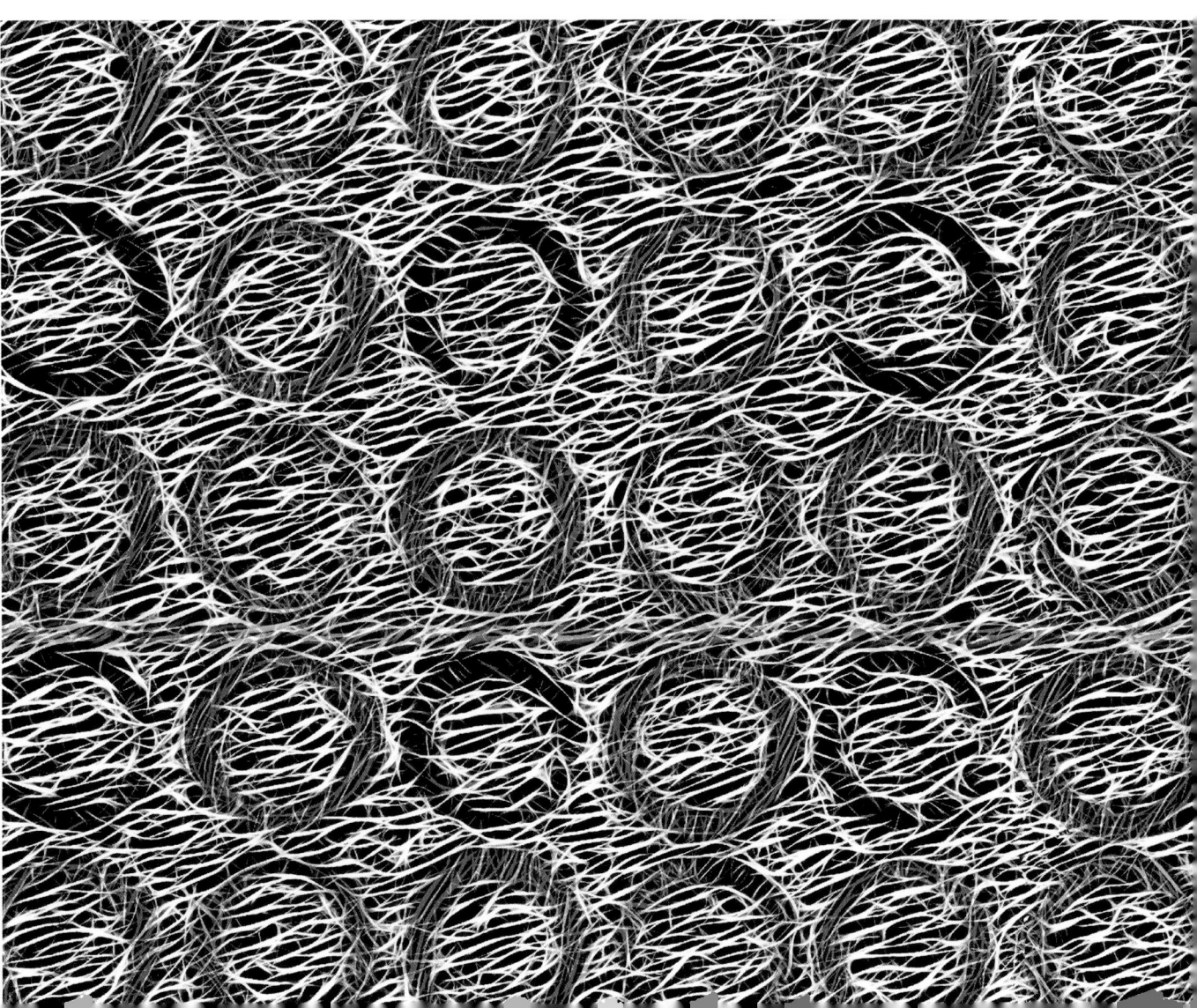

GGT0239
pattern size
50 cm x 50 cm
5906 x 5906 pixels
at 300 ppi in CMYK

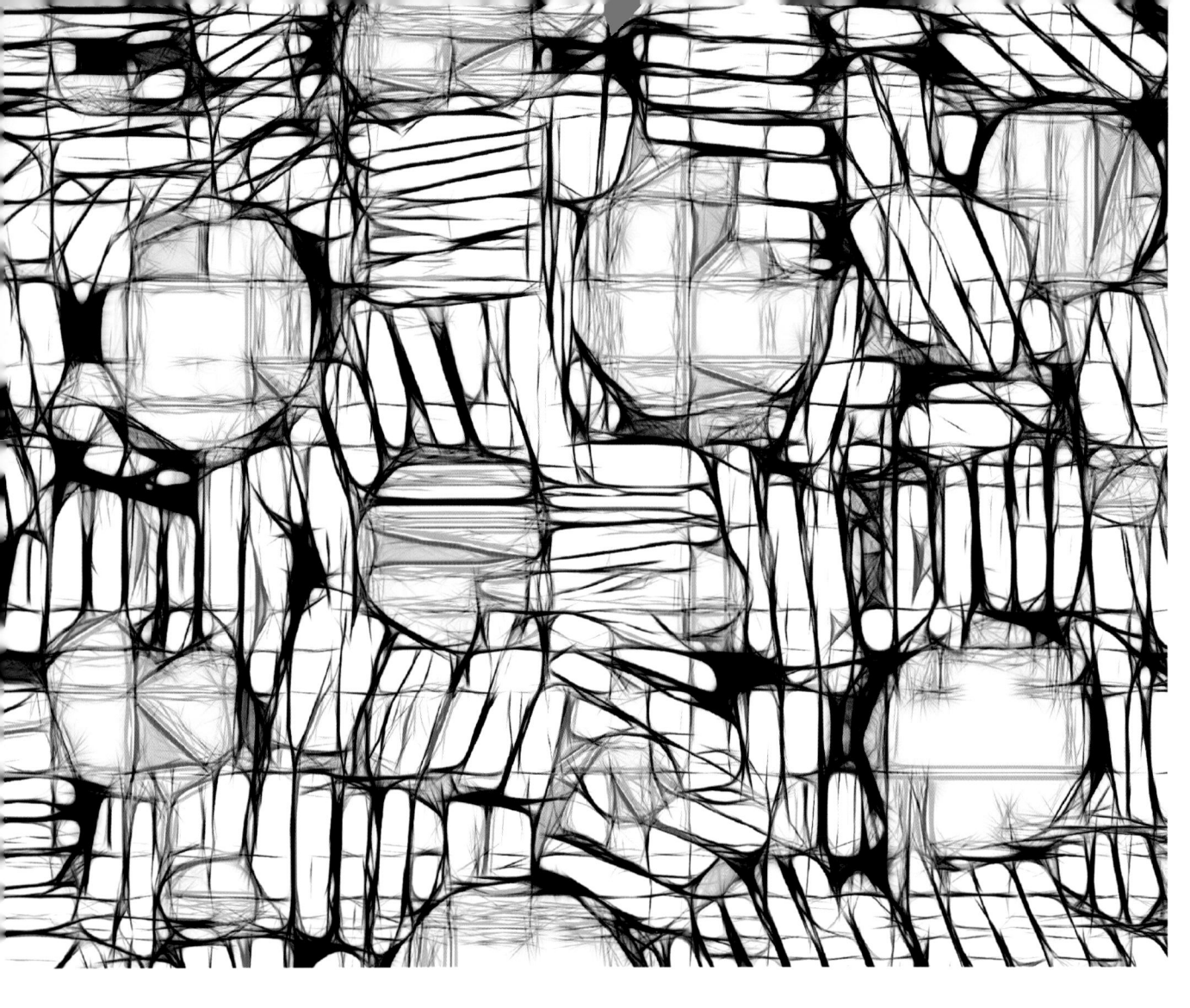

page 140

GGT0240
pattern size
50 cm x 50 cm
5906 x 5906 pixels
at 300 ppi in CMYK

GGT0241
pattern size
60 cm x 60 cm
7087 x 7087 pixels
at 300 ppi in CMYK

page 141

GGT0242
pattern size
60 cm x 50 cm
7087 x 5906 pixels
at 300 ppi in CMYK

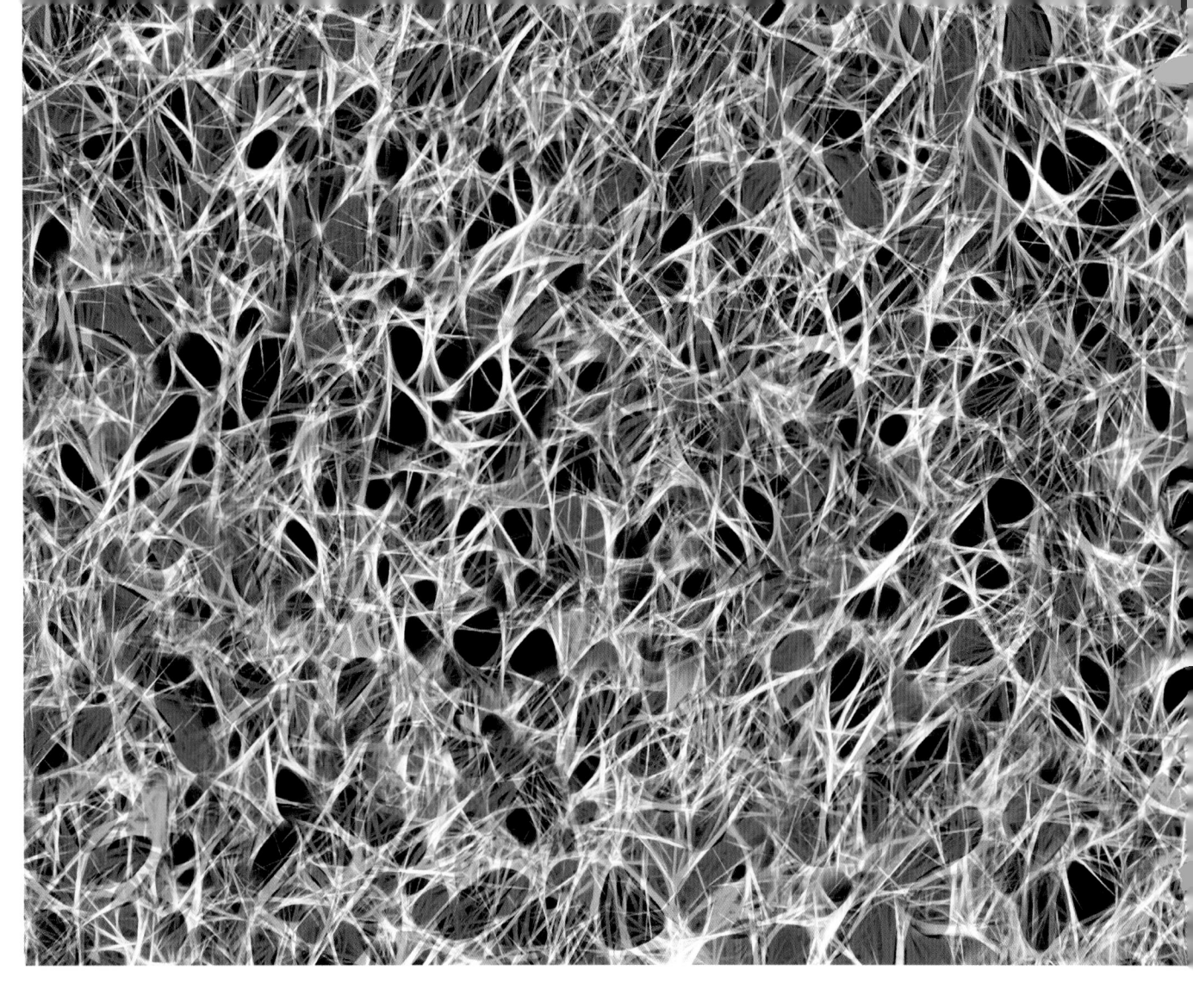

GGT0243
pattern size
60 cm x 50 cm
7087 x 5906 pixels
at 300 ppi in CMYK

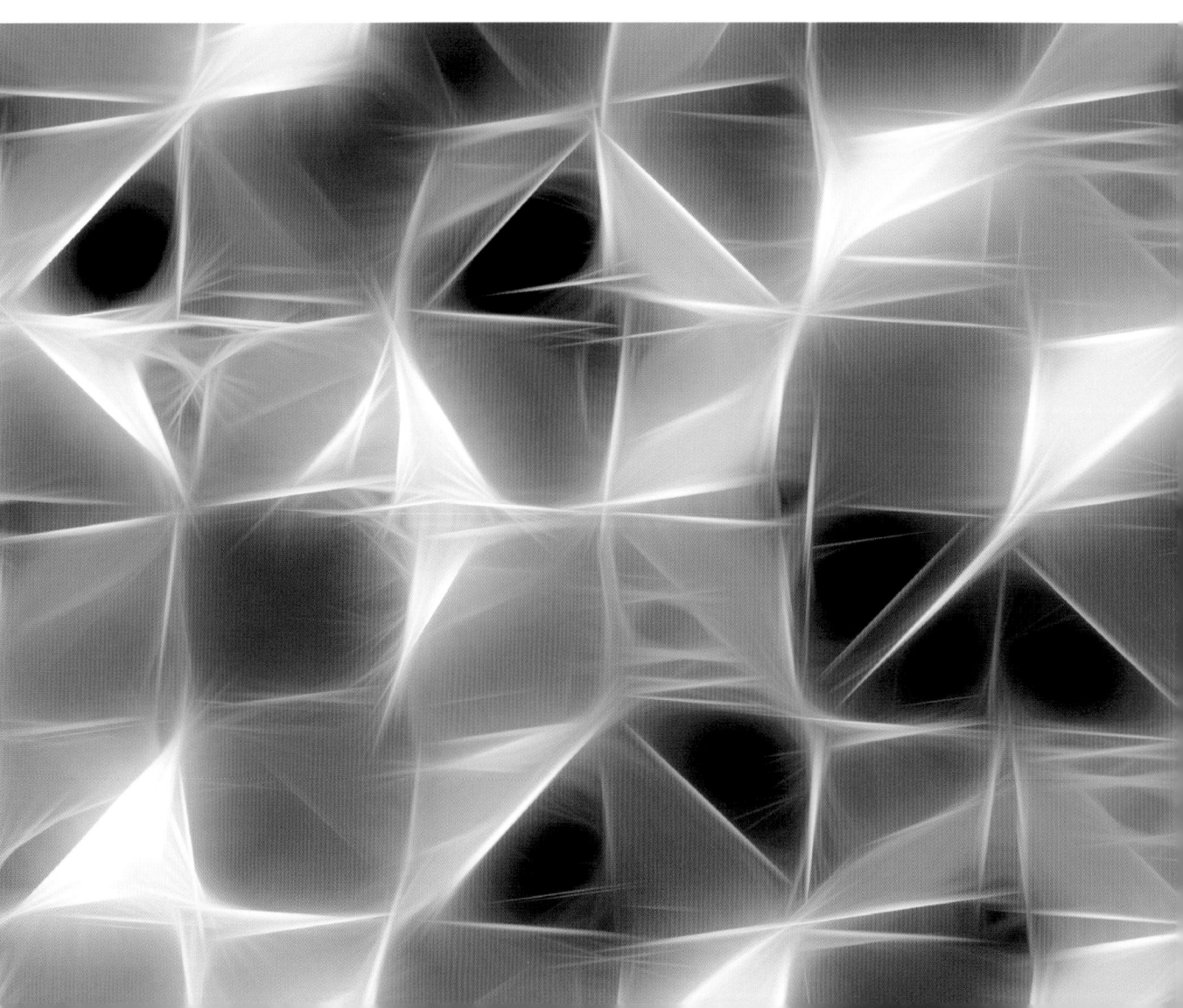

page 142

GGT0244
pattern size
60 cm x 60 cm
7087 x 7087 pixels
at 300 ppi in CMYK

GGT0245
pattern size
50 cm x 45 cm
5906 x 5315 pixels
at 300 ppi in CMYK

page 143

GGT0246
pattern size
50 cm x 60 cm
5906 x 7087 pixels
at 300 ppi in CMYK

GGT0247
pattern size
60 cm x 50 cm
7087 x 5906 pixels
at 300 ppi in CMYK

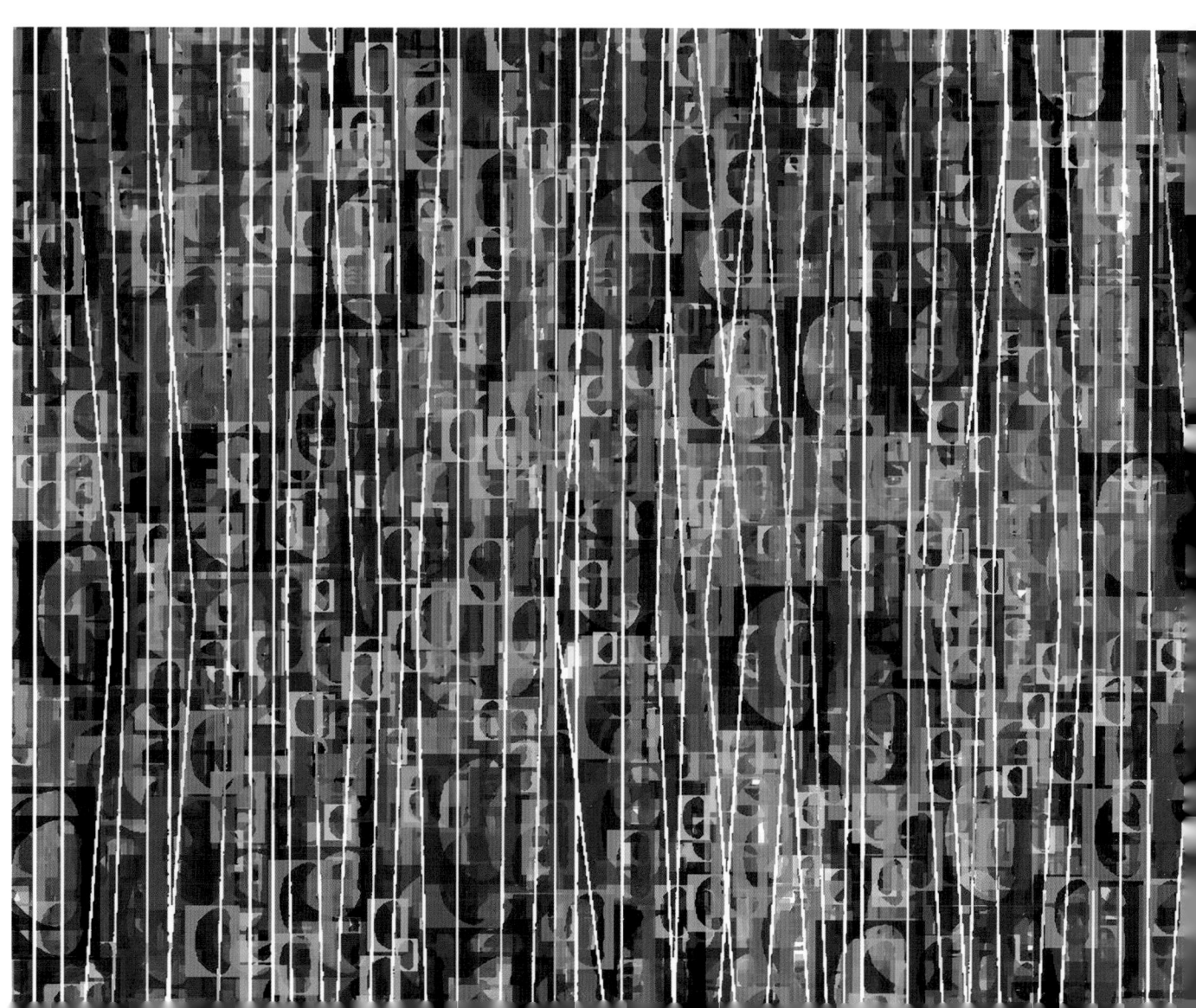

page 144

GGT0248
pattern size
50 cm x 50 cm
5906 x 5906 pixels
at 300 ppi in CMYK

GGT0249
pattern size
50 cm x 50 cm
5906 x 5906 pixels
at 300 ppi in CMYK

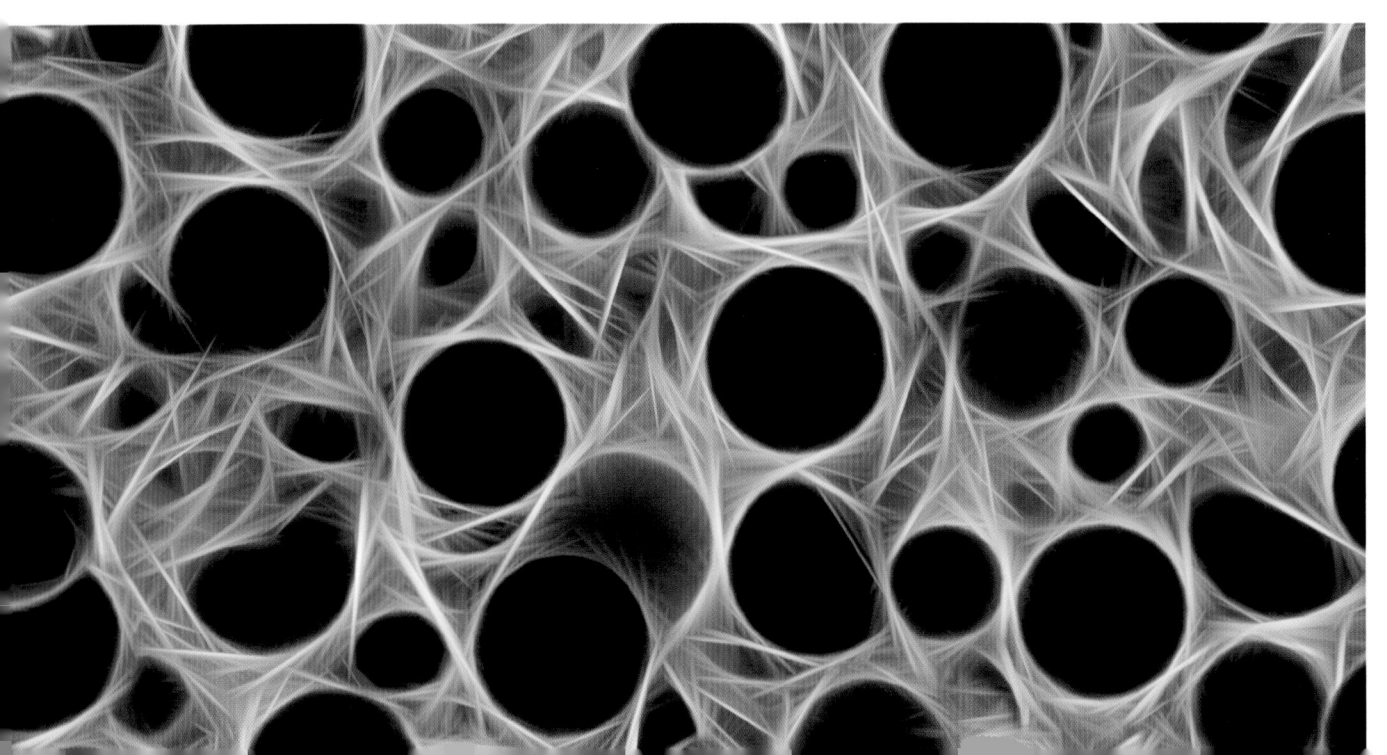

GGT0250
pattern size
50 cm x 50 cm
5906 x 5906 pixels
at 300 ppi in CMYK

arkivia books
collection

WHY ARKIVIA BOOKS?

For those who work as stylists or designers of product lines in various merceological sectors, one of the most important jobs is to determine the look that the line should have to attract clients and distinguish itself from others.

Research is fundamental, before any design can be made, research using books, magazines, samples of objects found all over the world. This results in a large quantity of ideas on which the marketing department works before starting to develop one of them.
A long and expensive process to reach the development of the designs, keeping in mind the production methods.

I have inserted into my books this kind of know-how:

1 - Research into a tendency theme
2 - Development of creative ideas that illustrate it
3 - Professional artworks for immediate production with
-    that look.

WHO FINDS ARKIVIA BOOKS USEFUL?

1 - Those who create products every day and need to -   -
-    document a single theme suitable to the product.
2 - Companies that with a small amount of money, very
-    low compared with the high costs of creative studios, --
-    can access material ready to be used and developed
-    by their internal staff.

In the recent past, Tendency Books have been produced for a restricted club of professional people who could afford the high cost of this sort of book
(around 1000/1500 euros).
I have decided to create books with the same spirit but within the reach of any professional in image.
As expensive as a good quality book but no more than is accepted in bookshops.

SOME TECHNICAL INFORMATION

All files in the CD or in DVD are in hi-res format:
PHOTOSHOP PDF format for bitmap files or
ILLUSTRATOR format for vector files, accessible by all programmes and compatible with WINDOWS and MAC.

All vectorial files are modifiable because they are the original graphics and the material is produced in a professional way and ready to use.

The designs are free to be used by those who buy the books in accordance with copyright terms present in each book.

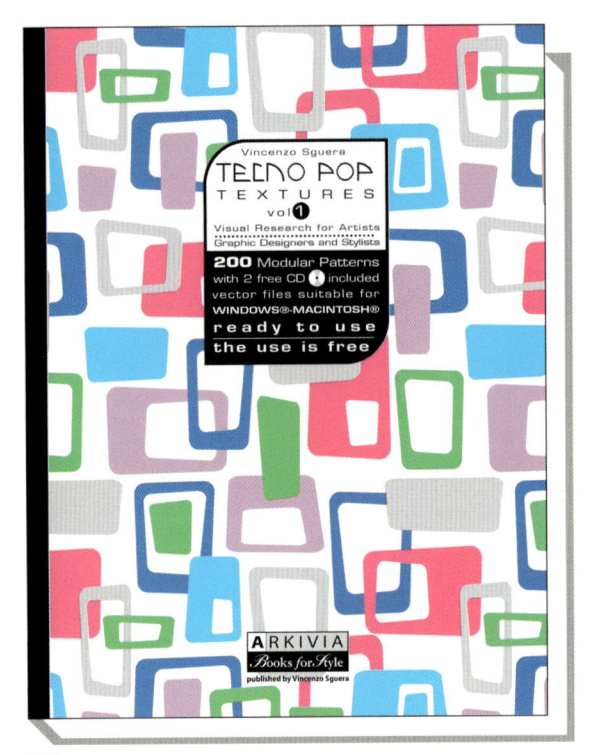

TECNO POP TEXTURES vol.1
ISBN 9788888766010

HARDBACK • 144 pages • size 24cm x 30.7cm
Contents:
200 Modular Patterns with 2 free CD included
Vector files in flat colors and CMYK

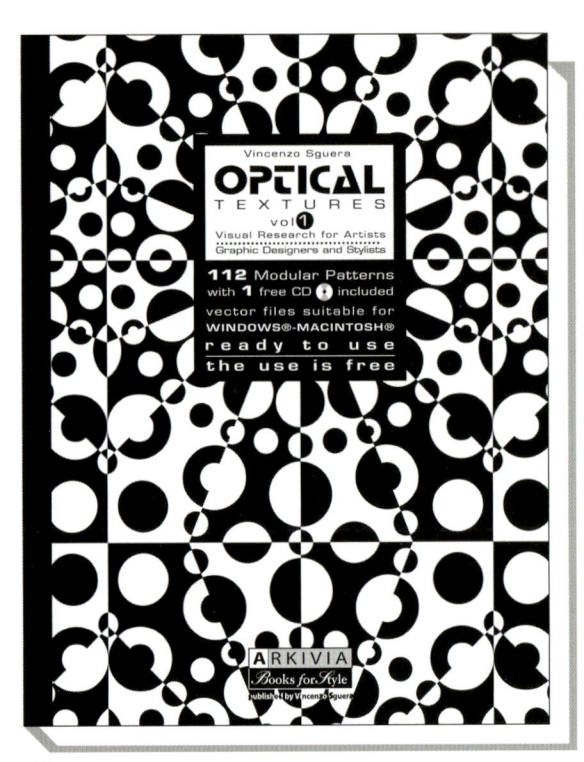

OPTICAL TEXTURES vol.1
ISBN 9788888766027

PAPERBACK • 128 pages • size 24cm x 30.7cm
Contents:
112 Modular Patterns with 1 free CD included
Vector files in flat colors and CMYK

STYLING BOOK vol.1
HB 9788888766034 • PB 9788888766515

HARDBACK (HB) • PAPERBACK (PB)
144 pages • size 24cm x 30.7cm
More than 600 designs with CDs or DVD included
Vector files in flat colors and CMYK

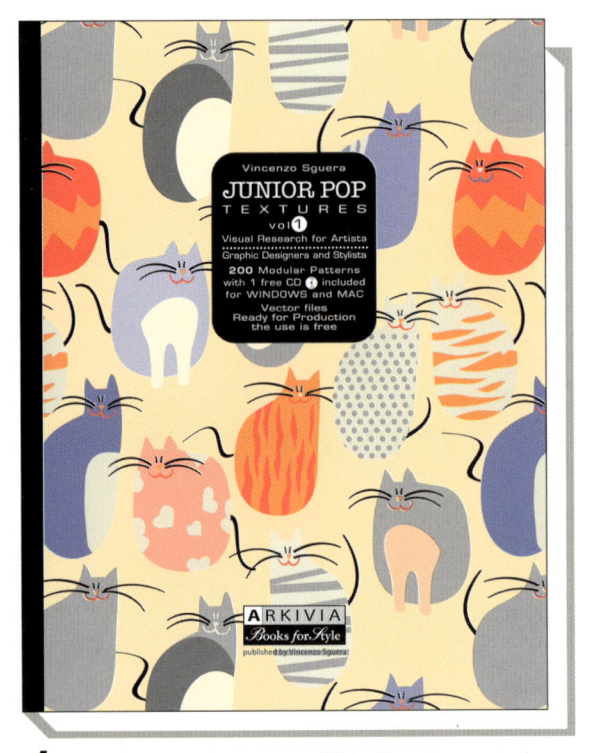

JUNIOR POP TEXTURES vol.1
HB 9788888766041 • PB 9788888766522

HARDBACK (HB) • PAPERBACK (PB)
144 pages • size 24cm x 30.7cm
200 Modular Patterns with 1 free CD included
Vector files in flat colors and CMYK

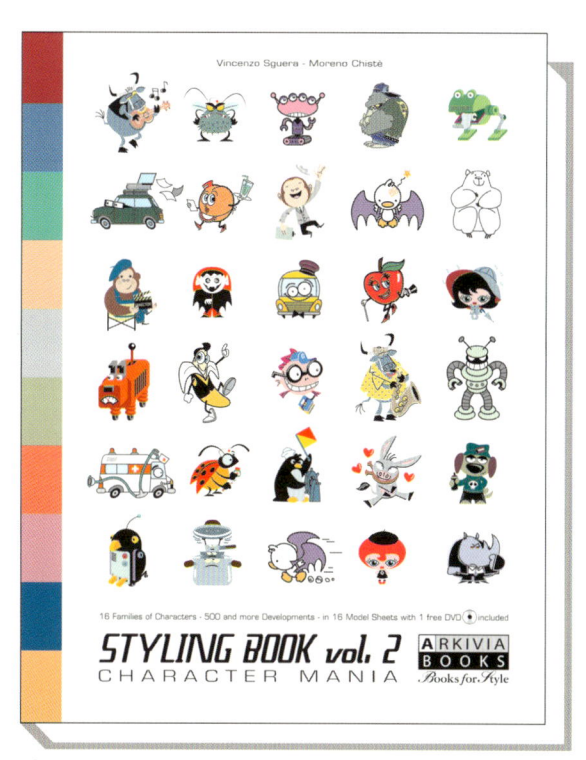

STYLING BOOK vol.2
HB 9788888766058 • PB 9788888766539

HARDBACK (HB) • PAPERBACK (PB)
160 pages • size 24cm x 30.7cm
More than 500 designs with 1 free DVD included
Vector files in flat colors and CMYK

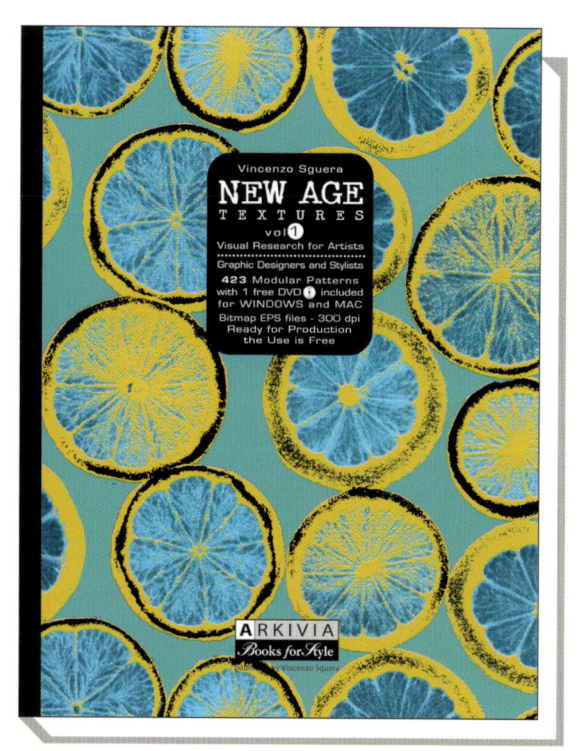

NEW AGE TEXTURES vol.1
HB 9788888766003 • PB 9788888766065

HARDBACK (HB) • PAPERBACK (PB)
144 pages • size 24cm x 30.7cm
423 Modular Patterns with 1 free DVD included
EPS Bitmap files - CMYK - 300 dpi resolution

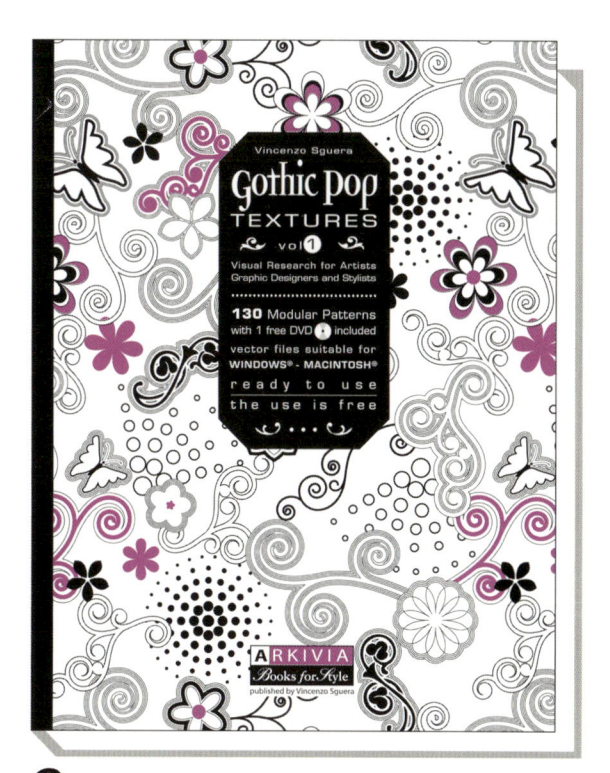

GOTHIC POP TEXTURES vol.1
HB 9788888766072 • PB 9788888766546

HARDBACK (HB) • PAPERBACK (PB)
144 pages • size 24cm x 30.7cm
130 Modular Patterns with 1 free DVD included
Vector files in flat colors and CMYK

GOTHIC POP TEXTURES vol.2
ISBN 9788888766089

HARDBACK • 144 pages • size 24cm x 30.7cm
Contents:
130 Modular Patterns with 1 free DVD included
Vector files in flat colors and CMYK

CHARACTER STYLING vol.1 - THE CAT
ISBN 9788888766096

HARDBACK • 72 pages • size 24cm x 30.7cm
Contents:
216 Designs (6 Characters) with 1 free CD included
Vector files in flat colors and CMYK

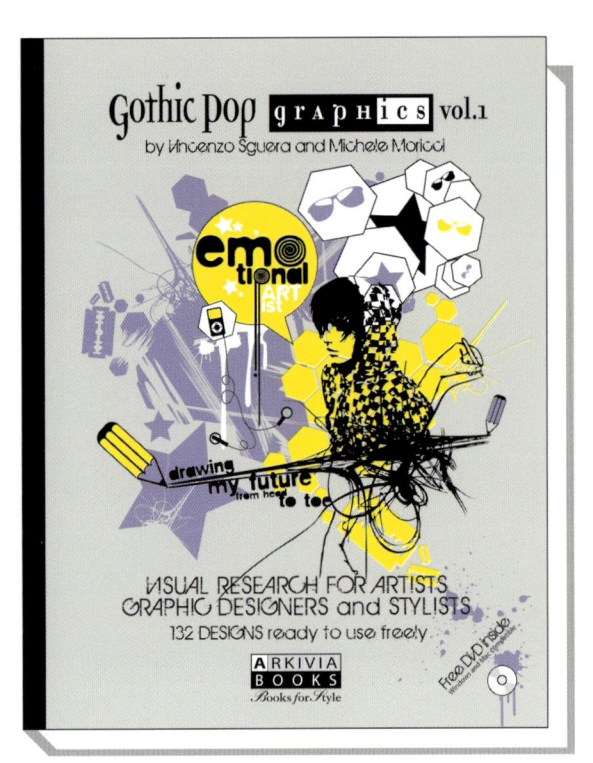

GOTHIC POP GRAPHICS vol.1
ISBN 9788888766102

HARDBACK • 144 pages • size 24cm x 30.7cm
Contents:
132 Graphics with 1 free DVD included
Vector files in flat colors and CMYK

NATURAL POP TEXTURES vol.1
HB 9788888766119 • PB 9788888766553

HARDBACK (HB) • PAPERBACK (PB)
144 pages • size 24cm x 30.7cm
130 Modular Patterns with 1 free DVD included
Vector files in flat colors and CMYK

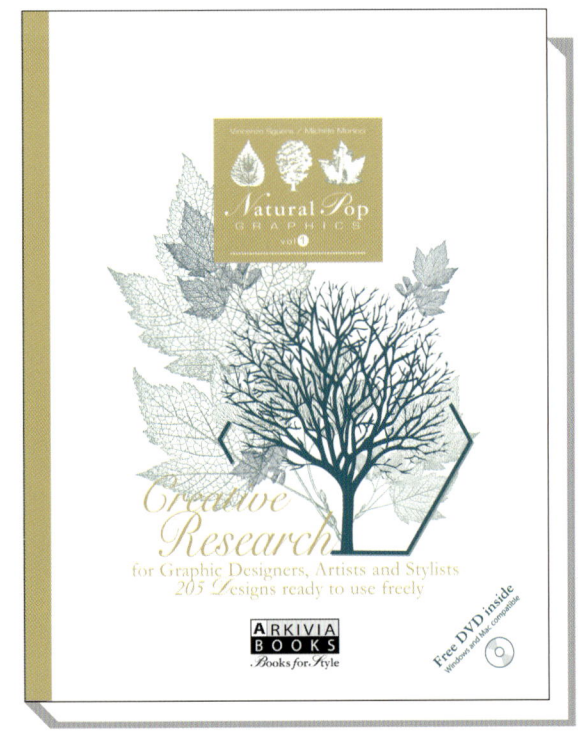

NATURAL POP GRAPHICS vol.1
HB 9788888766126 • PB 9788888766560

HARDBACK (HB) • PAPERBACK (PB)
144 pages • size 24cm x 30.7cm
205 Graphics with 1 free DVD included
Vector files in flat colors and CMYK

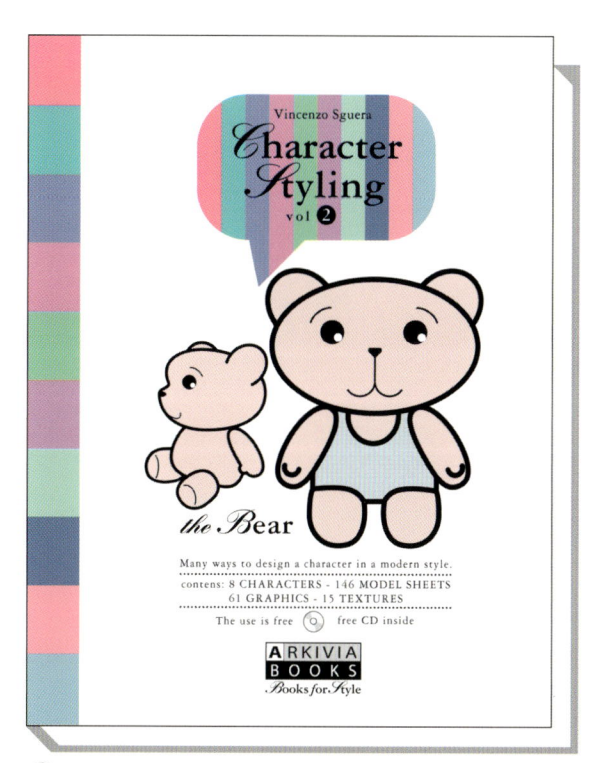

CHARACTER STYLING vol.2 - THE BEAR
ISBN 9788888766133

HARDBACK • 72 pages • size 24cm x 30.7cm
Contents:
222 Designs (8 Characters) with 1 free CD included
Vector files in flat colors and CMYK

BLACK & WHITE MATRIX 1
HB 9788888766140 • PB 9788888766577

HARDBACK (HB) • PAPERBACK (PB)
144 pages • size 24cm x 30.7cm
325 Modular Patterns with 1 free DVD included
Vector files in flat colors and CMYK

MATRIX GRAPHIX 1
ISBN 9788888766157

HARDBACK • 144 pages • size 24cm x 30.7cm
Contents:
250 Graphics with 1 free DVD included
Vector files in flat colors and CMYK

BLACK & WHITE MATRIX 2
HB 9788888766164 • PB 9788888766584

HARDBACK (HB) • PAPERBACK (PB)
144 pages • size 24cm x 30.7cm
275 Modular Patterns with 1 free DVD included
Vector files in flat colors and CMYK

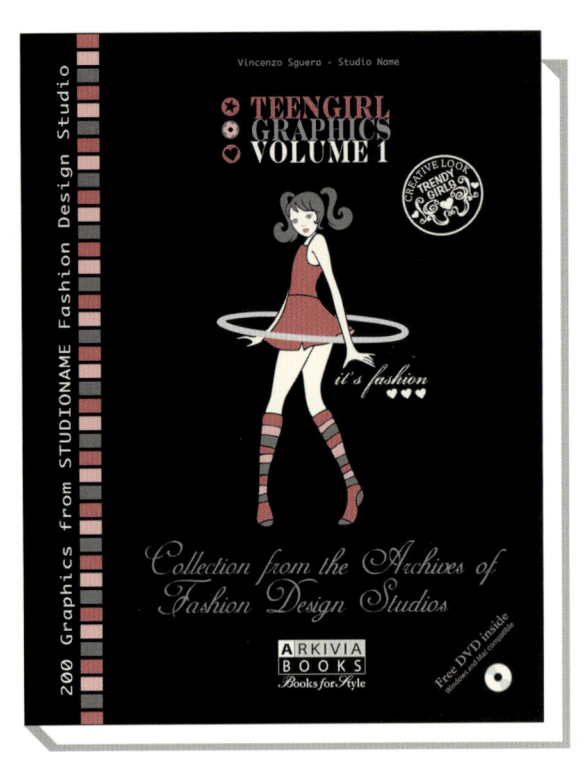

TEEN GIRL GRAPHICS vol.1
HB 9788888766171 • PB 9788888766591

HARDBACK (HB) • PAPERBACK (PB)
96 pages • size 24cm x 30.7cm
200 Graphics with 1 free DVD included
Vector files in flat colors and CMYK

ULTRA POP TEXTURES vol. 1
ISBN 9788888766188

HARDBACK • 144 pages • size 24cm x 30.7cm
Contents:
130 Textures with 1 free CD included
Vector files in flat colors and CMYK

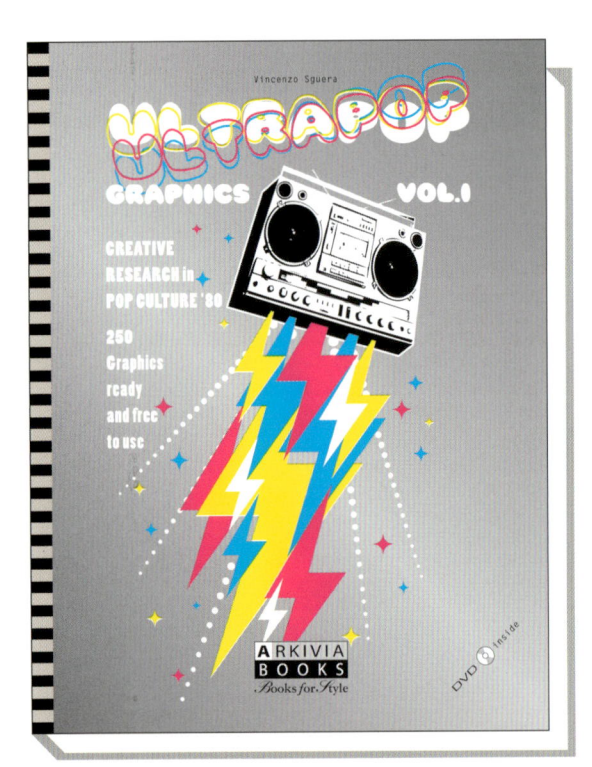

ULTRA POP GRAPHICS vo. 1
ISBN 9788888766195

HARDBACK • 144 pages • size 24cm x 30.7cm
Contents:
250 Graphics with 1 free DVD included
Vector files in flat colors and CMYK

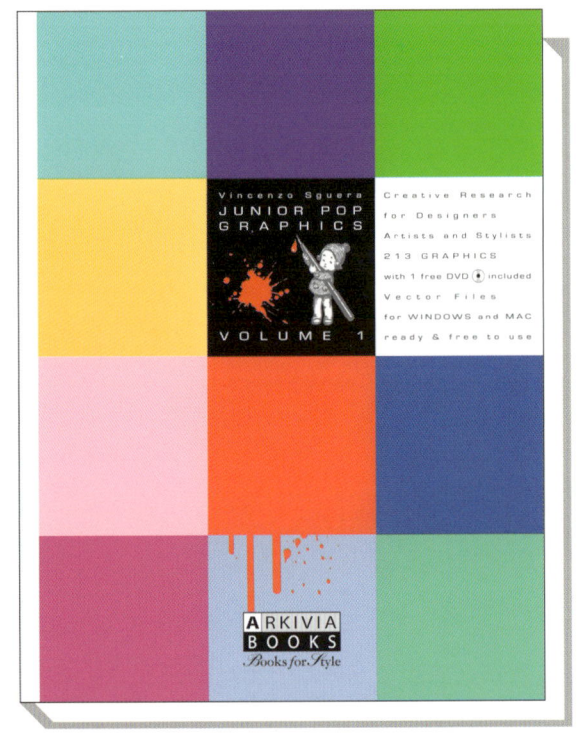

JUNIOR POP GRAPHICS vol.1
ISBN 9788888766201

HARDBACK • 96 pages • size 24cm x 30.7cm
Contents:
213 Graphics with 1 free CD included
Vector files in flat colors and CMYK

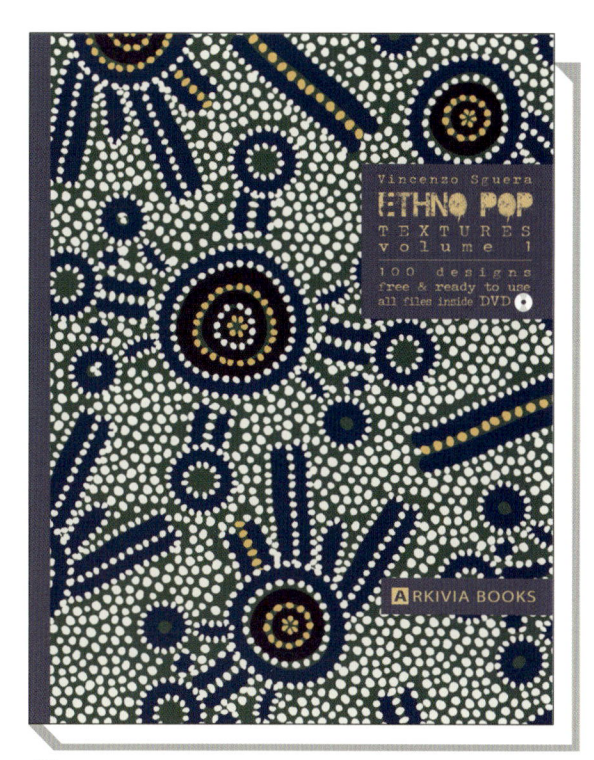

ETHNO POP TEXTURES vol.1
ISBN 9788888766218

HARDBACK • 112 pages • size 24cm x 30.7cm
Contents:
100 Modular Patterns with 1 free DVD included
Vector files in flat colors and CMYK

TEEN BOY GRAPHICS vol.1
ISBN 9788888766225

HARDBACK • 96 pages • size 24cm x 30.7cm
Contents:
200 Graphics with 1 free DVD included
Vector files in flat colors and CMYK

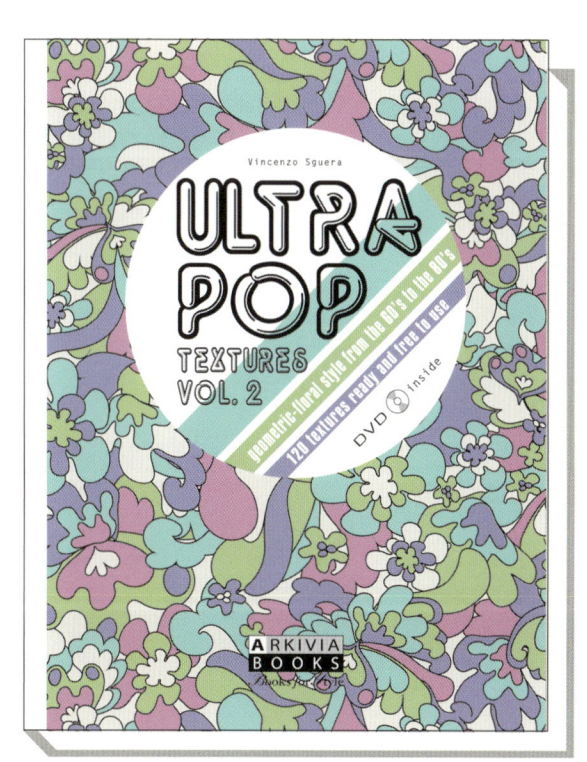

ULTRA POP TEXTURES vol.2
ISBN 9788888766232

HARDBACK • 144 pages • size 24cm x 30.7cm
Contents:
120 Modular Patterns with 1 free DVD included
Vector files in flat colors and CMYK

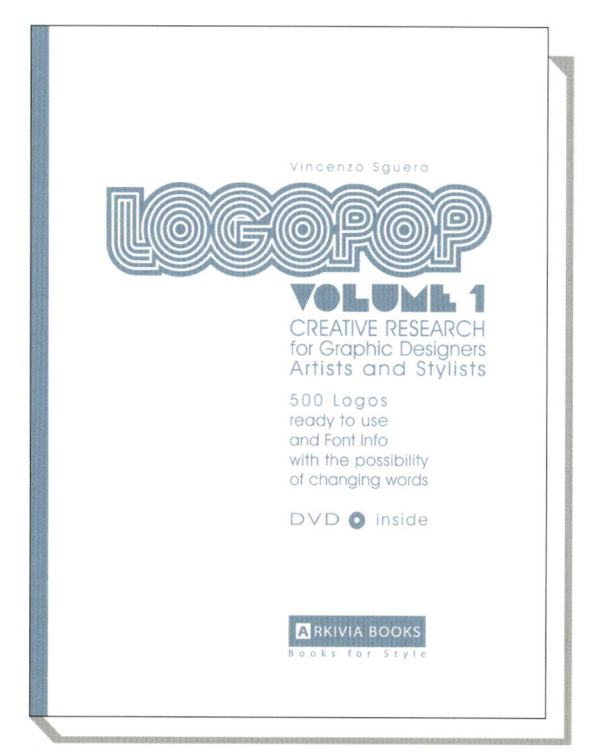

LOGOPOP VOLUME 1
ISBN 9788888766256

HARDBACK • 160 pages • size 24cm x 30.7cm
Contents:
500 Logos + Fonts Info with 1 free DVD included
Vector files in flat colors and CMYK

Grunge Textures vol.1

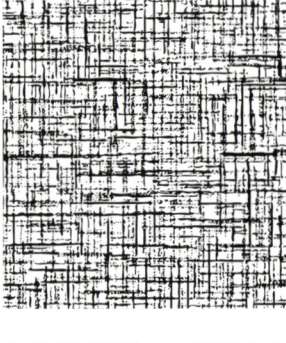

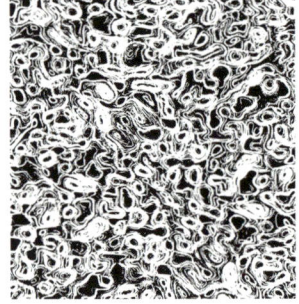

ISBN 9788888766249
PAPERBACK • 144 pages
size 24cm x 30.7cm
160 TEXTURES saved
in 5 ways-800 files in all

1 Free DVD included
for WINDOWS and MAC
Vector and Bitmap Files
Ready for Production.
The use is Free

"Grunge", a term intended to indicate something disorderly, casual or ruined.
The uses of this book are many, in decoration or to give a different touch to the image, creating movement where necessary.
At the same time it is a tendency book and also a very useful source book

---

Ethno Pop Textures vol.2

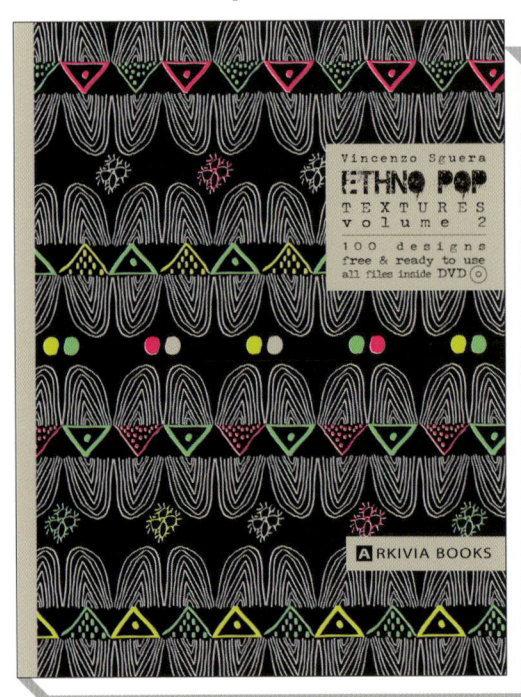

ISBN 9788888766263
HARDBACK • 112 pages
size 24cm x 30.7cm
100 TEXTURES saved
in 5 ways-500 files in all

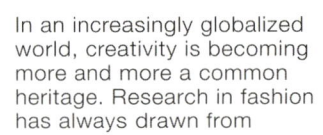

1 Free DVD included
for WINDOWS and MAC
Vector and Bitmap Files
Ready for Production.
The use is Free

In an increasingly globalized world, creativity is becoming more and more a common heritage. Research in fashion has always drawn from cultures all over the world, reproposing for itself designs from ethnic groups which are far away in time and space.

Natural Pop Textures Vol.2

ISBN 9788888766270
HARDBACK • 144 pages
size 24cm x 30.7cm
122 TEXTURES saved
in 5 ways 610 files in all.

1 Free DVD included
for WINDOWS and MAC
Vector and Bitmap Files
Ready for Production.
The use is Free

This second book develops
more soft and elegant designs
inspired by modern
North-European Design also
called Scandinavian Style.

New ideas in delicate colours
and graphic synthesis, clean
and essential, suitable for
home decoration, interior design
and fashion clothing textiles.

Kinetic Art Textures vol.1

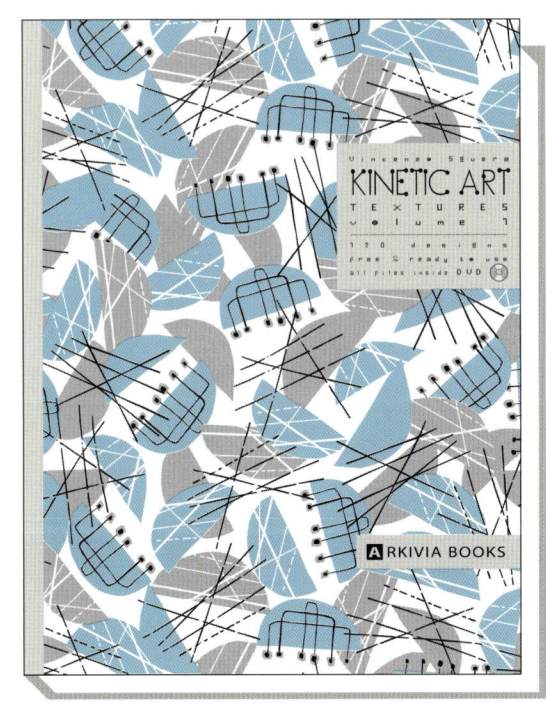

ISBN 9788888766287
HARDBACK • 144 pages
size 24cm x 30.7cm
120 TEXTURES saved
in 5 ways-600 files in all

1 Free DVD included
for WINDOWS and MAC
Vector and Bitmap Files
Ready for Production.
The use is Free

Beyond the image and the
meaning in every work, there
are rhythm and structure
to catch the aesthetics
abstracted from the meaning.

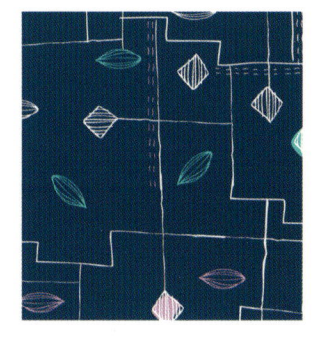

The geometries have their own
values apart from what they
represent and they do so in
a continuous and rhythmic way.
This style is "KINETIC ART".

Animal Style Textures Vol.1

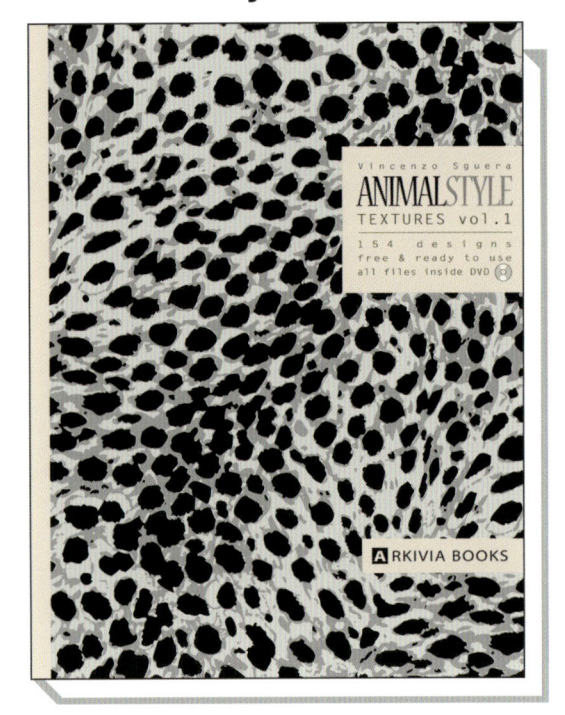

ISBN 9788888766294 HARDBACK Edition
ISBN 9788888766607 PAPERBACK Edition
160 pages • size 24cm x 30.7cm
154 TEXTURES saved in 5 ways - 770 files in all.
1 Free DVD included for WINDOWS and MAC.
Vector and BitmapFiles • The use is Free.

There is a tendency that has slowly but surely imposed itself: the style inspired by animal skins. Strong, essential and recognizable it has managed to renew itself, passing from a simple proposal of natural skins to mixing these in a fresh and new way.

Flower Fashion Textures vol.1

ISBN 9788888766300
HARDBACK • 144 pages
size 24cm x 30.7cm
300 TEXTURES saved
in 5 ways-1500 files in all

1 Free DVD included for WINDOWS and MAC Vector and Bitmap Files Ready for Production. The use is Free

The world of Fashion has always drawn inspiration from nature, colors and decorations. Small and large flowers with stripes and squares or provençal designs.

Roses and violets, poppies and daisies in a continuous flow of textures, making vectorial and synthetic designs following the trend of present graphics.

Black and White Matrix 3

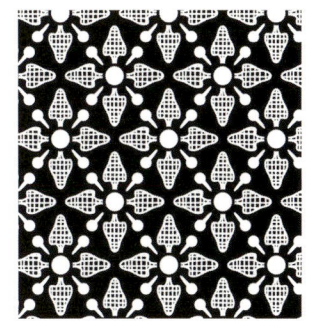

ISBN 9788888766317
HARDBACK • 144 pages
size 24cm x 30.7cm
250 TEXTURES saved
in 5 ways 1250 files in all.

1 Free DVD included
for WINDOWS and MAC
Vector and Bitmap Files
Ready for Production.
The use is Free

When decorative cultures from far away places meet. Europe and Asia with their traditions may coexist and adopt a mature look.

Various decorative layers, rich in detail, lead beyond the level of taste bringing a more graphic and essential pot pourri.

Geometric Textures for Fashion vol.1

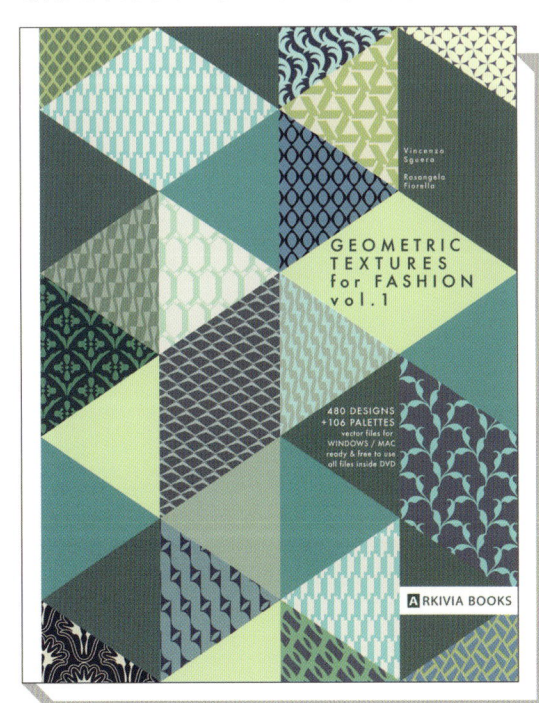

ISBN 9788888766324 HARDBACK Edition
ISBN 9788888766614 PAPERBACK Edition
144 pages • size 24cm x 30.7cm
480 TEXTURES saved in 5 ways +106 palettes.
1 Free DVD included for WINDOWS and MAC.
Vector and BitmapFiles • The use is Free.

This book offers vector designs of geometric fabrics, simple or structured with some elements in the Victorian or Liberty style, and with an emphasis on combinations of minimalist designs, which are useful for furniture and fashion.
The designs are divided into groups, coordinated together and harmonized each with the same colour palette.

Abstract Textures vol.1

ISBN 9788888766331
HARDBACK • 160 pages
size 24cm x 30.7cm
200 TEXTURES saved
JPG 300 ppi / JPG 72 ppi.

1 Free DVD included
for WINDOWS and MAC
Bitmap Modular Files
Ready for Production.
The use is Free

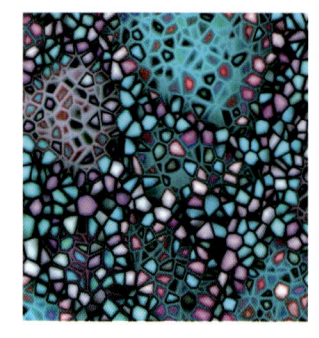

Abstract is real, as an idea, representing a world so vague, undefinable but equally real was the challenge for artists who wanted to break free from the shackles of codified reality.

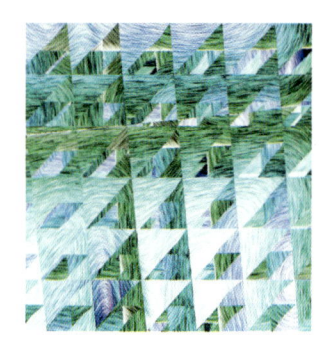

Entering into abstractionism reveals new form and beauty, where the rules of yesterday no longer apply to create others, transcend old visual cultures and generate new ones.

Simple Nature Textures vol.1

ISBN 9788888766348
HARDBACK • 144 pages
size 24cm x 30.7cm
123 TEXTURES saved
in 5 ways / 615 files

1 Free DVD included
for WINDOWS and MAC
Vector and Bitmap Files
Ready for Production.
The use is Free

Flowers are never enough, if they are in soft, pastel tones, as if drawn on a sketch pad.
Nature is a breath, a caress that covers you, interwoven leaves, flights of birds or dragonflies.

Suitable for timeless fabrics, collections that have the fragrance of spring, of a past time which we want to return.
Nature is tinged with nostalgia and becomes simple..

Grunge Flower Textures vol.1

ISBN 9788888766355
HARDBACK • 144 pages
size 24cm x 30.7cm
165 TEXTURES saved in
JPG 300 ppi / JPG 72 ppi

1 Free DVD included
for WINDOWS and MAC
Bitmap Modular Files
Ready for Production.
The use is Free

This book develops designs in the floral world with a particular imprint called GRUNGE in opposition to a synthetic, linear, geometric vision.

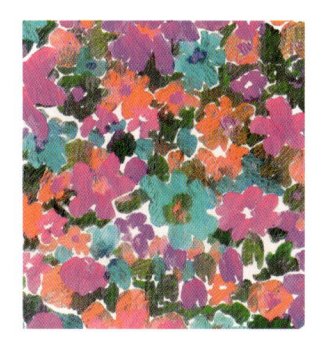

I have created designs where the broken, smudged, sketchy sign is predominant and the backgrounds are irregular to the limit of abstraction.

Liberty Style Textures vol.1

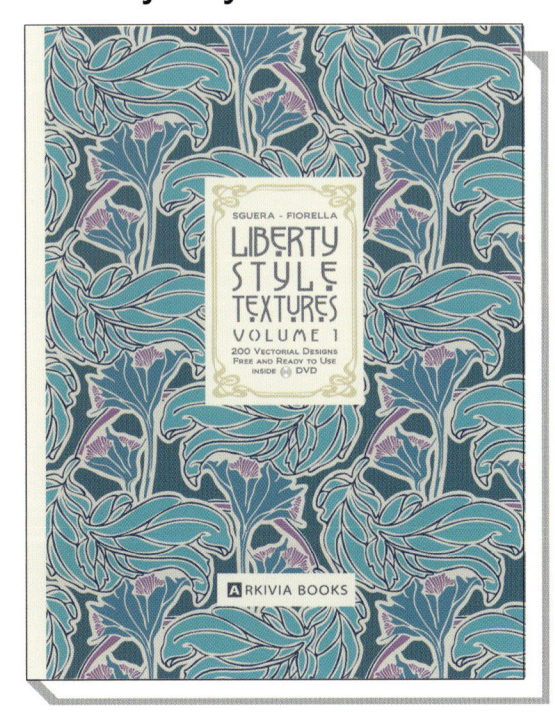

ISBN 9788888766362
HARDBACK • 144 pages
size 24cm x 30.7cm
200 TEXTURES saved in
5 ways -1000 files in all.

1 Free DVD included
for WINDOWS and MAC
Vector and Bitmap Files
Ready for Production.
The use is Free

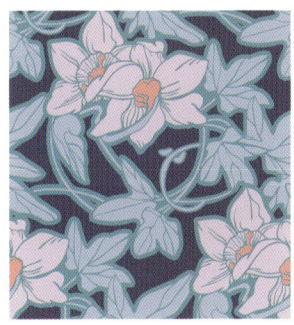

The Liberty Style or Art Nouveau has developed designs that have remained as art and decoration for their remarkable peculiarities: geometry and nature together.

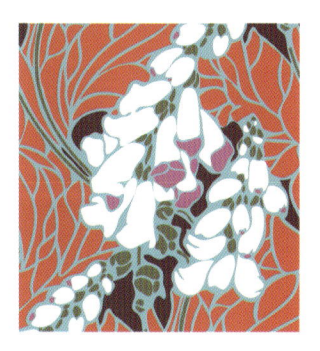

Features are the organic forms, curved lines, with ornaments made essentially of plants or flowers to decorate anything from home décor to clothing.

Abstract Textures vol.2

ISBN 9788888766379
HARDBACK • 160 pages
size 24cm x 30.7cm
137 TEXTURES saved
JPG 300 ppi / JPG 72 ppi.

1 Free DVD included
for WINDOWS and MAC
Bitmap Modular Files
Ready for Production.
The use is Free

Abstract is real, as an idea, representing a world so vague, undefinable but equally real was the challenge for artists who wanted to break free from the shackles of codified reality.

Entering into abstractionism reveals new form and beauty, where the rules of yesterday no longer apply to create others, transcend old visual cultures and generate new ones.

Grunge Geometric Textures vol.1

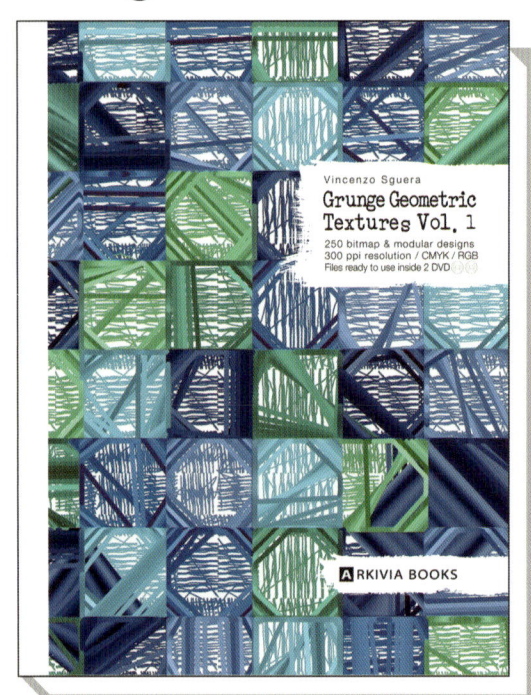

ISBN 9788888766386
HARDBACK • 160 pages
size 24cm x 30.7cm
250 TEXTURES saved in
2 ways -500 files in all.

2 Free DVD included
for WINDOWS and MAC
Bitmap Modular Files
Ready for Production.
The use is Free

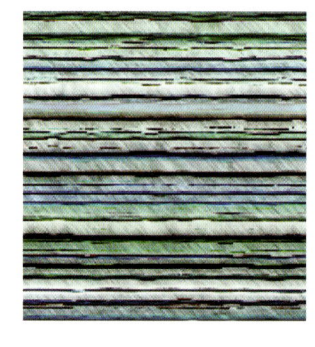

In this technological and global era between B&W miscellanea and Minimalism, the GRUNGE is a style opposed to these. It expresses a need the complex but at the same time is simple,

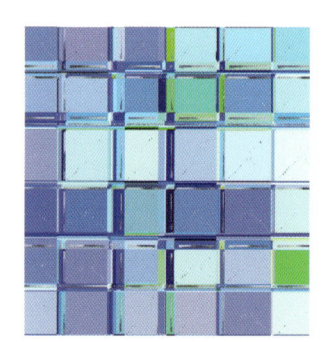

fresh and irrational, away from the constraints of current rules, from social and existential stress. In this sense a new geometry, starting from basic forms and classical fashion patterns.

Ethno Pop Textures - Black Edition

ISBN 9788888766393
HARDBACK • 144 pages
size 24cm x 30.7cm
200 TEXTURES saved in
5 ways -1000 files in all.

1 Free DVD included
for WINDOWS and MAC
Bitmap Modular Files
Ready for Production.
The use is Free

The charm of ethnic designs increases considerably if interpreted in Black & White. While taking away the magic of colours, typical of these designs, this gives them an added chance for greater use.
In fact, the graphical structure of these designs is suitable for all circumstances and so they become casual and elegant at the same time.

Geometric Textures for Fashion vol.2

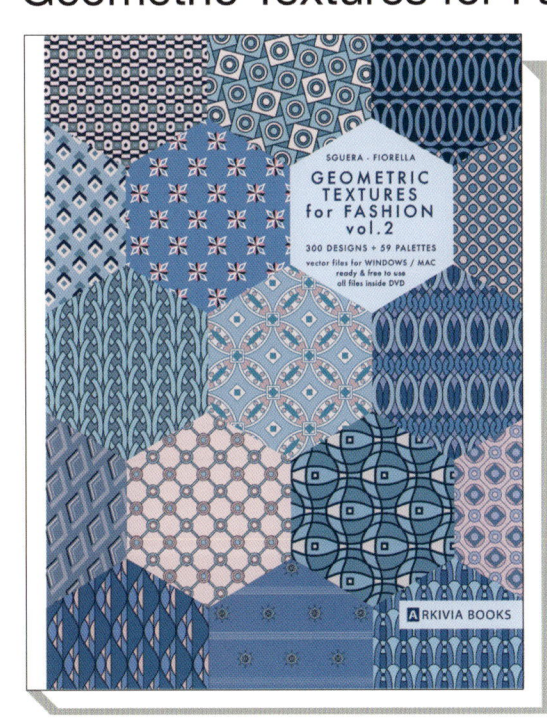

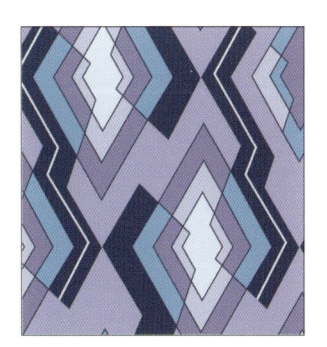

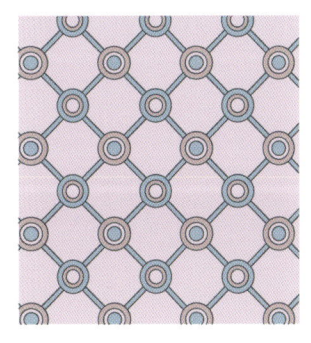

ISBN 9788888766409
HARDBACK • 144 pages
size 24cm x 30.7cm
300 TEXTURES saved
in 5 ways + 59 palettes

1 Free DVD included
for WINDOWS and MAC
Vector and Bitmap Files
Ready for Production.
The use is Free

In the second volume textures are more complex, sometimes with symbols and many colours to create sophisticated atmospheres. To do this I have used even more than the first volume paintings, all redrawn by me and adapted chromatically the textures combined. All palettes enclosed in this volume can to be used for other projects.

Structured Textures vol.1

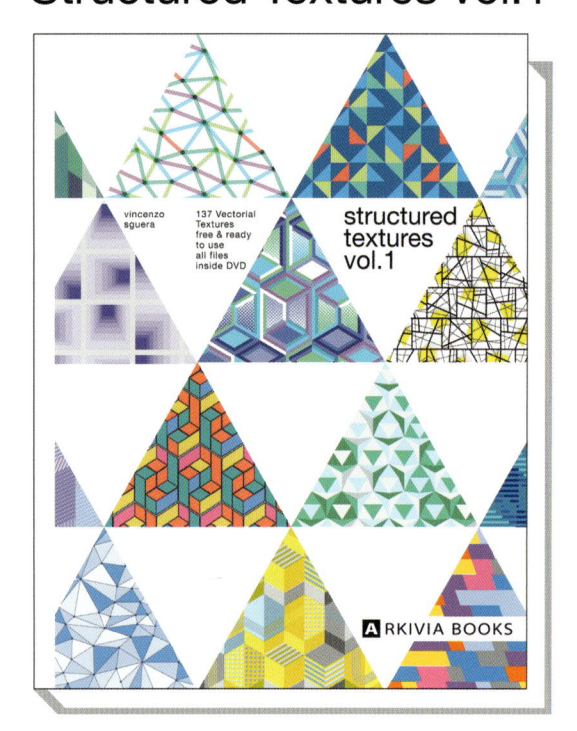

ISBN 9788888766416
HARDBACK • 160 pages
size 24cm x 30.7cm
137 TEXTURES saved in
5 ways -685 files in all.

1 Free DVD included
for WINDOWS and MAC
Vector and Bitmap Files
Ready for Production.
The use is Free

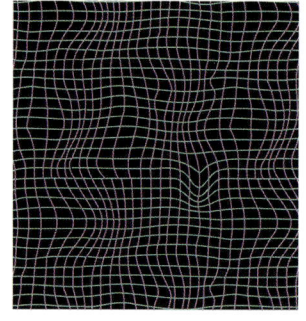

The modern side of those interested in style looks towards technology and architecture, to a certain type of repetitive geometries that goes under the name of "POLY" from polygon, exalting structure.

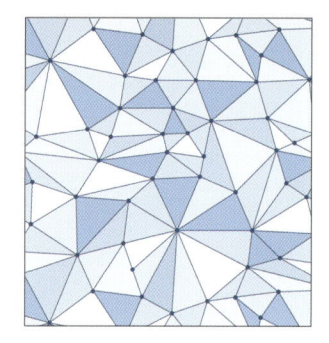

The inner part is as important as the external one.
Graphic artists and illustrators are already using these stylizations; it's time that the world of fashion too can access this contemporary style.

Grunge Textures vol.2

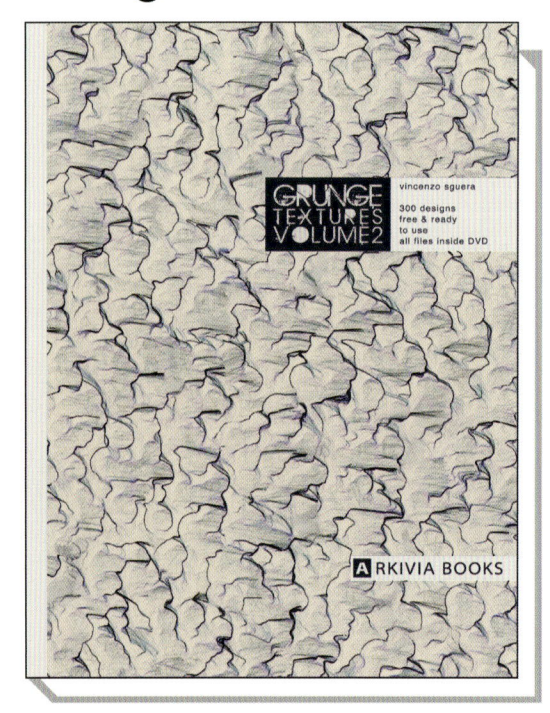

Available from January 2017

ISBN 9788888766423
HARDBACK • 160 pages
size 24cm x 30.7cm
300 TEXTURES saved
JPG 300 ppi / JPG 72 ppi.

1 Free DVD included
for WINDOWS and MAC
Bitmap Modular Files
Ready for Production.
The use is Free.

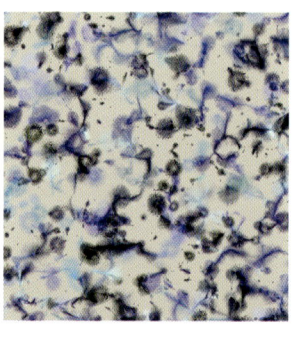

Nature and the world are full of beautiful grunge textures. The development of the designs in the grunge style has become increasingly detailed and complex.

Smearing of colours, shades and different digital skills has made it possible to give these drawings atmospheres and feelings less basic and essential than in Vol.1